Best
Wishes
For
Success

P
1995

# THEORY R MANAGEMENT

# THEORY R MANAGEMENT

## Wayne T. Alderson
## and
## Nancy Alderson McDonnell

THOMAS NELSON PUBLISHERS
*Nashville • Atlanta • London • Vancouver*

Published in Nashville, Tennessee, by Thomas Nelson, Inc., Publishers, and distributed in Canada by Word Communications, Ltd., Richmond, British Columbia.

The Bible version used in this publication is THE NEW KING JAMES VERSION. Copyright © 1979, 1980, 1982, Thomas Nelson, Inc., Publishers.

**Library of Congress Cataloging-in-Publication Data**

Alderson, Wayne.
   Theory R management / Wayne T. Alderson and Nancy Alderson McDonnell.
     p.  cm.
   ISBN 0-8407-9148-8
   1. Personal management.  2. Employee morale.  3. Affirmations.
   4. Recognition (Psychology)  5. Interpersonal relations.
   I. McDonnell, Nancy Alderson, 1956–     II. Title.
   HF5549.A548   1994
   658.3—dc20                           94–12159
                                         CIP

Printed in the United States of America.

1 2 3 4 5 6 — 99 98 97 96 95 94

# To

The many thousands of courageous men and women who have attended the Value of the Person—Theory R Seminar and who have committed themselves to implementing its principles not only at work but in the home

Sam Piccolo and the men and women of Pittron who took the first steps with us in the walk to change the face of the workplace into one that uplifts the value of the person and human dignity

All who labor and all who manage and all who are seeking a better way to do both

My wife, Nancy, who believed in me when no one else did. She has always been a source of encouragement and inspiration. I love her with a passion

Our friends and coworkers Lefty and Gloria Scumaci, Reid Carpenter, Tony Campolo, John Turyan, R. C. Sproul, and Guy Doud who have walked the walk with us

My mother who showed a special kind of love and made me tough enough to survive

My six brothers and sisters who shared the humiliating "tent experience" with me

Big John, my stepfather and friend who was always there

Dan Parisi, Jack "Doc" Gover, Willis Daniel, and the other young, carefree, fun-loving boys of Company B, First Battalion, Seventh Regiment, Third Infantry Division, who became old men overnight as they fought and suffered through unbelievable conditions

My close comrades, Will Barbour, Billy Weaver, and Joe Stankowski, who paid the ultimate price

And especially my best friend, Charles "Red" Preston, who sacrificed his life to save mine. He lived out and demonstrated the true meaning of the Value of the Person principles. I now understand the true meaning of these words: "Greater love has no one than this, than to lay down one's life for his friends."

—Wayne Alderson

———————————————

My husband, Pat, who is always there for me with support, encouragement, and love. He is a man of integrity who lives out his faith and commitment. I love him with all of my heart and am so proud to call him my husband

My mother, whose life has been an example of what it means to value people. She taught me how to love others by loving me unconditionally. I am so thankful for her guidance and want her to know I love her

My English professor, Hilda Kring, who taught me not only about writing but also about living life to the fullest

And Betty and Glen Sandmeyer, who not only opened their home for Bible study, but also their hearts at a time when my faith needed to be strengthened.

—Nancy Alderson McDonnell

# Contents

# Foreword

**E**very capable and conscientious person in a management position is aspiring to the same basic goal: to succeed. But many businesses continue to downsize, to restructure and reduce their workforces. Others seem compelled by their circumstance to settle for results far below their expectations. Why?

In *Theory R Management* Wayne Alderson and Nancy Alderson McDonnell offer an answer. They discovered many years ago that people do not fit neatly onto pie charts. Human beings resist being labeled. They rebel at being categorized and do not respond enthusiastically to the roles assigned them by a management ideology that suggests they are little more than machines that can speak.

Theory R goes beyond traditional management roles and boundaries. It is aimed directly at the individual, not the group. At first, this concept can be unsettling to those who have attended numerous employee relations seminars and have been taught to classify subordinates by apparent ability or perceived attitude.

The authors recognize that people will consistently outperform management's greatest expectations if they are allowed to feel as if their work, no matter how menial, is making a contribution toward the total success of the organization. Employees who feel valued will, in turn, do valuable work.

The premise of valuing the person, not the job is the foundation of Theory R Management. Its five principles (the "R" words) can be a blueprint for anyone striving for double-digit increases in profit and productivity, reduced absenteeism, and most important, customer satisfaction and long-term company growth. These are not empty promises. Wayne Alderson has proven the validity of Theory R Management.

A few years ago, when Wayne Alderson became vice president of operations at Pittron Steel Foundry in Pittsburgh, the company was failing. Managers and workers were in constant battle, operations were in chaos, and, of course, Pittron was losing money. The situation was so bad that many thought Wayne was there to oversee the dismantling of the company.

Then unusual things began to happen. Labor strife cooled, productivity increased, absenteeism nearly disappeared, and the company became profitable. In just twenty-one months the ugly duckling had become the graceful swan.

Pittron was the business proving ground for *Theory R Management.* Since then, hundreds of companies and thousands of Value of the Person seminar participants have embraced its tenets to forge people-oriented working relationships. Theory R Management is no longer a theory *because it works!*

We are not two persons, one at work and the other at home. What happens to us in one place overlaps the other. If you practice Theory R Management at work, you will find the benefits rubbing off in other areas of your life. Theory R can help you at home, at church, or anywhere you mingle with people. Everyone wants to be valued!

Read the book, apply the principles, and begin your personal and professional crusade to *value the person.* The results will be impressive.

Thomas J. Murrin, Dean
A. J. Palumbo School of Business Administration
Duquesne University
Pittsburgh, Pennsylvania

# Preface

This book is about relationships. That may seem to be an unusual focus for a book that deals with bottom-line results, double-digit productivity improvement, perfect quality excellence, and managing for the 90 percent. However, after twenty-five years of working with organizations across America and Canada, we are more convinced than ever that *internal relationships* are central to any successful business, and that they are the key to meeting the external demands of a global economy.

We have written this book to help the individual, and the management team, who is looking for a better way of doing business—a way that promotes the value of every individual and, in so doing, creates the vehicle for achieving a successful bottom line.

Theory R is a world-class approach

- to competing in a global economy.
- to meeting the health-care challenges facing this nation.
- to meeting and exceeding human relations development in manufacturing, technology, and education.
- to exceeding all expectations of growth and development in the service industry.
- to treating people with love, dignity, and respect.

At the core of Theory R is a very distinctive people-oriented, value-based leadership style. This book will give the basics for developing Theory R leadership as well as the hows, whys, and how-tos for making this style work not only on the job but in the home.

Most of us in the marketplace today are in the race to succeed, compete, survive, and win! The leadership style of Theory R calls for us to be winners and, in the process, to become builders of people.

**A New Direction**

As competition has accelerated and the global economy has become a reality, the general direction taken by most organizations in our nation has been to trim the fat, downsize, cut corners, and become lean and mean in preparation for economic battle. On the surface, the strategy may seem to be a good one. Too often, however, the methods used to achieve these results have been cancerous. The very people needed to make the organization successful have become alienated; bitterness and confrontation have taken root and spread in a malignant, out-of-control manner; and the net result to the organization is that it becomes filled with anger, frustration, and accusation. The emphasis falls on *mean* rather than *lean*.

When that happens, absenteeism, a drop of productivity, and a lowering of quality follow. If the downward spiral isn't reversed, an organization will soon find itself so lean and so mean that it no longer is in business. It becomes a casualty.

The forward-looking organization that truly succeeds in the next century will be one that identifies today its constant need to trim and pare and shape its business but, at the same time, is willing to change its corporate culture so that the people are both valued and empowered through the building of strong internal relationships.

It is no longer adequate for corporations to deal solely with the economic issues of the pocketbook. Priority must also be given to the noneconomic issues of the heart. The blending of the two needs will truly produce a world-class cadre of people ready to take on the challenge of a competitive national and global economy.

How does a manager or executive address the noneconomic issues of the heart? By developing a style of working with people that builds relationships. And how do you build relationships in the marketplace? By getting close enough to people to bestow value upon them—to truly affirm, appreciate, and recognize them. This style of living and leading results in reconciliation, not confrontation.

**Reconciliation Is a Must**

We are passionate about seeing people reconcile with one another. We see no advantage in confrontation—either in personal life or in work life. Confrontation demeans, destroys, and diminishes.

Reconciliation results in growth, dignity, and mutual benefit to both parties. It only makes sense that in the stress and pressure of the business world today, greater progress can be made if a business has an atmosphere of reconciliation where all parties work together for the mutual benefit of all.

**No Easy Task**

On the surface, achieving reconciliation may seem easy. In reality, it is perhaps the most difficult job any person ever faces. Reconciliation requires change, perseverance, vulnerability, and a shift from being me-oriented to being other-directed. Reconciliation is a constant challenge. It's tough work.

Does reconciliation truly make a difference? Yes! It produces by-products that may well exceed your greatest hopes.

**Reconciliation Works!**

As vice president of operations at the Pittron Steel Foundry, a division of Textron, back in the 1970s, I, Wayne, was able to experience firsthand what can happen in a work environment when conscious choice, effort, and priority are given to shifting a management style from confrontation to reconciliation. It was there that Theory R was first implemented as an alternative to a traditional style of management. The attitudes of separation and control were changed to ones of love, dignity, and respect—cornerstone principles that united the workforce. Pittron was a place where Theory R was tested and proven.

A dramatic turnaround occurred that affected not only the bottom line of the business but also the lives of the employees. The 64 percent increase in productivity improvement and the perfect quality excellence we experienced in a twenty-one-month period were dramatic, to be sure, but not as dramatic as seeing the impact that Theory R had on the families of the Pittron employees. The new emphasis on trusting relationships within the work environment also created and promoted trusting relationships in the home environment.

Since the days of Pittron, we have worked with countless organizations teaching the principles of reconciliatory management. Again and again, we have seen outstanding bottom-line, quality, and productivity successes in major corporations such as 3M, The Gillette Company, Ford, General Motors, and Owens-Corning, among others. At the same time, we have seen a tremendous impact on the families of the people who have come to our seminars. We have seen a new awareness take hold about what it means to be in relationship with others—truly to become people with eyes that see, ears that hear, and hearts that value.

**Not an Option**    We don't believe the message of this book is an option. It is a necessity for survival in a work world that is facing one of the most challenging times in history.

Our hope is that you will capture the vision for this new style of leadership in the marketplace, that you will truly learn how to value those around you, that you will make the commitment to implement these principles where you live and work, and that you will share the message of Theory R with every person you know.

Wayne T. Alderson
Nancy Alderson McDonnell

# Taking a
# Risk to Find
# a Better Way

1

*How can we compete and win in a global
economy?*

*What will it take for us to be a world-class
organization?*

*What more can be done to give us an edge over
our competitors?*

*Where can we turn to find a new stimulus for
growth?*

*How can I be assured that I am the best
manager I can possibly be?*

**T**hese questions are being asked by forward-thinking men
and women across America today.

The old standards of excellence are no longer high
enough. In nearly every industry, changes are rapid, and the pressure
to survive is rising. Something more must be done; something extra
must be added; something new must be implemented.

What can truly make a difference? Where can we get a few percentage points edge? How can we infuse our organization with new energy?

After more than two decades of working closely with literally
hundreds of businesses, in numerous areas of manufacturing and
service, we have come to a bold, strong, and heartfelt conclusion
that the answer lies with those who are doing the work—*the people.*

Technology, innovation, and new systems aren't where the greatest
changes need to be if America is to set tomorrow's standards of
excellence. The motivating focus toward excellence will not be external. Neither will it be in a tangible area such as design, cash-flow

**The Key Is
Building
Relationships**

management, acquisition of investment capital, or the installation of a new process. The key to total quality excellence in the next century will be the building of quality relationships—be they relationships between manager and manager, employee and employee, manager and employer, union leader and executive, executive and shareholder, or employee and customer.

We must regain, renew, and rethink the very heart of the way virtually any organization runs: a business is people working with people to create a product or provide a service. Regardless of the product being manufactured or the service being rendered, one finds relationships.

When relationships are allowed to disintegrate or focus is drawn away from the quality of relationships, the results can be devastating. Businesses close. Companies collapse. Even the best and biggest corporations crash.

**A Case Study**   Consider, for example, the case of Eastern Airlines. Most people look to Frank Lorenzo when placing blame for the demise of Eastern Airlines a few years ago. I, Wayne, don't. The kiss of death for that company took place long before Lorenzo was in power.

I am convinced that the reason Eastern Airlines went out of business is that two men—Charlie Bryan, president of District 100 of the International Association Mechanics union, and Frank Borman, president of Eastern Airlines prior to Lorenzo—developed an extreme distrust of each other, and I believe allowed their personal feelings to override their labor and management decisions.

**An Atmosphere**   Rather than focus on the legitimate issues before them, Bryan
**of**   and Borman allowed their relational dispute to degenerate into a
**Confrontation**   personal war. They began to attack each other in order to look right and to win with their constituencies. The two otherwise intelligent, strong, good men of integrity didn't realize that there really is no such thing as a win-lose situation in labor-management issues.

Frank Borman first heard about Theory R and Value of the Person concepts in 1983 from John Cordeiro, a thirty-two-year union mechanic and employee. He was interested in the Value of the Person but told John that Eastern Airlines was not ready for it yet. But I think Borman continued to see Bryan as the problem.

John also approached Charlie Bryan, who responded similarly, suggesting that getting rid of Borman was the solution.

During the 1980s, I had several meetings with both Bryan and Borman. I met with them independently, as a peacemaker. My message to each one was this: "Build a relationship of trust. The path you are on can lead only to greater and greater confrontation and, eventually, to intense conflict and perhaps great damage to Eastern. Find a way to put an end to your animosity before that happens. Seek to reconcile yourselves as two people who both want to see a company succeed."

I believe again that both Borman and Bryan refused to seek reconciliation or to develop an atmosphere between them in which compromise was possible.

The atmosphere of the relationship between the two men was indicative of a widespread feeling throughout the company. We have in our files a letter from an Eastern employee to his union leader and the company president. It says, in part,

> It's obvious that the reason most Eastern employees go
> A.W.O.L., show up late for work and abuse sick and injury leave
> (in order to skip work) is because Eastern is not a pleasant
> place to work and people naturally try to avoid unpleasant
> places. I personally used to enjoy going to work, but in the last
> few years the constant gloom and harassment have made East-
> ern a very unpleasant place to work and it shows up in em-
> ployee absenteeism and poor productivity. . . . If we do not
> cease the antagonism and become partners we may soon find
> ourselves without an airline to fight over.

How prophetic those words were!

Over the years, the antagonism was *not* addressed, and relationships were *not* reconciled. The distrust and disrespect grew more strident and entrenched.

Even after Borman resigned, the atmosphere of confrontation continued until, eventually, it came to the point of yet another strike. I met with Charlie Bryan the first week of February 1989, and for three hours, I pleaded with him not to strike. I said, "If you strike, it will be the final strike. Lorenzo has gone on record that if you

*A Last-Minute Attempt at Reconciliation*

strike, you'll put the airline into bankruptcy, and he'll close it down. Think about the forty thousand employees and their families, Charlie. Think about the effects that will ripple out through the communities of this nation where Eastern flies. You and Lorenzo need to start loving each other. You need to build a relationship of trust."

Bryan remained unyielding.

A few days later, I was asked if I would fly to Miami to meet with Phil Bakkes, president of Eastern. I said, "Phil, give me a chance to pull Lorenzo and Bryan together to meet face-to-face. These two men need to reconcile their differences for the good of this company. They need to begin extending love, dignity, and respect to each other so that they can work together on the problems they are facing in the airline industry. Agree to talk with the unions one more time."

Bakkes looked me in the eye and said in essence, What you are talking about is the only thing that makes any sense out of all I've heard in recent weeks. But I fear it's too late.

I said, "Phil, you have to try. I believe Eastern will cease to exist if an attempt at reconciliation isn't made."

**Too Little, Too Late**    No sooner had I said those words than we heard a commotion outside the building in which we were meeting. We walked over to the windows to see what was happening.

We were at the corporate headquarters in Florida, and the view outside the windows was of the Eastern hangars at the Miami airport. The commotion we had heard? The mechanics had just walked off their jobs and were forming a picket line with posters bearing the vilest kinds of statements against Lorenzo and the airline management. An illegal wildcat strike was happening before our very eyes! Even as I had been talking with Bakkes about the need for love, dignity, and respect, police cars by the dozens, with police officers outfitted in riot gear, were beginning to converge on the area just across the street.

It was too late. What had been one of the most reputable airlines in the history of America became insolvent within a few weeks. More than forty thousand employees, as well as their families and communities, were affected.

The collapse of Eastern Airlines is a classic case study of what can happen when issues related to employee dignity, respect, and value are ignored. Eastern Airlines began with a great tradition. The company was led by Eddie Rickenbacker, a World War I flying ace, who made great strides in aviation. Eastern Airlines was a state-of-the-art airline. Frank Borman took the helm after his years as an astronaut. Nothing seemed impossible to the company with a tradition of leadership from American heroes. Cooperation was a company hallmark.

We certainly don't mean to oversimplify what happened at Eastern Airlines because we are very aware of the external pressures being placed on the entire airline industry. But our contention is this: if the leaders at Eastern had expended more time and effort on addressing relationship issues between labor and management, the unfortunate outcome might have been averted.

Rather than begin a reconciliation in the spring of 1983, when the problems were just beginning to surface, the leaders of the airline and its major union began to entrench their positions. The more one side refused reconciliation, the more the other side pushed for concessions or benefits.

## With Confrontation, Everybody Loses

Who really lost?

In the end, everybody did.

The employees at Eastern Airlines lost. Their families lost. The managers lost. The stockholders lost. Air travelers lost.

Ultimately, America lost.

Who can count the cost of the demoralizing effect that the downfall of Eastern Airlines had on other airlines and on other American corporations? The sad fact is, many companies in America are in the same position that Eastern found itself in the early part of the 1980s. Confident of victory, yet in conflict with itself. And as a result, in danger of taking the same ill-fated flight that caused Eastern Airlines to go down in a fiery crash.

In labor and management struggles—as in virtually all relationship breakdowns—the result is one of lose-lose. Rarely does one person or group win decidedly and definitively, with the other person losing absolutely—especially if the relationship is ongoing. A spirit of confrontation remains, even in the wake of a decision, a signed contract, or a period of silence and separation.

**With
Reconciliation,
Everybody Wins**

The good news is that there's a fresh breeze blowing in many of our nation's largest and finest institutions—including such well-respected corporate giants as 3M and the Owens-Corning Corporation.

Executives, managers, and employees are coming together as never before and saying, "Let's work out our personal differences. Let's find a better way of relating to one another. Let's take our company over the top."

*True reconciliation is the only means of winning. It is the key to the excellence we must have in the coming years. It is the way in which American companies will find an edge.*

That is the cornerstone of Theory R.

# The Cry from the Workplace Is for Relationship

## 2

**T**he leadership principles of Theory R were not created on the drawing boards of the corporate boardroom, nor did they come out of the brain trust of the university elite. They were formulated in the marketplace where real people with hearts struggle each day to find a better way of living and working together.

For me, Wayne, the principles of reconciliation and the value of the person—principles I consider to be so vital to the life of corporate cultures in a globally competitive economy—had an early beginning. The principles were first developed when I, as a boy in the coal mining town of Canonsburg, Pennsylvania, near Pittsburgh, encountered circumstances in which there was no value of the person.

Canonsburg is perhaps best known as the hometown of Perry Como and Bobby Vinton. Both men received a lot of ribbing from the coal miners of Canonsburg, who encouraged them to get a "real" job in the mines.

One of the nicest things a person can ever say about me is that I'm the son of a coal miner. It is a heritage that has deep family roots. My father, Lank Alderson, worked in the mines as did his father before him and his father and grandfather before him. In fact,

Dad's father was killed in a tragic mine accident. My father's dream was that his four sons would follow in his footsteps and his three daughters would marry miners. Coal mining was not only my father's work; it was our life. We lived in a company town, we lived in company housing, and we shopped at the company store.

I can still hear my mother say, "We're living in slavery. We're living in bondage."

I always tried to be up in the morning to see my father off to work, and then I'd wait in the evening for him to return home. I'd listen for his lunch pail to hit against his miner's belt buckle—what I called the tinny sound. (Years later, when I was out on patrol in Germany as a young soldier, my uncanny ability to hear that tinny sound—this time that of an enemy rifle hitting against a belt—saved my life more than once.)

My dad lived mostly in darkness—leaving home at 4:00 A.M. before the sun came up, spending all day in the deep recesses of the mine, returning home after the sun went down. My father's words were branded on my mind as I heard him say to my mother time after time, "Edith, if they'd only value me as much as they value the mule."

In those days, mine mules were well trained and well kept. They were the high tech of the mines since they were the best advance-warning system a mine had against explosions. It was a known fact that the mine owners considered it much easier and cheaper to replace a miner than to replace a well-trained mule.

My father's desire to be treated as well as a mule left an indelible mark on me. Yet, even with all of the pain he experienced, Dad would say to me, "Son, someday, you're going to be a miner like me."

A mine accident brought disaster and humiliation to our family and only served to underscore my father's words about value. Dad suffered a compound fracture of his leg in a slate fall, and the injury made it impossible for him to go back down into the pit. His career as a miner was finished. Almost immediately, we were evicted from company housing. Feeling broken and defeated, my father left the family, leaving my mother to do her best to keep us together, sheltered, and fed. My mother was a single parent for the next twenty years, and she raised seven children. She was proud and very beautiful.

Having no place to go and no money to get there, my mother let her youngest baby stay temporarily with his grandmother, and she led her other six children to a vacant lot that was used as a ball field by neighborhood children. There, she set up a tent that would be our home for several months. We had no electricity, of course—no stove, no furnace, no plumbing, no toilet. There was barely room for two army cots. My mother worked nights in a bar named Steve's Place.

We children huddled together against the dark, the cold, the noise of trains that rumbled nearby throughout the night, the unrelenting dampness and its resulting mildew. Most of all, we huddled together against public humiliation. I remember looking out the tent flaps with my brothers and sisters and seeing houses on the hills of Canonsburg, aglow with electric lights, with curtains at the windows and cars in the driveways. It looked like another world to us, a world of warmth and security that was beyond our grasp but that we desperately desired.

Even after the tent was abandoned, the hurt lingered. Each of us children knew what it meant to be treated with indignity and to be shown no respect. We knew our mother loved us, agonized over our situation, and did her best to protect us and provide for us. We never would have made it without her. We received no love, no encouragement, and no respect from those we had once called friends and neighbors.

All the shame and the degradation of that period in my life led me to decide even before I was a teenager, *I'm never going to work in the mines. I'm going to escape from here as soon as I can. I want to find a place where people are valued.*

I left Canonsburg at the age of eighteen and exchanged my life there for a military uniform and a life in another type of tent—one on the battlefields of Europe. I never went to work in the mines. Even today, the words continue to ring out loud and clear in my mind: "If they'd only value me as much as they value the mule."

## Why a New Theory?

During the last twenty-five years as I have consulted with hundreds of businesses across the nation, I have discovered again and again that the mind-set I experienced those many years ago in Canonsburg is still very much alive, even though massive computers and space-age technology have replaced the dependency on pack animals.

Most businesses, industries, corporations, and organizations still seem to value their people less than they value many other things. When plant managers offer to give us a tour of their operations, they invariably say, "Let me show you the plant," rather than say, "Let's meet the people." They point with pride to this facility or that piece of machinery and say, "We just purchased this beauty," rather than say, "Meet Joe and Jane. They're our most highly prized employees."

The one thing that companies value the most is a positive bottom line. But too often they define winning as winning at any cost.

Winning, of course, is defined in terms of profit—which is an obviously vital component. Businesses do exist to make money, and the bottom line is the bottom line. However, when profit is the singular definition of winning, problems nearly always arise with the means of getting to profit. When profit becomes the sole concern of an organization at the expense of all other factors, very important aspects of running the business fall by the wayside.

---

- Customers become important only because they spend.
- Equipment is purchased only if the bottom line allows its purchase.
- Employees are the most expendable factor in the profit-generating equation. If the bottom line is suffering, most top-level managers turn first to a reduction in staff to reduce the head count.

---

The result is one that we see all around us: America's companies are not working primarily for the benefit of America or her people. Rather, American executives are working for money.

There's a very big difference between working for money and working for the people who make up that company and who buy that company's products. The two approaches are 180 degrees apart.

In working for the bottom line, everything becomes statistic-driven. Numbers replace people. Enterprise is reduced to formulas and ratios.

Conversely, in working for American people, business becomes people-driven. Top-level managers who adopt this approach—as precious and few as they may be—see their companies as existing for the benefit of three groups of people: customers, employees, and shareholders. The needs of those groups of people are given top priority. People-driven managers know that if the needs of customers, employees, and shareholders are met in a fair, equitable, win-win-win way, the bottom line will take care of itself.

Customers need a quality product—at the lowest possible cost—that makes their lives better or easier.

Employees need jobs that reward them emotionally, psychologically, and materially.

Shareholders need a return on their investment and a feeling of being involved in something bigger than themselves.

Is it possible to balance these three highly diverse needs? Yes! American businesses once operated this way, and the result was steady and persistent growth.

When a concern for the needs of any one group, however, takes over, the business moves in a direction that brings detriment to the other two groups. For example, if the return on investment—the bottom-line profit—becomes the almighty factor, those who suffer are usually the employees and the customers. Products are made with less quality so they can cost less. Workers are laid off so the bottom-line numbers can be met.

The triangle can be tipped in either of the other two directions just as easily. If employees win benefits in negotiations to the expense of the company's ability to produce a quality product for its customers, the customers will go elsewhere. Their lack of purchases will affect the company's profitability, and the result is that the employees may have negotiated themselves out of a company to work for.

If the concern about the customer's need for a low-cost product turns into an industrywide war, products will be pushed lower and lower in cost to the point that shareholders and employees lose out.

The balance is an economic one, to be sure. But at its heart—at its foundation—must be a concern for the people.

## The Need to Return to a Fair Profit

The ideal result is something we call a *fair profit*. The company makes money (which means that its owners or shareholders make money). The employees are rewarded fairly with part of the profit. The company invests in itself with part of the profit so that new research, development, and production factors can be improved to create an even better product at an even more competitive price. Business moves forward, finding new markets and creating new niches within them.

Fair profits are hardly the norm we're seeing in our nation's top companies today. You only have to take a look at the annual reports of a couple of dozen or more of the Fortune 500 corporations in this nation.

You'll find a number of companies losing money and yet rewarding one segment of the workforce (the chief executive officer [CEO] or the very top levels of management) with extravagant salaries and special benefits.

As reported in the April 26, 1993, issue of *Business Week*, CEO earnings in 1992 took a 56 percent leap over 1991—mainly from options in stocks. The average CEO of a big U.S. corporation was given a total compensation package worth $3,842,247. To make it to the Top Ten list of CEOs, an executive had to receive more than $22.8 million. By comparison, the average CEO earned $190,393 in 1960 and $624,996 in 1970.

Meanwhile, teachers in 1992 earned an average salary of $34,098; engineers, $58,240; and general workers, $24,411.

How do companies structure themselves to reward CEOs so generously? Massive reductions in staff are frequently required to make stock option and salary rewards possible for the elite—in some cases putting entire towns out of work. Many companies paying high compensation packages are in desperate need of retooling, and their shareholders are getting only a few dollars more per share.

Meanwhile, productivity improvement grinds to a halt. Productivity from 1943 to 1962 ran at 3.2 percent a year—a steady growth pattern. However, from 1963 to 1993, American productivity rose an average of only 1.5 percent a year.

What happened in Japan while America was experiencing this rate of slowed-down growth in the last three decades? Our competitors' productivity rose an average of 8.5 percent a year! In three decades—1963 to 1993—productivity in America rose about 45 percent, while our Japanese competitors increased their productivity by 255 percent. No wonder we're on the catching-up side of things today.

Not only did productivity decline, but quality also declined in America. Meanwhile, the Japanese were reversing their trend from poor quality to excellent quality. Prior to 1973, "Made in Japan" was virtually synonymous with "junk." In the last three decades, that trend dramatically turned around. "Made in Japan" is now identified with high quality and high performance.

The impact of these differences in productivity and quality has been staggering to our economy. Many corporations are still reeling.

Ironically, after World War II, Japanese businessmen came to the United States and asked the million-dollar question: "What do we have to do to be productive?" The answer given by their American counterparts was for labor and management to work together. Nearly fifty years later, American management and labor teams now flock to Japan in search of the secret to Japanese productivity and quality success. And what have they discovered? Involvement and recognition of employees . . . labor and management working together. The ways in which people are motivated and managed are just as important as the ways in which new widgets are being assembled.

In trying to adapt current Japanese models to the American economy, top executives have failed in several areas—one of which has been the adjustment of their personal goals and financial standards. The gap continues to widen between executive salaries and worker salaries, between management and employee. Personal winning is still at the core of what is being valued.

Something is wrong. The way we've been doing business just isn't working.

## An Obsession with Machines and Technology

Coupled with our national obsession over personal winning is a fixation about machines and technology.

Beginning with the birth of the Industrial Revolution, managers began to adopt a mind-set that said machines—and technology—are the key to unlimited organizational and economic growth.

With machines, operations could multiply their productivity; they could expand their factories to cover more city blocks. And with the increase in productivity, a company could hire on more people to run more machines so that more products could be produced and yet more people could be hired to run more machines. The boom was machine-driven.

Technological advancement—the creation and use of better and better machines—seemed to guarantee unlimited growth. Machines affected the bottom line in obvious, easy-to-calculate ways. They had purchase costs, maintenance costs, and material-use costs. They produced $X$ number of items or performed $X$ number of functions.

Bigger, faster, more efficient machines meant bigger, faster, more efficient operations.

And someplace along the upward spiral of technology, management lost sight of the growing needs of the people who ran those machines.

Ask virtually any top-level manager and that person will tell you that machines hold several advantages over people.

Machines are much easier to control. The more control a manager has, the more power. The more power, the more personal economic security for the manager.

Machines are much easier to maintain. Their problems can be fixed easily. They don't need to be motivated, nurtured, or communicated with (at least not in a dialogue). They can't walk away from the operation. They don't have to eat lunch or use a rest room.

Machines are much easier to justify as expenditures. Their performance is easier to measure and to talk about; their costs are fixed. Managers like the idea of adding material assets to their realms.

It's really no mystery why managers have turned to technology as the means of propelling their companies forward. Machines don't threaten, challenge, or even require very much ability on the part of the manager.

## Surprise! People Aren't Stupid

Ultimately, machines are stupid. The era of smart machines with artificial intelligence is just upon us. Yet even those machines have artificial intelligence—intelligence they must be given by their human creators.

People, on the other hand, aren't stupid. They know when they are being overlooked in favor of machines. They know when the bottom line is being inked to their disadvantage. Even if they don't have all the facts at hand, they can smell deceit, dishonesty, and a shift in priorities from people factors to machine-driven economic factors.

When people discern that they are being relegated to positions that are far less exalted than the machines they operate, a negative attitude sets in. Low morale pervades the workplace. A lack of trust for administrative policies sets in.

With lack of trust and low morale come a slackening of effort and a lessening of a worker's willingness to cooperate for the good of the company. After all, if the company values machines and bottom-line economic factors over people, why respect such a company? Why give that company your loyalty? Why think more highly of the company than it thinks of you?

A degeneration of loyalty begins to occur, and it spreads from both ends. Workers become less loyal to their companies. Companies become less loyal to their employees. Look around. You'll find that happening in businesses on every other street corner. Employees are coming and going in all directions. People don't count on their companies to be there for them twenty years down the line. Companies don't count on individual employees being there, either!

Now, if people are going to be coming and going, why get involved with them? Why hear them out? Why build a relationship with them? Why care what they think? Why pay them any heed at all?

## Human Resource Management Is Often the Problem, Not the Solution

The mushrooming cloud in business has become something known as human resource problems. The problems are growing bigger, not smaller. They are becoming more intense, not less intense.

To handle those problems, corporations across this nation have instituted in the last ten years an arena known as *human resource management* or *human resource development*.

At one time they were called personnel departments, industrial relations, or labor relations. The *human resource* tag apparently arose from a recognition that humanity and humane treatment were missing. The problem is that in many cases, human resource development is perceived by employees as being simply resource development, with employees as the resource.

Evaluations and needs analyses seem designed to assign numerical value to the products of human resource development. Why? So costs can effectively be compared to benefits. Does an employee who is paid a higher wage produce more? Does an employee who feels safe on the job produce fewer errors? Does an employee with an assigned parking space show up for work more regularly? The impact is nearly always drawn back to the bottom line of profit.

Furthermore, managers have come to assume that employee problems can be fixed in the same way that machine problems are fixed.

How are machine problems fixed? First, find out what's wrong.

In machine terms, find out what has broken. In human development terms, hear out the problem.

Second, find out what it's going to cost to fix the problem. In machine terms, get an estimate on repairs. In human development terms, find out what more the employees want. Usually, management goes into a problem automatically assuming that the problem can be fixed with an expenditure of money.

Budget considerations enter the process. Never mind that in human relations, money or benefits may not be a true fix-it. We must become aware that a real need can remain unresolved no matter how much money is thrown at it.

Third, find someone who can fix the problem. In machine terms, find someone to repair it. In human development terms, find a group process. Put together a committee. Name a task force.

Fourth, if the repairs aren't made satisfactorily, go back to square one. The goal: work at it until the machine runs. In human resource development terms, keep naming committees and keep forming small groups until employees are satisfied.

The problem is, employees aren't satisfied by group processes and added benefits alone. Neither one addresses the real root problem: managers are trying to fix human problems in a technological way. What employees truly want is not to be fixed but to be in relationship.

## Employees Don't Want to Be Fixed

Employees don't want to be an economic factor. They don't want to be a movable factor in the economic equation—one that is generally subtracted so others can have more money added to their pockets.

Workers don't want to be regarded as a component—just a piece in the puzzle. They don't want to be treated as less valuable than machines or lower than mules. They don't want to be manipulated or adjusted like dials.

Employees don't really want to be put into a position where they have to fight for recognition. They truly want to be working partners, not sparring partners, in building a better life for all Americans.

Employees want to feel that they are recognized as human beings, that they are seen as the life blood of any enterprise, that they count.

Employees want to be valued.

---

How would you describe your current relationship with

- your peers at work?
- your manager or supervisor?
- your company?
- your family?

What do you truly desire to be the nature of your relationship with each of these people or groups of people?

# 3

# Resolving to Move Beyond Confrontation

**F**ires burning in steel drums, workers huddled around trying to keep warm, trucks like silent sentinels lined up behind the chain-link fence in hopes of bringing out products, barricades and picket signs blocking their path, police standing where plant guards once stood—all depicted the bleakness of the situation at hand. Winter was upon us. The gates of Pittron were closed. The plant had been shut down. And I was the guy in charge.

The strike had begun on October 26, 1972. And for eighty-four days—through what turned out to be a meager Thanksgiving and dark Christmas season for the workers and their families, and on into the bitterly cold month of January—the fires in those drums stayed lit.

As bleak as the situation was for the employees, it was just as bleak for Pittron management.

Pittron was an old foundry. It opened in 1899 as the Pittsburgh Steel Foundry & Machine Company. It was then purchased in 1959 by Textron and renamed Pittron. From 1969 to 1972, Pittron's financial condition had deteriorated badly. The company showed a loss of nearly millions and was at the breaking point. It could not afford a lengthy shutdown. Nobody knew that better than I. I had been the financial man—the controller—during those three years. As controller, I would rate my skills with the best of those in my profession. But I had no administrative power.

Related statistics by the time of the strike in 1972 were grim:

- Productivity ................................. 0
- Absenteeism ................................ 25%
- Quality ..................................... Poor
- Grievances ................................. 1,200

Most people referred to the plant as a "junk shop." The three hundred employees were facing layoffs. Above all, the spirit of confrontation in the plant was so thick you could cut it with a knife.

Although I had no real administrative power, I had been bold in speaking up against what I perceived to be the dangers of management by confrontation at every possible opportunity. Just months before the strike began, I had attended an advanced management course cosponsored by Harvard University and Textron. There I had been rather outspoken in questioning current management operations and methodology. My comments had drawn the attention of Textron's board chairman, G. William Miller (who later was the chairman of the Federal Reserve Board and then secretary of the Treasury). I argued that practices that intimidated employees didn't work; rather, they had led to our thirty consecutive months of losses.

Just prior to the strike, Textron purged the management of Pittron, and Miller appointed a new president for the foundry. I was named vice president in charge of operations. Days later, the workers hit the bricks. As I watched the picket lines one day from my office window, I realized that the main operation I was going to administer was not managing the plant but very possibly dismantling and closing the foundry. Virtually nobody had any hope that Pittron would survive.

As the strike dragged on, Pittron's customers began to get uneasy. Orders were canceled, and customers began to seek ways to protect their vested interests, which were locked up behind Pittron's gates. One customer attempted to remove products from the plant, but as the driver crossed the picket line, violence erupted. In order to gain entrance, the driver rammed his way through the chain-link fence. The strikers, however, being just as creative quickly erected a barricade to keep him from driving out again. It took police to help the trucker escape—but without his truck.

In mid-December, Pittron's new president and I were invited to Providence, Rhode Island, to meet with G. William Miller and to present our financial and operating plan for the new year. I proposed what I called Operation Turnaround—a plan that focused on effectiveness rather than efficiency. I have long been convinced that there's a critical difference between the two. *Efficiency* is "doing things right." *Effectiveness,* on the other hand, is "doing the right things first." Theory R calls for managers to recognize that unless they are effective, all the efficiency in the world won't matter.

I said to Miller, a tough, no-nonsense CEO, "Don't evaluate the plan on paper. Give us a chance to be effective and then judge us on our bottom-line results." He agreed.

When I returned from meeting with Miller, I called my leadership staff together and presented Operation Turnaround to them as the outline of our new direction. I spoke to them about the vision I had for Pittron, the tough economic goals we faced and how I expected us to meet them. I expressed to them in strong, straightforward terms our need to create a new corporate culture—one *not* rooted in confrontation but founded on human value. In turning Pittron around, we faced the challenge of turning everything around, and that included the way we treated one another as human beings.

The changes I called for at Pittron ultimately required a personal commitment to change on the part of each individual in a leadership role. Business at Pittron was no longer going to be business as usual for any of us. I had recognized and faced up to that need for change in my personal life, and I challenged people working with me to take the risk, also. At no time did I feel as if I was abdicating business skills, executive toughness, or operational discipline. I developed a deep inner conviction that we needed to do the right thing in relating to one another as managers and employees. For virtually everyone at Pittron, that meant a radical change in management style.

Theory R and the Value of the Person principles will work for you, the individual, and for your workplace only if you are personally willing to face up to the fact that you presently aren't doing all the right things—that there's still room for improvement. Unless that realization is faced squarely, there's no inner conviction to push for excellence, no desire to see things get better, and certainly no compulsion to improve relationships with those for whom, and with whom, you work or whose work you supervise.

Not only was it critically important for me as a vice president and for my key staff members to make a change, it was also crucial that the rank-and-file employees become committed to a new day and experience a turnaround in their thinking. A line needed to be drawn in the sand; a mark needed to be made to launch a new beginning.

The necessity of this has been reinforced in me many times through the years. A management executive may make a decision to implement Value of the Person concepts, but this alone doesn't indicate change. It is only as rank-and-file employees and line supervisors are trained in the concepts and convinced of the need to change that a line is truly marked and the people in a company can begin to move forward together.

For us at Pittron, that line-drawing moment was explosive.

### Walking a Ledge on the Brink of Disaster

A message was handed to me while I was attending a church service in Pleasant Hills. The message said, "Piccolo wants to meet you. Now."

Sam Piccolo was president of the United Steel Workers Local 1306, a perennial thorn in the flesh to Pittron management. Most managers had the good sense to give Piccolo a wide berth. He was in his third consecutive term as president, and the workers hailed him as a hero.

I felt in no position to turn Piccolo down, yet I knew the meeting was unauthorized as part of the negotiations. Piccolo had set the meeting place as Room 8 in a nearby Holiday Inn, which in and of itself was a little suspicious. I talked the matter over with my wife, Nancy, who strongly urged me not to go, feeling that too many threats were in the air. I knew, however, that someone had to go, and I was the one who received the call. I had to respond.

### The Meeting in Room 8

When I knocked on the door of Room 8, Piccolo answered the door and motioned me in. As soon as I entered the smoke-filled room, I knew I had been set up. Six of Piccolo's men were there, and in surveying the room, I quickly spotted the evidence of heavy drinking. The atmosphere was charged with hostility.

Piccolo, with his massive barrel chest and hardened six-foot frame, glared at me and then shoved a piece of paper into my hand. "Here are our demands," he growled. "Meet them and we settle the strike."

I didn't even look at what was written on the paper. I crumpled it up and threw it at Piccolo's feet in defiance. "I'm not here to talk about demands," I said.

At that point, one of Piccolo's buddies jumped up, obviously drunk, and pulled a switchblade. He spewed forth a string of profanities and concluded, "I'm going to slit your throat!"

Using the most provocative epithet I knew, I threw caution to the wind and shouted back at him, "Either cut my throat, or shut up and sit down!"

Dead silence followed. Piccolo finally said, "OK, we'll settle."

Piccolo had already checked me out. He believed I was a man of my word. And in that moment, he decided that I was either the dumbest man he'd ever met or the bravest.

Piccolo and I started to communicate in earnest, the tension lessening only slightly. Our mutual toughness had been established. It was time to clear away the posturing and get to the core issues—eyeball-to-eyeball and man-to-man. I said, "Trust me. Judge me on results. I won't lie to you or to the workers. I won't cheat you."

Then I telephoned the professional team of negotiators and asked them to join the meeting. They initially refused, furious that I had met with Piccolo. From their perspective, I wasn't going by the book. They were correct. I was more concerned about doing the right thing to get the employees back to work and the plant into operation. I exploded, "Get over here fast. Forget the protocol. We're going to settle this strike now!"

They arrived minutes later, and we sat down and worked on the fine points of an agreement until well into the night. The next day the men and women voted to come back to work, and the foundry geared up for production. The eighty-four-day strike was over.

A line had been marked in the sand of Pittron, and from that point on, we faced a new beginning—tenuous but, nonetheless, a new start. I felt confident that a new attitude could take hold. I truly believed that Operation Turnaround could succeed. But I also knew that it would take a lot more than a showdown meeting and a rah-rah spirit.

Pittron's employees were grown men and women who had been hardened by years of growing mistrust and broken promises. They weren't about to put up with children's games or empty rhetoric.

If new promises were made, they needed to be kept. I knew that as well as anyone, and better than some around me. I announced in rather bold ways—so that no employee could miss them—that "we shall be different." We *all*—managers and employees—needed to be different if we were going to turn things around at that foundry.

The first steps, however, needed to come from management. It was our responsibility to help heal old wounds and to start building a bridge across the long-standing hostility in the plant. In my heart of hearts, I held to a belief that, ultimately, the employees and managers at Pittron were on the same side, and they wanted the same thing.

Ultimately, the goals of both labor and management are very similar—more similar, perhaps, than either would like to admit. Both want higher productivity. Both want increased sales. Both want better quality of goods and services. Both want a positive work atmosphere. Both want a safe environment. In part, they want these things for the same reason: so the plant or office or school or hospital will stay open. Above all, both hope for and desire a relationship that is beyond confrontation. Both want to be valued.

We had discovered on that day in Room 8 a basis for establishing some degree of agreement rather than disagreement at Pittron. We both wanted to be valued as individuals and treated with love, dignity, and respect.

Every person has a need for relationships. Relationships encompass a give-and-take with other people. They include communication, care, shared experiences, and a feeling of commonality. A person's need for relationship doesn't stop at the factory gate or cease to exist the minute the person steps off the elevator into the department. Relationships make any enterprise meaningful and fulfilling.

Furthermore, the strength of the relationship always has a definite impact on the human being's ability and desire to do relationship-related tasks.

Leave the workplace and think about a marriage for a moment. The spouse who is in great relationship with the partner in marriage may not like taking out the trash or doing the laundry, but the person is a lot more willing to do the tasks that are related to the relationship if the relationship itself is a good one—marked by mutuality and a shared commitment—than if the relationship is sour.

Within the workplace, the same dynamic is evident. Employees who enjoy working with their colleagues, bosses, and subordinates and who have an ongoing healthy relationship with them are a lot more willing to work, even at tasks they may not find pleasurable.

All the money, all the benefits, and all the added features of the workplace can't create relationships. Small groups may provide a means of putting people together, but even they do not in and of themselves create relationships.

People create relationships. And *create* is the operative word. Relationships are not engineered. Those that are engineered usually turn out to be big disasters. Relationships are built by people who find ways and means of sharing things, experiences, ideas, feelings, and processes that are mutually meaningful to all parties involved.

Relationships are also fragile. They take work to make them strong. They require time and effort. They don't emerge full-blown and strong overnight. And even the most solid relationship can be shattered by uncaring actions or hurtful words.

Above all, relationships are valuable. They are the true stuff that makes life meaningful.

## Fear Flows from a Broken Relationship

Fear is one of the main things that creeps into a person when a relationship is damaged or when a relationship is never forged.

A person who finds the marriage or other valued family relationships disintegrating nearly always begins to feel fearful. When a person at work feels that the relationships with others are on shaky ground, fear also manifests itself.

Perhaps the greatest fear we see in the American workplace today is the fear of losing one's job. People are genuinely fearful that their jobs aren't going to be there tomorrow. They suspect rightly or wrongly that economic factors are going to swamp their company's boat and they are going to be swept overboard or that a new machine will come along and replace them on the assembly line or that the organization will be restructured and they will be squeezed out or that a new technology in which they aren't trained will overtake them and they will be discarded as obsolete. Just look around. Take the fear temperature of your workplace. The vast majority of corporate America is feverish.

Fear is not motivating—a fact that seems to amaze a number of managers we've met. People in fear cower down, keep quiet, and lie low. Employees who are afraid of losing jobs become cautious, not creative. They make a diligent attempt to keep all the rules and, in so doing, test none of their personal limits at producing excellence or beating previous highs. Employees adopt a "don't make waves" attitude; they don't make new suggestions or offer fresh ideas.

Fear—and its resulting lowering of motivation—isn't a situation we see in just one company. It's a problem we see in every type of organization we work in, from border to border and sea to sea:

- Nurses are afraid to give their opinions to doctors. Physicians are afraid to share their power with nurses. And who suffers? All involved, including the patients.
- Teachers are afraid to challenge principals. Principals are afraid to challenge school board policies. And who loses? The students.
- Employees are afraid to question their line supervisors. Supervisors don't speak with candor to their managers. Managers are afraid of losing the respect of their executives. Who loses? Everybody! Customers and stockholders included.

Being a part of human development small group programs or team-building efforts doesn't alleviate fear, either. It often builds in a little more fear—the fear that the individual employee might be blamed for the failure of the team to solve the company's problems!

## Fear and Hate Produce—Just Not the Right Things

Fear and hate aren't innocuous emotions that exist in some type of labor vacuum. They are deadly live viruses in an organization.

Fear is accompanied by frustration and unrest. Employees are upset. They frequently become more obsessed with holding jobs than with doing them. They miss more work because the workplace isn't an enjoyable place to be. Their productivity drops. They let quality slide. Their anger—or their withdrawal—creates relationship problems with fellow workers and supervisors. And all the while, the employees feel less and less human, less and less valued.

The typical management response to this lessening of quality and productivity is to turn to material and technological development. Find a better machine. Find a better way of working. Find better (more skilled, harder working) people. Replace components. Update units.

Once again, we come full circle to the desire on the part of managers to fix things—including fixing people just as they fix machines. Corporations have spent vast sums of money on think tanks to help them develop ways of fixing people. And thus, we have a number of theories circulating that are designed primarily to help managers get more out of workers so that the company may experience a bottom-line gain. The three most popular of these theories are Theory X, Theory Y, and Theory Z.

**Theory X**   This theory is founded on the premise that people are fundamentally lazy and irresponsible. They need to be watched constantly. A heavy hand is required if a manager is to get the most out of an employee.

**Theory Y**   This theory says that people are fundamentally hardworking and responsible. They need only to be supported and encouraged. Show the employee what to do and how to do it, and then a light touch is all that is needed to get that employee to perform to full potential. A manager need have only minimal involvement with an employee.

**Theory Z**   This theory says that employees perform better if they are involved in the company process. Find trusted (and trusting) employees, and slot them into committees, groups, and task units where they can voice their opinions and help make decisions.

Out of Theory Z have come a number of popular programs, such as Total Quality Management, Quality Circles, Quality of Work Life, Labor-Management Participative Teams, Management by Objectives, Employee Involvement, and others of like ilk.

What we must recognize at the outset about these theories and their resulting programs is that to a very great degree, all of them are aimed at programming employees into the organization's set design. The employees are being no less controlled by being made a part of a group. They are simply being controlled in a little safer, less threatening manner, with the outside possibility that the employees will actually contribute something to the company.

All of these programs are designed to make the employee produce better, even though they may be cloaked in a guise of making the employee feel better, or they may be presented as ways to produce a manager-employee relationship.

The new hot team approach is Total Quality Management (TQM), which is widely heralded as today's savior of corporate America. While it's true that TQM may be implemented to great benefit, it's equally true of TQM—as with virtually all other similar programs— that the protocol will not work unless it is firmly rooted in quality relationships first.

Unless quality relationships are established, TQM is a form without any real substance. The goal setting is empty, the self-directedness is shallow, and ultimately, worker involvement and commitment are weak and short-lived. As one seminar participant said to us, "TQM? As far as I'm concerned, it's just another management idea that's supposed to become my idea. What I'd rather have is a manager who would recognize me as a person. If she doesn't value me as a person, why would I think she was going to value my ideas?"

## Replacing the Old Style of Confrontation

All of these theories—X, Y, and Z—are rooted in confrontation as opposed to reconciliation. Theory X openly advocates confrontation. Workers are lazy and irresponsible. Managers must confront these traits to get maximum productivity and quality out of employees.

Theory Y, however, is really no less confrontational—the confrontational style is simply wearing kid gloves. Cajoling replaces coercing. Employees are still on the opposite side of the invisible fence that separates them from managers. Employees who fail to respond to *support* and *encouragement*—two key words in Theory Y—find themselves being confronted.

Theory Z may deny confrontation, but the fact remains that managers set up all the rules by which trusting employees are involved. The street is not nearly as two-way as the language of the theory might suggest. Managers require from employees just one more result: involvement. Meetings and group involvement become more conditions of employment. And if productivity and quality fail to improve according to management expectations, groups are quickly disbanded or rearranged as a management directive. In sum, employees do what managers demand, and if employees fail to perform, managers take action.

## The Theory R Challenge

Theory R responds to theories X, Y, and Z in this way. Most people want to contribute unconditionally to the environment in which they live and work. They want to be wholly a part of something. There are pleasure and fulfillment in feeling needed, wanted, useful, and connected. Each person has a basic human need to serve because a life that encompasses nothing beyond oneself becomes barren.

## Control vs. Leadership

This argument is sure to arise: "Companies need someone to be in charge. Someone must make decisions, chart the course, and give directives."

True. We have no argument with those statements.

The matter is one of style. Is the style one in which managers assert, "We say you must," or "Let us"?

There's a very big difference in the two approaches. In the "we say you must" style, one finds an implicit underlying conviction: "And if you don't, we will make you." Blame flows downward from managers to employees. Control. Power. They are expressed as much in how managers relate to employees as in the words actually used.

In the "let us" style, the underlying conviction is this: "And if *we* don't, *we'll* fail together." Blame flows two ways. Control and power over the situation—over productivity, quality, and other measures of performance—are viewed as being shared. The environment is one of conciliation and cooperation, not a war zone that pits managers against employees.

Confrontational management is usually marked by rigid lines, distinctions in rank and position, that dictate communication. A manager on one rung of an organizational ladder dare not leapfrog over a rung to talk to employees or move laterally to communicate with employees in another area—even in informal, non-task-related ways. Neither does that manager dare bypass a step upward in communicating toward the top. Confrontational management requires that channels be observed at all times.

In other human relationships, channels are not nearly so enforced.

**THEORY R SAYS,**

*People have a fundamental desire to work hard and take pride in what they accomplish.*

*When placed in an atmosphere that is sensitive to Value of the Person principles, employees will be cooperative, creative, and productive. Employees are neither lazy nor irresponsible.*

*Teamwork and problem solving are to be encouraged but always within an atmosphere of mutual trust and responsiveness.*

Think about it. Children, for example, frequently talk directly to their grandparents without going through Mom and Dad. The principal talks to children on the school ground without first getting their teachers' permission. Managers talk to customers in a store without going through clerks. Senior pastors minister directly to parishioners without consulting their associate ministers first, and parishioners write to bishops without their pastors knowing it.

In nonwork areas, a confrontational style in a relationship tends to be regarded as an abusive or inhumane one—in other words, an undesirable style. We've become so accustomed to this style at work, however, that we have come to regard it as the norm.

It needn't be and shouldn't be.

When confrontation is the norm, persons on both ends of the teeter-totter—in the business realm, managers and employees—place greater and greater conditions on their relationship. You do *A;* I do *B.* You mess up; I come down on you. Unless you do *C,* I will do *A.* And so it goes. Rules are put in place that define the relationship more and more narrowly. Workers and managers get to the place where everything must be put into writing, everything must be contractual, and everything must be spelled out in terms everybody understands. **Great and Greater Chances of Failure**

What happens to trust? It walks out the door. Without trust, we're back to fear.

Even managers and employees who recognize the process rarely look in the right direction for the answer. **There Must Be a Solution Out There**

The statement is nearly always made, "Go find a better way." The implication is that there's a solution out there somewhere. We suspect that somebody somewhere must have figured it all out and that somebody can tell us how to fix our relationship problems. We seek out counseling—in business terms, the word is *consultants.* We try to find persons who are external to our situation to tell us what we are doing wrong and how to fix our problems. (When the consultants fail to give us the answers, we then run to Japan for the solution!)

The fact is, the solution to most employee-manager, worker-worker or manager-manager problems lies within the organization, not without. The answer lies in the way that employees at all levels of the organization treat one another—which brings us squarely to the fundamentals of Theory R.

## THEORY R AT WORK

Think about a recent confrontation you have experienced or witnessed.

What happened to the value you felt as a person during the confrontation?

# The Fundamentals of Theory R

4

**T**heory R has five fundamental concepts. They work together, each vital to the other. Furthermore, they are progressive. Although we will be expanding upon each fundamental concept as the book progresses, we have listed them in summary for easy reference and as an introductory overview.

**CONCEPT #1
The
Fundamental
Motivation and
Guideline:
Doing What
Is Right**

***Doing what is right*** is a power—a drive—that when released

- transforms and redirects natural human energy.
- is extremely valuable, although money cannot buy it.
- is other-directed, not inward-directed.
- is at the heart of any individual's "doing more than what is expected."
- paves the way for the establishment and the growth of relationships.

It is the fundamental motivation for and guideline of Theory R. In other words, it is the overall attitude that must exist for Theory R to work. Any other motivation becomes manipulative.

The Theory R manager does what is right for one reason alone—because it is the right thing to do!

**CONCEPT #2**
**The**
**Fundamental**
**Principle:**
**Building**
**Relationships**

What happens as the result of doing the right thing to and for other people? Relationships are built.

Theory R calls for every person within an organization to view every other person in that organization as a person with whom a relationship is desirable and with whom a relationship can be built.

This is not to say that presidents and line workers will become buddies, or that managers and employees will immediately begin to socialize with one another. Factors such as proximity, neighborhoods, mutual experiences, and mutual likes and dislikes play a part in how close any two people can become as friends.

It is to say that if both parties are doing the right thing by each other, there is no reason why a relationship should not be desired or achieved.

*What is the hallmark of a relationship? A mutual recognition of the other person's worth.*

When relationships are at the core of what you desire in your life, you will become much more sensitive to people. You'll begin to see their needs, feel their hurts, be aware of their struggles, know something about their families and their history, share experiences with them (which results in sharing memories with them), talk to them, and rejoice with them in moments of victory or personal triumph.

Even before my wife, Nancy, and I were married, we made a decision that we would not leave our home city of Pittsburgh. We decided that we would remain Pittsburghers—that we would build a relationship with the people of our city. We've attended the same church for more than forty years. Many of our friends and associates are ones we've had for that long and longer.

Relationships are at the core of our Value of the Person—Theory R Seminar team. Lefty Scumaci and I have been friends for more than thirty-three years; Reid Carpenter and Tony Campolo, who frequently speak at our seminars, are men with whom we've been in relationship for eighteen and fifteen years, respectively.

Relationship is more than just knowing someone. Relationship is sharing something of yourself with the other person.

Too often, we believe, people are too quick to give up on relationships or to think that they can trade them in on a better one. The fact is, the person who goes from relationship to relationship never has any relationships.

A relationship requires a mutual responsibility for keeping it going. The primary responsibility for a relationship, however, rests with the person who is perceived to have the greater authority. This holds true both at home and at work. The primary responsibility for the relationships within a family rests with the parents, not the children. The parents have the authority to set the tone and create the atmosphere in which healthy and satisfying relationships occur. If the relationship between the parents is rocky, the entire family will be kept off balance.

In the workplace, the primary responsibility for a relationship rests with management. Managers must create the environment in which relationships can flourish.

Once established, however, both parties must take a share of responsibility in keeping a relationship alive. A relationship is not a one-way street. It must be marked by mutuality.

Show us a company that's strong and we'll show you a company where the relationships among various employees in that company are strong. Show us a company that's weak, or weakening, and we'll show you one where there's strife or conflict or where a majority of the people are new to one another and relationships haven't had time to build.

## CONCEPT #3 The Fundamental Goal: Reconciliation

If the fundamental principle is one of building relationships, the fundamental goal is that those relationships be healthy and strong. That requires reconciliation.

People sometimes ask us, "Why is confrontation wrong?" It's wrong because it alienates. It compromises, diminishes, or destroys relationships.

Confrontation drives a wedge between two people. It separates. Persons in an argument know that they are moving farther apart the longer and more heated the argument becomes. What do we do when we reconcile with a spouse? We kiss and make up. We draw closer. We reconcile the differences that have pushed us apart.

### Reconciliation must be:

- *genuine*. Just saying you're sorry doesn't mean that you are. Actions must support words.
- *ongoing*. Disagreements may arise, but if they arise in the framework of understanding that the relationship will go on and that reconciliation will emerge at the end of a disagree-

ment, the overall direction of the relationship will be one of harmony and growth.

• *mutual.* It isn't enough for one person to admit a fault, offer an apology, or extend a hand of friendship. The desire for reconciliation must be mutual for both parties in the relationship.

Reconciliation must be desired because a relationship is desired. It must be rooted in *right* behaviors.

**CONCEPT #4**
**The**
**Fundamental**
**Response:**
**Responsibility**
**by Everyone**

Theory R calls clearly for each member of an organization, family, or community to take responsibility for personal actions toward others. It is not up to the other person to express value first. It's up to you.

Value of the Person is not a trickle-down attitude. Value of the Person behaviors can and should flow freely in all directions within a workplace, home, or city—up, down, and laterally.

Theory R does not require management initiative. It can begin any place within an organization.

**CONCEPT #5**
**The**
**Fundamental**
**By-Product:**
**Positive Results**

When the fundamental motivation and guideline is doing what is *right* and the fundamental principle is building good *relationships* and the fundamental goal is bringing about *reconciliation* and the fundamental response on the part of everyone is *responsibility,* the by-product will be positive *results* for all persons involved.

It is critically important that you recognize one key element about these results. They are not the beginning point for Theory R. They are the end point. They are not the motivation. They are the automatic outflow of the process.

In many ways, we wish there were no need to speak of results. It's too easy for a person to say, "Aha! We're back to the bottom line." Or for a person to say, "I like these results. Let's see, to get them I just need to bring about reconciliation, and to do that I just need to value my people, work on relationships"—backtracking up the chain of concepts but with the overriding thought, *What can I get out of this?*

The motivation behind Theory R isn't what you'll get. It's in why you act the way you do to others. ***The motivation for Theory R is doing the right thing.***

When you do the right thing, however, you'll build relationships. You'll seek reconciliation. And when you do that, you *will* get results. We prefer to call them by-products because the implication is one of inevitability. They are part and parcel of doing the right thing.

***What are the by-products?***

The foremost one is ***growth.***

Growth in personal relationships is sometimes described as deeper or stronger. We frequently comment that a friendship is growing deeper or that a marriage is growing stronger. In the workplace, growth manifests itself not only in stronger bonds among employees at all levels but in increases of other types:

- Growth of output—or increased productivity
- Growth of excellence—or increased quality
- Growth of participation—or increased presenteeism or group morale

When a relationship is reconciled, a flow of energy begins between the two people that affects other relationships. Reconciliation between two people can result in reconciliation between two departments or between two divisions. It can cause others to want to reconcile. In other words, it's contagious.

Theory R sets up a win-win situation. In true reconciliation, each person wins. In a broader sense, when employees and managers are reconciled, winning is also mutual. That winning mind-set compels the growth.

We see reconciled people growing in their abilities to produce more, produce better, and be more willing to be part of the team process because they are made to feel like winners.

In a win-win situation in which both parties feel like winners, the outcome is high morale. And high morale causes people to want to grow, to pursue growth, and to relish in growth.

This growth is virtually unlimited. It can be measured, but it rarely can be forecasted effectively. In virtually all cases we know, managers who have implemented Theory R and have begun to put Value of the Person principles into effect have experienced results that were far greater than they initially expected.

How great can a friendship be? How strong can a marriage be? The answer can't be calculated. The same is true for the growth in a factory or an office in which reconciled relationships are at the core of the organization.

Again, the lofty, desired, and grand result of growth begins with the planting of a vital seed: doing what is right.

# THEORY R AT WORK

For which of these five concepts—doing what is right, building relationships, reconciliation, responsibility by everyone, positive results—do you believe you have the greatest understanding at the present time?

Write a few of your opinions for each *R* word:

- Right
- Relationship
- Reconciliation
- Responsibility
- Results

Think about an incident in your life where someone did what was RIGHT in a problem situation. What kinds of by-products resulted? How did they affect relationships and attitudes?

# Doing the Right Thing

5

**D**oing what is right takes many different forms. Very often a manager must first determine what is wrong, but what is wrong may also vary. And sometimes what is wrong is not the most obvious thing.

At Pittron, the most obvious thing that was wrong to the casual observer may have been that it was a filthy place to work.

The foundry covered seven blocks along the banks of the Monongahela River on the edge of Glassport just south of Pittsburgh. Inside, the foundry resonated with loud sirens from overhead cranes, the clanging of chippers' hammers, the rumble of rolling cars, and the reverberations from riveting machines.

The light that managed to filter in through the soot-covered windows high on the outside walls at Pittron managed to cast only a twilight look on the foundry's interior. The floors were nearly always strewn with cigarette butts and wrappers, discarded soup cans, and other odd bits of litter. The air was filled with the acrid smell of sulfur and grease.

But the darkness of Pittron's physical appearance was not the real problem. It was not at the core of what was wrong. The real wrong was not any one specific item on the latest set of labor demands. The real issues were matters of trust and value—

*not* factors related to wages, benefits, or other statistical standards:

---

- "Many times when I came in here I wanted to punch a foreman in the mouth."
- "Best a black man could do was chipping. Make a long story short—all the dirty work."
- "We were considered second-class citizens."
- "I was considered a bum. They made me that way."
- "It was a jungle."
- "If I had a little grievance and wanted to talk it out, they would tell you no before you even opened your mouth."
- "You walked past the boss. He didn't care if he talked to you or not. Drop his head. You were nothing."*

---

To me, those expressions by the workers at Pittron were symbols of a deeper-seated emotional current. They were saying, "We are being treated with indignity and disrespect, as if we are of no value. How can we trust you—indeed, why would we want to be in a relationship with you—when you treat us so poorly?"

Their words were backed up by symbolic actions that had very real meaning: high absenteeism, poor quality, and a massively high number of formal labor grievances.

What is the antidote?

Actions that become symbols of an opposite attitude!

Consider for a moment a marriage that has gone bad. Angry words—or stone silence—are acted out. Property or personal belongings might be damaged or destroyed. Behavior is exhibited that conveys the message, "I don't want to be around you," or "I don't like you." The deep underlying feelings driving the words and actions are ones of distrust and a loss of feeling valued.

One evening of candles, roses, and a moonlight stroll doesn't erase years of pain and aggravation, but the direction of a marriage can change in one evening of candles, roses, and moonlight if one or both persons truly express a deep inner change or desire for love to bloom again.

As vice president of operations at Pittron, I was determined to

---

*These are actual comments recorded by Robin Miller, a documentary filmmaker—comments made by workers about Pittron in the film *Miracle of Pittron*.

engage in symbolic actions that would signal a change in the direction of our attitude toward doing what was right.

## Symbolic Actions Send Strong Signals

*Symbolic actions arise from answers to questions such as these:*

- What might I do to send a signal that I desire a fresh start in a relationship?
- What more might I do to convey that I value this person?
- What might I do to communicate respect of this person?
- What might I do to initiate a change in the way I treat this person?
- How would I like to be treated?

A symbolic action arises from an innermost attitude. It expresses a true feeling—in the case of Theory R, a true feeling of value, affirmation, dignity, and respect.

*A symbolic act is doing what is meaningful to the other person—taking a step that the other person perceives as reflecting a positive, genuine move.*

Symbolic acts are real behaviors—real actions, real words. They embody and thus symbolize the intent of the heart.

Symbolic acts vary from setting to setting, person to person. There are no pat behaviors. On the other hand, a symbolic act is nearly always understood on a universal level as being positive and appropriate.

Here are some examples of symbolic actions I chose to take at Pittron:

- I positioned myself at the company gate during shift changes and offered my hand to any worker who would shake it. Not every one would shake my hand, but I personally thanked each one who shook my hand for the day's work.
- I stayed an hour after the day shift went home so that I could greet people who worked the second shift. Frequently, I came to work an hour earlier than the day shift so that I could spend a little time with people who were coming off the midnight shift. I sent a signal that I valued the work of all shifts equally. Periodically, I visited the other shifts during their work period.

- I made a decision to learn the names and something about each of the slightly more than three hundred employees who were at the plant at that time.
- I began walking through the plant daily, stopping to chat with various workers. I became highly visible.
- I sprayed my manager's white hard hat black, the color of the workers' hats.
- I gave the union president, the leader on the floor, a real office, not just the cab on his crane.
- Unlike many who claim they have an open-door policy, I truly created an open-door policy. Employees knew that I would receive them and hear them out.

All of the acts sent a strong and immediate signal that I was intent on seeing a turnaround in attitude, one of valuing all employees and upholding the dignity of each employee, no matter what the position.

Perhaps one of the most potent symbolic actions that I chose to demonstrate happened spontaneously the day I attempted chipping.

**Trying My Hand as a Chipper**

Chippers have one of the most difficult jobs in a foundry. Their work is dirty, and it requires brute strength and endurance. A chipper uses a large chipping hammer—like a jackhammer—that weighs about thirty pounds to chip away defects from large steel castings. Some of these castings weigh up to three hundred thousand pounds and are the size of a small house. A steel defect on the casting may be quite sizable, and no easy task to chip away.

I said to the man I was watching, "Hey, Deacon, what are you doing?"

He responded curtly, "Chippin'." The obvious had been stated.

"Looks like hard work," I said, determined to communicate with him.

He gave me a weary glance and said, "It is."

I said, "Let me have a crack at it."

I removed my suit coat, rolled up my sleeves, and climbed onto the casting. Then I asked for his hammer, which he handed over in disbelief. He watched, stunned, as I hammered furiously for all of three minutes, making very little progress at chipping steel but working up quite a sweat. Gasping for breath, I finally gave up and handed the hammer back to him. I asked, "How much money do you get paid for this job?" Deacon told me, and I said with a sigh and a handshake, "This is tough work. You earn every cent the company pays you."

Within five minutes every man on that floor had heard what I had done. By being willing to walk in the moccasins of one worker for just a few minutes, I had dignified the least respected task in that plant. I might as well have been a surgeon cleaning a bedpan or a bank president sweeping out a washroom.

For many, the demonstration of symbolic acts is a risky matter. It means stepping into the realm of the uncomfortable—trying something new, doing something that alters perceptions and reputations.

In nearly all cases, however, the bold, gutsy move that arises from a heart genuinely intent on expressing value is greeted with admiration and gratefulness.

## A Symbolic Act Is No Less Real

Through symbolic acts, you send signals indicating your motivation and intent to convey love, dignity, and respect. They stand for—or are examples of—what you really think and feel. They are not insincere.

Symbolic acts are unexpected. Because of that, they stand out. They have added meaning because they draw attention to themselves. They actually raise the consciousness level of those who see them and respond to them.

As in all Value of the Person principles, symbolic acts must be rooted in a desire to do the right thing. They are acts intended not to manipulate but to convey an attitude of genuine valuing.

The genuine nature of a symbolic act is directly related to a leader's overall quest for excellence. The leader who desires maximum performance, the best operational policies and procedures, perfect quality, and the greatest productivity possible should also seek excellence in relationships. Just as the corporate leader does the utmost to exact from others what is required for economic success, so the leader should be willing to require what is necessary for personal relationships in the work, home, and community environments to be rooted in personal affirmation, dignity, and respect—even if it requires personal risk, a willingness to change, and a commitment to try the previously untried.

Symbolic acts tend to have two highly divergent results: the rank-

and-file employees tend to love them, but the palace guards tend to hate them.

## Getting Past the Palace Guards

There's a group of people in just about every organization that the top-level manager must reckon with. We call them the *palace guards.*

Palace guards are persons in management who choose to consciously insulate the top person from the heartbeat of the organization—they tell the leader what they want him to know. They block contact with the people. They do not permit the people to get to the leader but through them. They neutralize the top person by making him believe he can't do without them. They are into power and control. They don't want change, and they don't want Theory R management. They are afraid to give up power.

They can be the administrators, managers, assistants, bureaucrats—people in power—who tend to insulate and isolate top-level administrators from the people who do the work. They operate as gatekeepers, who let the gate swing both ways. It is generally to their political advantage to keep top-level administrators from mingling with employees and vice versa. Problems that might be solved within five minutes in a face-to-face conversation between the president of a company and a worker on the line can be tied up for months in round after round of meetings and memos.

The reason for having the palace guards, of course, is primarily one of time. Top-level administrators don't have the time that they might like to spend with each employee. Tradition also has its place. Employees have frequently been trained to be uncomfortable around top-level administrators. Thus, the bigger the organization, the larger the cadre of palace guards tends to be.

The palace guards are not limited to corporate America. You'll find them in every church, hospital, school, social club, and union.

At Pittron, many of the symbolic actions I demonstrated resulted in my having direct contact with the frontline supervisors and the employees. Those managers who were palace guards weren't comfortable with my non-conventional style, circumventing at times the organizational chart. I intuitively understood, however, that if the company was to succeed we had to reach the heart of the organization. I forged ahead and chose to walk among the people and to identify the needs of the rank-and-file employees and the frontline supervisors.

We've encountered numerous executives who are neutralized by their palace guards. They are afraid to ruffle the feathers of their subordinates for fear of upsetting the organizational etiquette entrenched in so many organizations. The results are ongoing isolation, status quo and an inability to effect real change. At Pittron, I refused to be intimidated by my palace guards.

One of the foremost actions that I took—and it upset the palace guards a great deal—involved Pittron's supply of gasoline.

## Free Gasoline Just for the Asking

Pennsylvania—as many areas—was hit hard by our nation's gasoline shortage in 1973. Within weeks, we became aware that a number of Pittron employees with excellent attendance records were having difficulty getting to work because they lacked access to fuel.

We had substantial gasoline reserves at the foundry, and I made a decision that was actually one of the easiest, fastest, and best of any I made at Pittron: "Beginning today, we'll make free gasoline available to any employee who needs it to get to work."

My palace guards fought the decision vehemently. The objections were voiced in the form of questions:

- "Who will monitor this to make sure the gasoline is distributed fairly?" Answer: Nobody. We'll distribute gasoline on an honor system. No one will keep track of who gets what. We won't ask any questions.
- "How will we distribute the gasoline?" Answer: Workers will request what they need. We'll give them what they request as long as our supply lasts.
- "Why not sell them the gasoline?" Answer: Absenteeism costs us more than gasoline. We'll give it away.
- "What if someone abuses the system?" Answer: We'll deal with that if it arises.

The employees also questioned the new directive. One of them said, "If you think we're going to pay one dollar a gallon for gasoline, you're crazy." The automatic assumption was made that management was out to take advantage of the employees. (The going rate for gasoline was thirty-one cents a gallon.) They could hardly believe that the gasoline was being made available free.

When employees asked, "Why are you doing this?" I responded, "Why not?"

More than one manager said to me, "This is going to cost us a lot of money."

Looking back, we found the facts showed just the opposite. We spent far less on gasoline than we would have lost in production had our employees not been able to get to work.

Those who feared the "give an inch, take a mile" syndrome were proven wrong. So were those who thought that management was becoming soft or that riots would occur with mobs of workers fighting for gas.

The flow of gasoline was an amazing thing to watch. Some employees requested one gallon or two gallons or five gallons. A few requested a fill-up but then used that gasoline to travel to and from work for two weeks. The employees requested what they truly needed. A few of the workers were so low on gas they ran out before they reached the pumps and had to be pushed the final few yards.

The worst fear, however, did come to pass. Pittron ran out of gas. One of my colleagues came bursting into my office one day with the news: "It happened. We ran out of gas. Now what do we do?"

I didn't have a good answer, but fortunately, I didn't need one. The phone rang at precisely that moment, and the voice on the other end asked, "Are you the guy giving away free gasoline to your employees?"

"Yes," I said.

"Look, I have two thousand gallons of gas on hand. Do you want them?"

Those were sweet words. We replenished our supply, and by the time we needed gasoline again, the national shortage had eased to the point that free gas was no longer needed.

In all, we gave away about six thousand gallons. In their place emerged a corps of people with much higher morale.

What kind of message was sent to the employees?

We value your presence here. We need you. We're counting on you. We're doing everything we know to do to help you do the job we all need for you to be doing. Freely sharing the company's gasoline with its employees was the right thing to do.

In one organization, an employee experienced a fire in her apartment, and she lost most of her personal belongings. The people in her department banded together, and within days, her fellow employees and the managers had provided all of the essentials she needed: sheets, towels, cooking utensils, and so forth. Some gave furniture; others, cash to help restock her cupboards. The company even went to its warehouse of office furniture to see what might be given to her. They were doing the right thing for those circumstances.

In another situation, a young man received word that his mother was gravely ill in New Zealand, thousands of miles away from his current home and place of employment. His fellow employees and the managers passed the hat to help him purchase a ticket home, and the company suspended its vacation policy to allow him to take two additional vacation days in advance of his earning them.

In yet another situation, a frontline supervisor became seriously ill with what is now defined as chronic fatigue syndrome. She was unable to stay at work longer than four hours at a time. Her superiors allowed her to work flextime, and they encouraged her to take the time off she needed to recover her health. For nearly six months, other supervisors and managers pitched in to help with her workload. They were doing the right thing.

There's no set formula for determining when something is right. There are as many variations on the theme as there are individuals and circumstances. The amazing thing, however, is that virtually everybody knows when the right thing is being done by a person. A universal sense of fair play and generosity manifests itself if given the opportunity. A manager who questions whether something is the right thing to do for an employee need only sincerely ask some of the other workers. They'll have an answer, and in nearly every case, they'll be right.

**Doing the Right Thing Takes Many Forms**

We all know when things aren't right. We may not be able to describe what is wrong or tell why, but we have a feeling that it's wrong. We collectively know some things are wrong:

**What *Isn't* Right—Seeing the Group and Not the Individual**

- Being dishonest
- Lying
- Stealing

- Abusing
- Exhibiting uncontrolled anger

These behaviors are subject to human will—not just a collective will but a very personal will. A dishonest group is made of dishonest individuals. An angry mob begins with one angry person. What's right and wrong comes down to the individual level very quickly.

Theory R speaks directly to the person. It is not something that aims to influence only a segment of an organization or a department, division, or management layer. It is not a group-oriented theory. Rather, it is a concept that directly involves, relates to, and depends on the recognition of the individual. Again, this focus on the person is not a focus on the boss or the leader. It is on each person as a person, not as a title—such as manager, laborer, executive, white collar, blue collar, union boss, or any other title.

"How," a manager may ask, "can I address individual issues when I have a hundred people for whom I'm responsible?"

**THEORY R SAYS,**

*Do what's right for the person. It will invariably be what's right for the group.*

Value of the Person behavior is a perspective, an attitude, a style of living—not a format or formula. In each person's life, numerous windows of opportunity for giving an affirmative word or doing an affirmative deed present themselves each day. That word or deed may be to the secretary every day, a janitor one day and a mail delivery person the next, the boss one week, and a sick employee the next. Look for moments that arise in the normal flow of each day. Be aware of people you encounter as part of your daily routine. Regard each encounter with an employee as an opportunity to give a word or take an action that expresses value.

**Team Recognition Doesn't Replace the Need for Individual Recognition**

In our years of doing Value of the Person—Theory R Seminars in major corporations across this country, we've found that a number of the managers who are interested in introducing their employees to Theory R have already tried one or more other programs designed to improve morale in their operations.

Most of these programs are aimed at involving employees in a group process, such as self-directed work teams. The thinking seems to be that if employees have an opportunity to voice opinions and be a part of a team, they will think more highly of their jobs. To a certain extent, this thinking is valid.

What's often askew, however, is the underlying belief that if people are involved in teams, they will automatically feel they are more valuable. That isn't always the case. (Just ask any third-string football player who warms a bench. He may take a little pride in a team's victory, but he certainly wouldn't feel nearly the pride felt by his first-string colleagues who scored the points and made the great defensive plays of the game.) Just being a part of a team isn't what counts—being made a *valuable* member of the team is what counts.

If you are a manager or executive, don't assume that just by naming a committee, appointing a task force, or setting up a quality performance group, you are going to be expressing value to the individual employees named to that group. In some cases, employees are going to feel as if you've given them just one more thing for which they are responsible—just one more area in which they might fail.

What tends to be even more wrong is the undergirding motivation: *why* management wants to include employees. Generally, the reason is so that morale will improve, employees will feel more involved, they'll be more loyal to the company, they'll be more concerned about quality, they'll work harder to achieve goals, and so forth. The reasons are bottom-line motivated.

Nearly all people programs in corporations are result-driven. Managers see a need for better results, and they attempt to use or manipulate employees into participation to get those results.

One way to identify this motivation is to observe the frequency of programs that come and go in an organization. If the programs don't work—which means if they don't produce the results that management desires—the programs generally are dismantled or replaced, or they fall into disrepute. The eye is always on the bottom line and the impact that the programs are having on productivity, quality, and the generation of profit. Programs that fail to produce according to the standards preset by management are eliminated.

Theory R takes a radically different approach.

Theory R doesn't call for managers to begin to show value as some type of manipulation or gimmick that will affect the bottom line favorably. To be sure, we feel confident the bottom line will always be affected in a positive way but as a by-product. It is not the motivation driving the theory. The motivation is person-driven.

Becoming person-oriented is a style of leadership—a style that not only can be but must be transmitted to others around you.

**THEORY R SAYS,**

*Be concerned about and involve your employees solely because it's the right thing to do. Period.*

We come now to a critical question: What *is* the right thing to do for an individual? Is there anything that we know is always the right thing to do for every person? It is *always* right to value another person and to show love, dignity, and respect.

# THEORY R AT WORK

Can you name at least three actions that you can take immediately to show your fellow employees that you value them?

Is there a specific wrong you can name that needs righting?

# Always Right: 6
# Valuing the
# Person

**A**s I look back on my years in operations at Pittron, I recognize that Sam Piccolo and I didn't agree on management or union matters. We didn't agree on politics. We didn't dare discuss church affiliation. We didn't play the same games, hang around with the same crowd, go to the same places, or live in the same neighborhood. At times, it seemed as if we didn't even speak the same language.

The same things hold true in virtually every organization across our nation. People doing the work and people managing the work very often have different interests, purposes, and goals.

Yet even as Sam and I found a basis for agreement, so, too, have countless others—whether waiters and restaurant owners, janitors and building engineers, or rocket scientists and laboratory vice presidents. The three points of agreement are the same:

- Both want to be loved.
- Both want to be treated with dignity.
- Both want to be respected for who they are and for what they have accomplished in their lives.

Love, dignity, and respect are the three basic elements required for the growth and development of the human personality. Woven into every human relationship, whether in the workplace or in any other area of life, is the desire to have others acknowledge and affirm our presence, appreciate the fruits of our labor, and recognize and respond to the contributions we make.

*Love, dignity,* and *respect* are not considered to be respectable business terms. Nevertheless, they are critical terms for creating a successful environment for any business we've ever encountered.

---

**I Learned About Value from a Guy Named Red**

Where did I learn perhaps the most potent lesson in my life about what it means to value a person? From a guy named Red. He taught me more about the value of the person in a more dramatic way than anybody else in my life.*

In February 1945, as an eighteen-year-old green recruit panting for action, I found myself at the front line of the European initiative. We were at Colmar in the Alsace-Lorraine region of France, our ranks significantly thinned by heavy artillery bombardment from 88's (88 millimeter cannon shells).

The company commander called an assembly and said to us, "I need a point man."

All around me, men shuffled their feet in embarrassed silence, hoping someone would volunteer. To be a point man was to accept one of the most dangerous assignments of war, a job that had one of the shortest life expectancies of any job in the infantry.

Point men served their units as advance scouts. They would isolate themselves from the main body of soldiers, moving in front of the troops to observe, penetrate, and probe the placement of enemy combat and reconnaissance patrols. Point men were usually considered guys who had more guts than brains. They were the first exposed to enemy activity and were prime targets for enemy sniper fire.

The job, however dangerous, is also critical. A point man becomes the eyes and ears of a group. If a patrol or platoon can't trust their scout, their commitment falters.

The commander repeated his statement: "I need a point man." And I volunteered, "I'll go."

*Much of the material here on the war was excerpted from *Stronger Than Steel,* written by Dr. R. C. Sproul.

Charles "Red" Preston volunteered as second scout to back me up, reluctantly to say the least. "You're crazy! Why did you volunteer? Now I have to do it, too. If you go, I go."

Red and I were friends. Red was a wiry redhead who drew girls like a magnet because he radiated such life and vitality. He was fun loving, but he had very carefully thought-out opinions. Red was the first soldier I met when I came to the front, along with Lt. Will Barbour, Billy Weaver, and Joe Stankowski. He taught me lots of tricks of survival.

"Point men out!" With that command, Red and I would push our way into enemy territory. I'd go out farther than the commander required just to gain the respect of the older, more seasoned soldiers in our unit. And for several weeks, Red and I went out almost daily (or nightly) and made it safely back unharmed. Once we were shot at as we paddled our tiny rubber raft across the Rhine. Numerous times we were close enough to enemy soldiers to hear the tinny sound that their rifles made as they clanked against their belts. A close call with a grenade had left me trembling. Both of us had smelled death, had seen bloated bodies, and had experienced our moments of inflicting death. But at no time did either of us request to be called off point.

Red and I valued each other as friends. We were a team.

In March 1945, our unit had advanced forward into German territory, and by midmonth, we were facing the dreaded Siegfried Line. Billy and Joe had been killed the night before.

The Siegfried Line was the first line of defense for the Third Reich, and it was awesome. The outer perimeter was lined with solid concrete barriers that barred the path of tanks or other armored vehicles. The concrete pillars were called dragon's teeth. Backing them up was a complex maze of deep trenches arranged in a zigzag fashion. The trenches were manned by German infantrymen backed up by elements of the elite Seventeenth S.S. Panzer Division. At strategic points along the Siegfried Line, carefully engineered pillboxes provided a base for machine-gun and artillery fire against any soldiers who attempted to attack on foot.

The only way to get through the barrier effectively was by means of hand-to-hand combat. Red and I knew that. We also knew we would be at the head of the charge as point men.

The night before our scheduled assault against the Siegfried Line,

I had a premonition that it would be my last day in combat, although I really wasn't sure if I would die. Red felt no such ambiguity. He felt sure he was going to die. We talked into the night, and we made the customary foxhole vow to each other that if either of us was killed and the other survived, the survivor would visit the other's family after the war.

As the sun burned away the mist the next morning, we heard the words, "Scouts out!" and Red and I broke out of the forest in a run, our company following close behind. Expecting a barrage of bullets, we were surprised to be greeted by silence. When the storm of battle finally broke, the shelling was deafening. Rifle and machine-gun fire from the trenches was so intense that dust and metal fragments hurled around me. I was hit in the thigh as I ran, but what I instantly had feared as a mortal wound turned out to be a wound in my canteen! It wasn't blood soaking my pant leg; it was water. The moment of comic relief was short-lived.

Red and I made it past the dragon's teeth. Firing our machine guns wildly, we jumped into the end of a trench. We were joined by a handful of other GIs who had also made it across the open field. Our intrusion into the trench isolated us from the rest of our battalion, and we quickly realized that we were alone. Our radio had been knocked out in the firefight. In other words, help was *not* on its way. Peering over the lip of the trench would have been suicide. We knew that German machine gunners and snipers already had their weapons trained on our ragged remnant of Company B. Furthermore, we knew that the other end of the trench was occupied by Germans. We were facing a standoff and most likely a deadly counterattack.

We had three options, equally deadly. We could attempt to retreat back across the field we had just crossed. The likelihood of surviving two trips across that field was very slim. We could wait for help, which might never come. Or we could attack the other end of the trench in an effort to take the entire trench.

We chose option three, the only one that offered any real hope of our coming out of the day alive. Our goal was to conquer the trench, come out the other end, then outflank the pillboxes and knock them out of commission.

We started our march through the trench. I was on point, backed up by Red and Barbour. We felt as if we were waging war in a tunnel.

We knew that only I could dare fire my weapon. They were backing me up with grenades.

We began to move through the trench, winning precious yard by precious yard. Red and Barbour lobbed grenades over my head, and then I followed with bursts from my machine gun. We quickly realized that spider trenches had been cut as branches into the main zigzag line. We knew that ambush could await us at any turn. Even so, we pressed forward, forcing the enemy to retreat deeper and deeper into the labyrinth.

Instinct told me that the Germans were retreating too quickly and that we were being sucked into a trap, but we had no alternative but to keep moving forward. It was obvious that the Germans were mounting a counterattack to overrun our position and we were the only ones in a position to keep them from succeeding. Furthermore, the only way to stop them was to move forward and to attack.

A fierce firefight erupted that resulted in many German casualties. The Germans began to retreat.*

Then suddenly, I found myself staring into the eyes of a German soldier. We both froze. The German was a big man, his rifle trained on my head, and in his hand, he held a grenade with the pin already pulled.

Within an instant, the German threw the grenade, and with little regard for it, I instinctively responded with a spray of machine-gun fire. The German crumpled to his death, and I found myself staring at a grenade I couldn't escape. I literally watched it explode in my face. I can still recall the heat emanating from its epicenter, the shrapnel flying toward my face in what seemed like hideous slow motion.

When the shrapnel hit, I felt as if my brain exploded. And yet, somehow I realized I was still standing, still conscious, still alive. Numb, stunned, disoriented, I stood there with blood gushing from my head. Red rushed toward me, and with the gentlest of bear hugs, he turned his back to the enemy and embraced me, shielding my body with his own. Red had moved to point position.

Red didn't say a word, but his eyes spoke volumes, "Don't be afraid. I won't leave you."

*The details of this military action have been documented by Private First Class Daniel Parisi. Because of Wayne Alderson's heroism in combat, he has been recommended for the Medal of Honor.

He never saw the bullet coming. Death was so quick for Red that he probably never felt it. A bullet penetrated the back of his head, and his blood blended with mine. Red started to sink, sliding down my body, grasping my jacket, then belt, then pant leg, until he lay at my feet. When I saw the blood oozing from his head, a violent stream of crimson clashing with his bright orange hair, something inside me snapped. At that time Barbour was also killed by a sniper's bullet. I began to scramble like a wild man—clawing, crawling, and scraping my way back along the trench, shouting orders to myself to keep myself moving, until finally I turned a corner and came face-to-face with my company commander. He recoiled in horror at the sight of me and then shouted for a medic.

Miraculously for me, some of our troops had made it across the field to our trench, and they handed me from soldier to soldier like a bucket in a fire brigade, speaking words of encouragement: "We'll get 'em for you. We won't take any prisoners." I finally was passed to the medic, and within a matter of minutes, his shot of morphine took hold.

By midafternoon, the medics made a decision to attempt to evacuate the wounded back across the open field. I refused to be carried on a stretcher—a decision that turned out to be a life-saving one. No sooner had the medics started across the field with their stretcher than they were chopped to ribbons. Feeling no pain because of the morphine, I charged ahead on my own, crawling, screaming, and stumbling toward the tree line into the arms of GIs who took me by jeep to a first aid station, where an ambulance then transported me to an evacuation hospital somewhere in the interior of France.

Why am I alive today?

Because a twenty-two-year-old redheaded kid named Charles E. Preston, Jr., gave his life for me. In one split second, Red's true nature came shining through. He turned himself inside out and selflessly gave his life so that I might live. No person has ever valued me more. Nobody ever will.

## Valuing—It's Always Right Because It's Always a Need

What is so right about valuing another person? Every person has the need to be valued. It's a basic part of our humanity.

There's not a person in any organization—executive, manager, supervisor, worker—who doesn't have that need. We generally don't, however, recognize that everybody has certain intangible, emotional, human needs, or admit them openly to one another. Theory R openly recognizes that *everybody* needs and desires

- love.
- dignity.
- respect.

We value people we love, and we love people we value.

We value people when we treat them with dignity.

We value people we respect, and we respect people we value.

Love, dignity, and respect aren't words that you'll find in most management textbooks or books about business. They are words that seem more common to the bedroom than the boardroom.

Theory R contends that every person in the workforce—manager and employee—has a deep-seated human need to be loved, to be treated with dignity, and to be respected.

## The Need to Be Valued Is Universal

Human needs don't evaporate over time. They don't dissipate if ignored. If anything, human needs for love, dignity, and respect grow stronger with age. Furthermore, the needs tend to be more keenly felt the longer they go unmet.

Consider Fred, a worker who is twenty-five. He has been on his job as a medical technician for two months, and he is eager to learn his job and to be out on his own for the first time in his life. He has a need to be loved and to be shown dignity and respect by persons with whom he works. He may not even know that he has this need, but he has it nonetheless.

When his performance goes unrewarded, his accomplishments go unnoticed, his race is demeaned, or he begins to feel overlooked or used by others around him, he—like all workers—feels affronted. Fred would have no reason to feel affronted, disappointed, angry, frustrated, or otherwise miserable about the lack of reward, praise, or recognition or the occasional snide remark or slang comment if he didn't have a need to be valued and to be shown love, dignity, and respect. Why be bothered by such behavior if those things don't matter, or if they aren't really universal needs within every person?

Fred soon realizes that he isn't alone at the hospital. Joe and

Linda and Sam and Sally feel the same way. None of them likes to be overlooked, unaffirmed, mistreated, or unfairly classified. They feel hurt by ethnic jokes or demeaning language.

Bill, who is sixty and who has been employed for twenty-five years at the hospital where Fred works, can do his job as well or better than anyone else in the medical technology area. The work hours and the stress related to the job don't bother him. He enjoys putting in a full day and going home with satisfaction about a job well done. He has a strong sense that lives are improved and even spared through the work that he does.

But insult Bill, snub him, treat him unfairly, fail to reward his efforts, or fail to recognize him, and Bill is going to feel mistreated far more than Fred. Many in management might assume that because Bill has been at the hospital longer, he needs fewer positive strokes and less affirmation than the new hire, Fred. Bill's longevity and job loyalty may be misinterpreted as a tough skin, and in many organizations in which we have consulted, we see the Bills put into something of a no-need-to-pat-on-the-back category. That's not where Bill—or any employee—belongs.

The longer an employee has been with a firm or company, the *more* that employee needs to be shown love, dignity, and respect. The need grows with the passing of years and the loyalty that the employee has vested in a job well done.

Furthermore, if devaluing behavior has been going on for a long time—years, perhaps even a decade or more—an employee's need for love, dignity, and respect may have been bashed to the point that his anger and frustration turn into an inner seething hatred just waiting to erupt. In those cases, the need for love, dignity, and respect hasn't gone away. It has only gone underground.

## THEORY R SAYS,

*Managers and employees do not and should not leave their basic human instincts, needs, and desires for love, dignity, and respect behind when they show up for work.*

*People need to be valued. They need love, dignity, and respect to be shown to them.*

*Because these needs are basic to everyone, actions aimed at meeting these needs are always right.*

## Feelings Gone Underground

Human needs cannot be legislated away, dismissed with a new procedure, or overcome with an ingenuous gesture. But most traditional managers refuse to face the facts about the needs for love, dignity, and respect.

Most traditional managers also refuse to recognize that human needs drive human behavior. When certain basic human needs aren't being met, behavior turns sour and becomes disruptive. And such behavior affects work performance and morale. Maybe not today but definitely sometime in the future.

Ask yourself, "Do I feel a need for love, dignity, and respect in my life? How do I feel when I'm not given those basics in a relationship? Doesn't everybody feel that same way?"

## People Are Hungry to Be Valued

Sometimes people in a business are so hungry to hear someone speak to them about value, they'll endure extreme situations.

At the height of the 1992 L.A. riots, in the aftermath of the Rodney King verdict, we were conducting a Value of the Person—Theory R Seminar at a major manufacturing plant in Compton, just south of Los Angeles. The hotel where we were conducting the seminar had been set up as something of a command central by the police, who were facing a major problem with sniper fire in the surrounding community.

What a contrast! Outside, the world seemed to be degenerating into conflict and hatred. Inside, we were talking about love, dignity, and respect. Outside, the value of the person was dropping like a lead balloon. Inside, the value of the person was being elevated to its proper position.

At the end of the first day, we questioned whether we should continue with the second day of the seminar, but we decided to forge ahead. The next day we lost our lights in the ballroom, and we moved out into the lobby area where we could take advantage of natural sunlight. We also lost our air-conditioning; it was a hot day so the heat built up inside the building.

As sirens wailed by outside, we could almost feel the people inside clench, wondering if the police, ambulances, or fire engines were on the way to their neighborhood, their block, their homes. The sponsoring company announced permission to its workers that they could leave if they had serious concerns about the safety of their families. Only a handful left. That was a strong indicator to us about how much the people wanted to hear about the value of the person. People are desperate to hear that their need for value is valid.

If the need for value is so universal, why do we see so little evidence of value for the person in the workplace?

## Why Is Valuing So Difficult?

As much as people desire to be valued, not everybody chooses to give value to others, to give it openly, or to give it in an unqualified way. Why? Most likely because we're afraid of losing something.

We're afraid that people may perceive us as being less strong, less capable, less sure of ourselves, less in control. We suspect we may be accused of groveling.

Those fears are unfounded 99.9 percent of the time. The person who is truly capable of valuing others and expressing that value in a genuine, honest way is nearly always a strong person, and a person who is receiving high-value statements and behavior from someone else.

A sense of valuing, therefore, can spread through a company person by person by person. But it takes one person to begin that process. And it takes another person willing to receive that person's statements of value and then to pass them on to others.

Valuing others isn't difficult. ***Expressing*** value for others is.

## Conducting a Personal Inventory

Take stock of your relationships today—those you have at work, at home, in your neighborhood, and in groups to which you belong:

- Are you expressing value for others?
- How are you expressing value?
- What more might you do?

Value of the Person principles require an ongoing commitment. Nobody ever affirms continually, upholds dignity always, or expresses respect perfectly. The goal of even greater excellence must always be pursued as an individual and as an organization. This requires true intentionality. Theory R must be made to happen, day in, day out, month in, month out.

One must choose daily to value others. The alternative is not a void but a negative: to devalue.

## Thinking the Right Thing Is Not *Doing* the Right Thing

Valuing others is not a matter of thinking. It's a matter of doing.

Theory R doesn't merely call for employees to think their peers are valuable. It doesn't challenge managers only to think workers are worthy of love, dignity, and respect.

Theory R calls for action.

It calls for managers and workers to:

- do the loving thing.
- do the respectful thing.
- do what upholds the dignity of a person.

Thinking requires only awareness and an adjustment in attitude and feeling.

Action requires courage. It means putting your reputation on the line for someone else, putting yourself between a bullet and a friend, putting another person's needs before your own.

Theory R challenges every person in every organization, institution, or relationship to *do* the right thing, not just think about it.

## THEORY R AT WORK

Is there a person who has truly made you feel valuable? How did that person convey value to you?

Are you a person who is conveying love, dignity, and respect to others?

- If so, in what ways?
- If not, can you isolate the fears that keep you from doing so? What more might you do?

# 7 The Most Revolutionary Concept in the Business World: Love

**T**o demonstrate truly loving behavior, actions need to be marked by these two traits: steadfastness and without condition.

*Steadfast love is love that is constant over time.* Your willingness to care for a fellow employee should rise above circumstances, moods, or any other fluctuation experienced in the workplace.

Do you cease to love a person because she is promoted into another department? Do you fail to care for a person because you don't feel like love on a particular day? Do you quit communicating with a person because he has started wearing flamboyant ties? If so, your love for the person isn't steadfast.

*Unconditional love is "nevertheless" love.* It says, "I love you in spite of"—or nevertheless—in spite of your bad mood, in spite of your change in circumstances, in spite of your color, sex, race, nationality, religion, age, or cultural differences. If your love is contingent on a person's willingness to conform to your idea of perfection, it isn't unconditional love.

We all desire to experience steadfast and unconditional love. Most of us find it difficult, however, to give love in this manner. Giving love of this quality requires that we genuinely care—that our loving behavior isn't an act but is truly an expression of the heart.

Giving steadfast, unconditional love also requires that we have a degree of vulnerability toward others. We're willing to take their guff, ride out their moods, and be hurt by them along the way.

Everybody likes to talk about love. Truly living out love is a much more difficult task. It requires a willingness to walk the talk.

Do you want to be loved with steadfast, unconditional love? Then give that kind of love.

Do you claim to be a loving person? Then live it out.

## The Language of Love: Affirmation

Love in action in the workplace communicates, above all else, "I'm for you."

- "I believe in you."
- "I support you."
- "I'm working for your best."
- "I desire to see you win."
- "I hope for your highest levels of achievement and your best possible performance."
- "I'm your fan."

When we affirm others in these ways, we encourage them. Affirmation is always a building-up process.

To build up people is to affirm their positive traits and to encourage them to continue to pursue excellence. Affirmation does not deny that people have weaknesses; rather, it puts the emphasis on their ability to overcome weaknesses or to transform them into strengths.

False flattery may temporarily leave a person feeling high, but in the end, it rings hollow. Affirmation must be genuine and honest for it to be true affirmation.

Affirmation has a lasting quality. It endures and grows over time. False flattery is but for the moment. When it evaporates, it leaves in its wake a negative aftertaste.

What happens when affirmation abounds in the workplace?

## First, There's an Immediate Rise in Trust

Too often, people see only the bad in us. We know that we have some negative traits in our lives; we don't need others to harp on them. Most of all, we don't need other people to see only our negative

*We Tend to Trust Those Who See the Good in Us* traits or our faults. We don't trust those who do. We know they aren't seeing the whole of us, and thus, we don't trust their appraisal to be accurate. When we don't trust people's appraisal of our personhood to be accurate, it's difficult to trust their appraisal of anything else to be accurate.

We all know managers or spouses who

---

- put only negative comments in the file, literally or figuratively.
- give only negative feedback to persons under their supervision.
- harp only on a person's faults.

---

On the other hand, we know that if other people see good in us and affirm that good, they choose to see good. Surely, they don't see only good. (If so, they're off base, and we are suspicious of their sanity.) The fact that they choose to emphasize the good, however, says that they are for us and that we can trust them to be on our side if push comes to shove.

*Second, When Affirmation Abounds and Creates Trust, Communication Begins to Flow* We tend to talk more to persons who affirm us than to those who negate our value. We tend to communicate more freely with those we trust.

*Third, the More We Have Communicated with People Who Affirm Us and Whom We Trust, the More We Are Loyal to the People* We are more tolerant of them. We stand by them in crisis situations. We speak up for them. They have become our friends, not only our colleagues or colaborers.

What happens when a workforce is marked by these traits? Loyalty to associates is readily transferred to the entire company. And the more loyalty employees have toward a company, the less likely they are to jump ship and help a competitor, the more likely they are to give their best to the job (effort, skill, time, and talent), and the more willing they are to ride out tough times (in the company or in the industry in which that company operates).

Time and again we consult with organizations in which these three words repeatedly stand out:

---

- *Trust*
- *Communication*
- *Loyalty*

---

Every executive wants them in an organization. They are the keys to a healthy operation. Yet, in most cases, they are lacking or are at the low end of any scale.

Too many managers aren't doing what is required to engender trust. They aren't communicating with their employees. They aren't doing what will build loyalty. And therefore, they have created no reason for their employees to respond to them in a trusting, openly communicative, loyal manner.

A human resource manager, new to her position, told us of a meeting with a representative group of employees in her plant. They were supposed to discuss the results of an opinion survey. She said, "I was so frustrated. I kept asking for input, but nobody would talk! They were like stones. Nobody would say anything!"

We asked, "Why do you suppose they were silent?"

She replied candidly, without much forethought, "I guess they don't trust us." Even as she gave her answer, she had her problem clearly defined.

"What can you do to *grow* trust?" we asked. That key question should be asked in virtually all corporations today. Programs won't fix trust. A new orientation toward valuing others and toward building relationships that are rooted in value will build trust. How can managers instill trust in their employees? By first demonstrating acts of trust. Trust grows trust. And out of trust, communication and loyalty will grow.

---

Of the three terms that represent the value of the person—love, dignity, and respect—love is probably the least understood. We talk about love as being acceptable and respectable at home, in the family, at church, and even in the community—but not at work.

The principle that holds true for love outside the workplace, however, holds true for love within the work environment: we can exist without love, but we cannot truly live without love.

**Love Is a Universal Need**

Love adds vibrancy to our lives and to our behavior. Without love, we simply go through the motions—no matter where we are.

We don't turn off this need for love the second we punch the time clock or the minute we cross the threshold of the office. The need is still there. It still dictates the degree to which we put energy, vibrancy, and a positive flair into our behavior—in this case, our work.

What does it mean to love another person in the workplace? It has nothing to do with soupy, smarmy, overly sentimental behavior.

It also has nothing to do with sex. When we say, "Bring love into the workplace," we are *not* saying—as some people seem immediately to conclude—"Bring sex into the workplace." Sex and love are two distinct things, yet in our culture, they frequently are regarded as synonymous. If that happens, many vital aspects of expressing love fall by the wayside.

The need for love in the marketplace is the need for the best, purest, and highest ideals of love to be displayed.

## Love Is an Action

We can define love by considering the ways in which we complete the statement, "If you love me, you'll . . ." In conducting Value of the Person—Theory R Seminars across the nation, we frequently ask groups of people to complete that sentence, and the answers that we receive—whether from busboys, engineers, accountants, nurses, or students—are nearly always the same. Here's how one group responded:

*If you love me, you'll . . .*

- care for me.
- respect my uniqueness as a human being.
- trust me.
- share with me.
- be polite to me.
- talk to me.
- listen to me—really hear me.
- really see me.
- appreciate my distinct qualities.
- try to understand me.
- give to me.
- pay attention to my needs.

How many times have you heard a spouse say one of these phrases to you? How many times have you heard a friend bemoan the lack of these behaviors from a loved one?

Is there anything about any of these behaviors that employees don't also want from fellow employees, managers (or those above them on the organizational chart), and workers (or those below them on the chart)? Read the list again. We all crave these behaviors from other human beings.

All of these are operational definitions of love. They are behaviors, not feelings. They are examples of love in action. It's this type of love that we envision as a hallmark of value and that we call on Theory R leaders to display.

## Love in the Marketplace

Love in the marketplace is action. It's showing others that you care about them, respect them, and trust them. It's being willing to share with other persons, talk to them, listen to them, really see them, and make every attempt to understand them. It's going out of your way to give something to them that is meaningful—even if it's just a friendly greeting.

This type of behavior requires change and a willingness to do what may initially be uncomfortable. Most people discover, however, that the more they do what is uncomfortable but right, the more comfortable they feel!

Moreover, a loving attitude and loving acts in the workplace are not behaviors that can be learned solely from a textbook. (To be certain, ways to express love and build healthy relationships in the workplace are rarely taught in our nation's schools of business.) Love is learned fully as one expresses love.

The impact of love in the workplace is so great, it's worth the risk, a few qualms, and even a little embarrassment at times.

## Love Makes Time for No-Agenda Listening

Dr. Sharell Mikesell, vice president for science and technology at Owens-Corning World Headquarters, recently sent a copy of a memo to us. One of his scientists, whom Sharell described to us as an "extremely talented and fundamental research scientist," had attended one of our Value of the Person Seminars.

The scientist wrote,

*I have always believed that my first supervisor at DuPont was the finest supervisor I have ever had (no offense to the other fourteen or so previous or present supervisors intended) because of the way he interacted with me and other chemists in his group. One of the most significant and symbolic things he did was to walk into our labs unannounced, and provided one had somehow indicated time was available and one was inclined to have a conversation, he would sit down with his cup of coffee at the conference table separating the two desks in the lab, put his feet up on the table and ask, "What's hot?"*

*What ensued could be a technical discussion of current research (what was boiling in the hood), "Did you see the article on . . . ?" "What did you think of X's seminar yesterday in Central Research?" or "Do you need any help to get Y to let you use his explosion proof hood to scale up the diazirene synthesis for the patent application verification?" I do not recall any conversation ever starting with "I think you should . . ." or "What is the status of . . . ?" It has only been in recent years that I realized how symbolic it was that conversations almost always took place on my turf and not in his office.*

One of the greatest expressions of love that a person can make is to listen without an agenda and to do so intently, with full attention and interest.

A young minister, who spends a great deal of his time listening to church members with problems, tells this story: "I came home from work one day and asked my wife how her day had gone. For the next half hour, she went through a long list of problems, including a problem with the car, the development of an earache by our younger son, and her frustrations at not being able to get an appliance fixed.

"I listened and then immediately began to problem solve—saying in rather crisp administrative style just what I thought she should do 'first thing in the morning' about where she should take the car, our son's health problem, and how she should handle the people at the appliance repair department.

"She just looked at me and sighed. 'I've already taken care of all that,' she said. 'You have?' I asked. 'Sure,' she said. 'Then why tell me about it?' I said.

"'Because you asked me how my day went,' she replied very sweetly. 'I don't need for you to solve my problems, but I do like it when you are interested in knowing what I've been through.'"

The young minister concludes his story: "I learned a lot that day. Many people don't really want to have their lives fixed. They simply want the opportunity to tell what they've been through and how they are going about fixing or improving their own lives."

One of our associates in the Value of the Person seminars, Tony Campolo, tells about an eight-year-old boy who was asked to describe God's job. The boy said that one of God's main jobs was to make people. And then he said, "God's second most important job is listening to prayers. An awful lot of this goes on, and some people like preachers and rabbis pray other times besides bedtime. God doesn't have time to listen to radio and TV because of this."

People need to tell others what they are doing, how they are feeling, and how they are responding to life's circumstances—not only at the dinner table or in prayer but on the job. It's a part of how employees see themselves as workers, and good managers will recognize that giving employees an opportunity to "tell what's hot" is going to be far more valuable than it may appear on the surface.

Listening is rated as one of the top qualities in managers by nearly all employees we've polled after our seminars. An employee at Gillette noted, "Value of the Person allowed us to listen more to each other so that we could hear what the problems were and get to the heart of the issues." No-agenda listening frequently reveals the real issues underneath surface incidents.

An employee at the 3M Cordova Oxide Plant said in high praise of his supervisor, "Jerry will always listen to you. It doesn't matter what it is, he listens. What he does with what he hears is up to him." What a great example of an employee who has come to equate listening with trusting! The employee who is truly being heard by a manager is likely to place far greater trust in that manager than the employee who feels he is being only partially heard.

Listening with love:

- yields information.
- reveals underlying issues.
- builds relationships.
- builds trust.

This kind of no-agenda listening leads to a second aspect of love in action.

## Love Sees the Whole of a Person's Life

A manager who takes time for no-agenda listening, whether in a hallway, over coffee in an employee's office, or on the plant floor, will discover numerous things about employees, and a good percentage of those things will relate to the employees' lives away from work.

As a result of conducting our Value of the Person seminars in many cities and in many kinds of work environments, we receive on a regular basis a number of *VOP Newsletters* that departments or companies have introduced to keep the principles of Value of the Person alive in their offices or plants. These newsletters do something that plant managers sometimes fail to do: they provide profiles of "whole people." Traditional managers tend to see their employees as living job descriptions—slots on the chart, spaces to be filled, duties to be assigned. Employees and Value of the Person managers strive to see people as unique, fully functioning family members and community residents.

Bob was congratulated for twenty years of service with a cake decorated with a motorcycle—Bob's favorite mode of travel.

Bill, a woodworking enthusiast, voluntarily made a set of shelves in his workshop at home for the control room.

Phil and Nancy recently purchased a new house.

Larry races scale-model cars.

Walt had surgery.

Joanne's son, Alton, graduated with a 4.0 GPA and in the top 5 percent of his high-school class, and he is headed for college on an academic scholarship.

Love doesn't separate one aspect of life from all others; it recognizes that when someone is hurting or rejoicing in one area of life, that emotion spills over into all other activities and relationships.

## Love Means Going a Second Mile

How many employees today will see a person struggling under a load and do nothing to help?

How many phones will ring and go unanswered because the person at the next desk says, "That's not my job"?

Many employees believe that if they momentarily do another person's job, a manager will spot them doing the work and will assume that they have the time and energy to do the job all the time. Before they know it, they've got themselves double the work and rarely double the pay. In a traditional management organization, this happens more often than not.

As managers, we need to encourage mutuality of help rather than say to ourselves, "That person apparently doesn't have enough to do if there's time to help someone else." Certainly, there's room to draw that conclusion if a person is continually or constantly helping someone else. That's not what I'm referring to here. The employee who puts forth an extra effort and offers a helping hand or goes a second mile for another employee should be rewarded for that effort, not reprimanded or punished for it.

We've got to get beyond the mentality of "I do only my job all the time" if our nation is truly going to progress and regain its number one status in all areas of manufacturing, marketing, and service. We've got to get to the place, instead, where we can say to one another, "Here, let me lend you a hand," and believe that in time, that helping hand will be extended back to us when we need it. The morale of the overall workforce, not to mention productivity and quality of performance, benefits from mutuality of help.

**THEORY R SAYS,**

*Love belongs in the workplace.*

*Love is positive behavior toward another in action.*

*Love means going the second mile to care for, respect, share with, communicate with, and give to another person.*

## The Ultimate Loving Action Is Giving

You can't truly show others you love them without doing something for them. Love ultimately comes down to giving—and giving without expecting anything in return:

- Giving a compliment
- Giving a helping hand
- Giving a boost or a lift
- Giving a word of encouragement
- Giving moral support
- Giving advice that is helpful for growth and fulfillment

## Giving Love Sometimes Means Giving a Wake-Up Call

Love means not waiting for a manager to take the initiative in showing love but jumping in and doing what you can do.

Our associate, Lefty Scumaci, tells the story about a group of employees who banded together to show love in action to a fellow employee who had a great deal of trouble getting out of bed in the morning. He had such a terrible absentee record that he was on the verge of being fired.

The five said to themselves, in essence, "What's our friend worth to us as a colaborer? What can we do creatively to help, to show our love for him?" They decided to take turns giving their colleague a wake-up call. They did that for months until he developed a new habit of getting up on time.

They loved him enough to help him develop a new incentive to get to work. He eventually became a model employee.

Love sometimes means making a decision that requires a little extra effort. The easiest route for the five may have been to let a fellow employee get fired. In the long run, salvaging a friendship was far more rewarding.

Let's ask ourselves, "What is a relationship worth?" Very often in the home or workplace, we are faced with choices about what we might do for others. Too often, we take the easy way out. The more rewarding approach is to ask, "What is the *best* I can do?" not, "What is the least I can do?" We need to ask ourselves, "What *more* can I do?" not, "How little can I get by with?"

Love in the workplace affirms the good of others.

Love in the workplace means cutting others some slack occasionally, overlooking some of their faults and, at the same time, encouraging their growth and improvement.

Love means helping a person get qualified for a better job.

Love in the workplace means hanging together rather than hanging separately. It means caring for others on your team.

## Love Sometimes Means Buying a Gizmo . . . or Flowers

Today's electronic information environment offers unique challenges to a manager—as well as unique opportunities to value trusted employees.

An accountant named Charles came to his supervisor, Lynn, one day and said, "Do you think it might be possible for me to have a modem?"

"A modem?" Lynn asked. "What do you need to transmit?"

"Well," Charles hesitated a little, "I have a computer at home, and sometimes ideas hit me at two o'clock in the morning. I find that I can't get back to sleep until I try to resolve the problem or put my ideas down on paper. But sometimes I need a piece of information that I have in my computer at work. I have a modem for my machine at home but not on the one at work. If I had one on the computer here at work, I could get some work done."

"At two o'clock in the morning?" Lynn asked. "That's way beyond the call of duty, Charles."

"Actually, I think I'd get *more* sleep," Charles said with a grin. "I could deal with my ideas faster, and I wouldn't stay awake as long trying to sort things out."

"All right," said Lynn. "We'll give it a try."

Those two-in-the-morning ideas paid off in several ideas that streamlined two time-intensive processes in the accounting department, saving hundreds of work hours a year.

In other companies, we've heard of managers allowing workers to have company-owned typewriters, computer terminals, and facsimile machines at home. In one office, virtually no productivity has been lost to sick-child care this past year, primarily because parents who stay at home with their sick children are still able to put in a full day's work using machines and hookups provided by the company.

In another instance, Leslie came to her manager, Geri, with this suggestion: "Do you think we might have a copy machine right here in our department?"

"I don't know," Geri said. "Talk to me a little about it. The company is really tight right now on capital equipment purchases, so I'd really need to justify the expenditure."

"Well," Leslie explained, "as it is right now, we have to go to the department next door, and nine times out of ten that machine is being used or is out of service. Some of the people I send over there have to wait ten to fifteen minutes to get copies made. A few have gone on to yet another department to use a machine. When the clerks are gone that long, the phone calls and messages really back up. I think we'd save a lot of time and effort if we had a small machine that would handle our copy work."

Geri agreed to give the idea a try, and so did the upper managers. The copy machine they leased didn't have a lot of bells and whistles like the ones in the adjacent departments, but the employees hadn't used all the extra features anyway. Both morale and workload increased greatly.

In Peter's department, employees asked for stamps. The company had a tight policy on postage, and for employees to mail items, they had to fill out forms, hike to the centralized postage meter, and often wait in long lines for their request to be processed. The procedure was designed with large bulk mailings in mind, but for those who needed to mail only a few letters a day, the system was cumbersome.

Peter bought three rolls of stamps from central services and allowed one of the secretaries in his department to issue them as needed. The stamps lasted a month, and no abuses of the new system were noted. Overall, the "bending of company policy" resulted in dozens of hours saved and much more efficiency within the department.

Hector tried to find a way to bridge the gap between the workers in the plant and those in the office where he worked. He collected five dollars from every employee in the plant and, on Secretaries Day, bought flowers in bulk and made arrangements for each secretary in the office. The gesture formed a bridge of kindness that opened a door to much greater communication and understanding between the two entities of the company.

Acts of love can be very practical, very inexpensive, and very straightforward. Virtually any action that meets a need can be considered a loving act.

## Love Means Being There in Times of Trouble

Caring doesn't run by the clock.

There are two main times when loving actions outside the work arena will have monumental impact: death and serious illness.

Has one of your employees lost a loved one? Why not take a moment on your way home from work to stop by the funeral home and extend your sympathy to the family?

Is one of your employees at home because of a long-standing illness or an accident? Why not stop by occasionally to see how she is doing and to bring greetings from others in the workplace?

Is a family member of an employee hospitalized with a serious ailment? Why not stop by the hospital and give a word of encouragement to the family? The person who is ill may be your employee. If so, spend a few minutes at the person's bedside encouraging him and envisioning the day when he will be well enough to return to work.

Your presence should lift a person's spirits. Don't put pressure on the ill, troubled, or grieving person. Let her know that you miss her presence and that, above all, you want her well and whole. Assure the person that the job will be waiting for him when he is able to return. Do what you can to ease concerns about absenteeism.

When visiting those who are grieving, in pain, or sick, put yourself in their shoes momentarily and ask yourself, "What would I like to hear?"

---

- You'd probably like for the visit from your boss to be short and very positive.
- You'd like to hear that the person cares or is concerned, that the person is sorry you are feeling ill or have lost a loved one, and that you can expect brighter days ahead.
- You'd probably like to know that your boss is willing to walk through this or ride out this incident with you.

---

Convey to your employee what you'd like to hear.

If you are on the road and can't attend a funeral or if the funeral is out of town, call the person who has suffered a loss. There's no more important time to convey your care and concern for a person than at times of death.

A manager's visit to a hospital or funeral home is interpreted by employees as a special gift of time. Every worker knows that a manager regards personal time as a jealously guarded possession. Workers closely guard their personal time, too. To take time out and give it to an employee sends an added message of value.

I, Nancy, experienced this in a very personal way when I was doing my student teaching as part of my college degree program. I had been given sole responsibility of a classroom to teach a unit on mythology. The students in the classroom, mostly boys, had a reputation for behavioral problems, and they generally had low academic records.

The first few days, I overheard several teachers in the teachers' lounge talking about one particular young man who had just recently returned to school after a suspension. They all talked about what a disruptive influence he was in their classes. I couldn't help wondering to myself about the real underlying cause of his problems, so I made an attempt to learn more about him.

I discovered that he had been abandoned as a baby—literally left on the doorstep of his grandparents, who had raised him as best they could with very few resources. His upbringing was one of poverty and displacement.

One day when the young man didn't show up for school, I asked one of his friends where he was, and he told me that the young man's grandfather had died. I knew that must be a terrible blow to him since his grandfather had been the only father figure he had known, so I made plans to stop by the funeral home on my way home from school the following afternoon.

The funeral home was dark and dismal. Only a few family members and neighbors were there. I felt somewhat awkward walking in alone, but when I saw my young student consumed with pain and hurt, I was moved to put my arms around him. I didn't say much or stay long, but I could tell my visit was very meaningful to him.

From that day forward, the young man was a changed student, at least in my classroom. His grades went up, he paid attention in class, he was respectful, and he actually came to my defense on more than one occasion when other students tried to give me, the student teacher, a hard time. Yes, love means being there in times of trouble.

I came away from that experience thoroughly convinced that a wonderful thing happens when teachers truly value their students. The students not only behave better, but they perform better. They try harder. They give their best effort to the learning tasks. They cooperate better in group assignments. In all, they achieve more!

And what about teachers? They respond to a principal's expression of value in much the same way. Show me a teacher who has a principal providing love, dignity, and respect, and I'll show you a teacher who goes the second mile for students.

## Where Will the Extra Time Come From?

Many people ask, "How will I find time to add more people encounters to my already overbooked schedule?" Theory R calls for managers to have a shift in orientation—from paper to people.

Today, the traditional manager is likely to say, "I've got to get my paperwork done, no matter what." We suggest those managers switch gears and say, "I've got to get my people work done, no matter what." Those who make the switch will likely find that they have less paperwork to do because they will have dealt with a number of paper-based issues face-to-face.

There's a great likelihood of fewer memos, fewer reports, fewer forms related to absenteeism or discipline, and fewer proposals to write on the subject of resolving human relations crises.

Rather than take home a briefcase of reports to read or spreadsheets to analyze, the Theory R manager is more likely to spend

**THEORY R SAYS,**

*Become people-oriented, not paper-oriented.*

after-hours time going to a hospital or funeral home or running an errand that helps an employee. Rather than take home a list of business calls to make, the Theory R manager is more likely to be on the phone giving words of encouragement to an absent worker or a worker in need.

In some cases, managers may be able to reapportion their time to accommodate a greater percentage of valuing behaviors. In some cases, people time may be shifted to after hours and paper-shuffling chores that were once done at home may be shifted to in-the-office hours.

"But," you may say, "there are only so many hours in a day. If I am required to spend more time caring for employees, where do I get that time? Something is going to have to take less time. What gives?"

As managers, we frequently spend a great deal of time resolving people problems but very little time attempting to prevent them. Substantial savings in time frequently can be made, however, in preventing problems and, thus, in preventing the need for rework. Theory R managers usually find that they spend less time:

- fixing problems.
- sorting out miscommunication.
- resolving errors.
- playing referee in disagreements.
- coordinating activities between people who should have been able to coordinate their own tasks (with good communication).
- reconciling differences of opinion.
- engaging in damage control.

**THEORY R SAYS,**

*Wise managers cultivate love among employees. They exhibit love in action toward all with whom they work, regardless of position or personal characteristics. They are steadfast and unconditional in love. They affirm employees at every opportunity.*

*In return, they experience love in the form of trust, loyalty, and high quality of job performance.*

Bob Wood, human relations director for The Gillette Company, once juggled as many as seventy grievance cases at one time. That's an amazing workload, filled with lots of tension and strife.

After the valuing principles of Theory R had taken root in his organization, he saw a 90 percent drop in grievances. Rather than seventy grievance cases, he faced seven. Problems were being resolved where and when they started.

Where did the shift come in his use of time? He spent vastly more time in preventive human relations than in resolving grievances. The time spent in prevention was far more satisfying personally to him than the time spent in arguments with his union counterparts. He spent time loving his employees, and in so doing, he had fewer hate-rooted problems to resolve.

# THEORY R AT WORK

Recall a time when you felt love in action.

What was the last thing you did for someone at work that you consider to be a truly loving action?

What more might you do to show love at work? At home?

# Showing Regard for a Person's Dignity

8

**S**ome years ago, a report came over the news wires about a man who had committed suicide at his place of employment. What made the report unusual was the note that the man left to his boss. The note was placed so that it would be found as his body was found. It read, "I have worked for you for more than thirty years, and in all those years, you never once told me anything I did good. You only told me what I did wrong."

Psychologists might have a field day with such a note. But one conclusion is certain: the man had no sense of being appreciated.

***Expressing appreciation for who a person is and what a person does is the language of dignity.***

Most of us have a much stronger sense of what it means to be treated with indignity than to be treated with dignity. All of these behaviors are ones we readily classify as expressions of indignity— regardless of our profession or status:

**The Value of Dignity**

- Being ignored in your struggle
- Being cut out of the communication loop when all of your other peers are included

- Having an idea stolen or in some other way being ripped off
- Being called names
- Being given no place—perhaps no locker, perhaps no seat at the lunch table
- Being made to feel that you don't fit—perhaps being given a uniform that doesn't match or being assigned to a group of beginners when you've been doing a task for a year
- Being called, or considered to be, expendable

Showing disregard for a person's dignity is behavior that says, "I don't appreciate you. I don't regard you as being worthy of my appreciation."

Whether union or nonunion, in a manufacturing plant or a service organization, wearing a white collar or a blue one, employees agree that being treated with dignity might be best defined in operational terms that are, in tenor, the opposite of those conveyed previously:

- Being counted in
- Being given a place
- Being helped to fit
- Being considered a vital part of an operation
- Being called by your name (instead of being called a name)
- Being recognized for the valuable contributions that you, and you alone, make to the whole

Showing regard for a person's dignity is behavior that says, "I appreciate you and what you do."

Whether one is a garbage collector or a corporate executive, the person deserves to be treated with dignity. The job is vital. It contributes to the welfare of all. It is a contribution that is welcome. And while it does not define the whole of that person, it does speak a great deal of that person as one who is working, producing, giving, and relating to the whole of our society.

**Dignity Is Vitally Linked to Work**

Our jobs are important to our dignity not only in a sense of having a job and keeping a job but in feeling that we are winning at our jobs. It's one thing to lose a job. It's another thing to feel that you're losing on the job or that you're a loser at a job.

A manager once said to us with a laugh in his voice but a real depth of sincerity to his words, "Oh, I don't disrespect the person.

I don't even know the person. I just don't think very highly of the position."

Three things are violently wrong with that manager's attitude:

- First, he doesn't know the person. Why not?
- Second, he thought he wasn't showing disrespect for the person. Chances are very high that the person in question felt that he received no respect.
- Third, he separated a position from an employee. Disrespect for a worker's position still feels like disrespect for the person to the person! Most people are their jobs to a very great extent. Their work defines a big part of who they are and requires a big part of their time, energy, and concern.

When we dignify work, we dignify the employee. When we show value to a job, we show value for the person who does that job.

A ripple effect begins to occur when we feel unappreciated or ignored, or when we are the victims of indignity. This ripple effect begins with our feeling insecure.

**Indignity and Insecurity Are Closely Related**

When we feel insecure about ourselves and our positions, we tend to become extremely cautious. We don't act out of fear of making a mistake or of acting inappropriately. We don't speak up because we're insecure about saying the right thing. We retreat and become uninvolved.

The uninvolved employee tends to become increasingly uncooperative. She'd rather go it alone than work with others. If the situation isn't turned around, she's likely to become apathetic about her performance because she's apathetic about her role in the company.

The more apathetic and uninvolved an employee is, the more likely he is going to be reprimanded for being uncooperative and uninvolved. His relationships with other employees and with his manager are going to deteriorate, and with the breakdown of relationships come confrontations and anger. Eventually, the job implodes on the person. Everything that he is trying to keep at arm's length, out of insecurity and a fear that he won't succeed, comes crashing in on him.

Job, the man of great troubles in the Bible, perhaps stated it best: "The thing I greatly feared has come upon me, and what I dreaded has happened to me" (Job 3:25). We've seen it happen dozens of times—the dignity of employees is undermined, causing them to fear the loss of their jobs, and their subsequent behaviors actually set them up for failure and job loss.

The situation is the exact opposite, of course, when dignity is upheld.

## Dignity in Action Is Appreciation

You may ask, "How can I as a manager (or a staff worker or a professional) extend dignity to my employees?"

We come back to the premise that began this chapter. The language of dignity is appreciation. We say, "I appreciate you."

To appreciate others means to value their ideas. It means to respect their opinions. It means to include them as part of the group.

The traditional manager says, "Good job."

The Theory R manager says, in effect, "Good you." The Theory R manager sees and applauds the link between quality performance and the self-satisfaction an employee takes in a job well done.

The Theory R manager also finds creative ways to include every person in the larger group. Consider what it might mean in your organization to:

- cycle rank-and-file employees into management meetings.
- ask questions or solicit spontaneous input from employees.
- sit down occasionally to have lunch with the employees (or order in pizza for the entire group to share).
- visit the employee's office rather than insist that the employee come to your office.
- pour a cup of coffee for your assistant rather than ask your assistant to pour coffee for you.

After attending a Value of the Person—Theory R Seminar, Dr. Sharell Mikesell, vice president of science and technology at Owens-Corning, felt challenged to find a way to personally extend value to the hundreds of people who report to him. He decided to focus on affirming the accomplishments of his engineers and staff employees by sending personal handwritten notes of praise and appreciation to them. He set a personal goal and proceeded to send an average of about thirty notes a month. In extending appreciation, he is receiving appreciation. He told us not too long ago that an uplifting attitude has taken hold, and that others in leadership are also finding unique ways of expressing appreciation. Appreciation can be contagious!

Appreciation means letting others know that you value them as individuals. What does it mean to an employee to see his name posted—as a surprise—on a bulletin board along with a memo citing his accomplishments (which may very well be outside the workplace)? What does it mean for a worker to be complimented genuinely and sincerely by a manager in the presence of others? What does it mean for a manager to give a worker a hearty handshake while handing her a Christmas bonus and to say, "I really appreciate you"? A great deal! Far more than can be calculated on cost analysis sheets.

Appreciation, like love, must be consistent. It must be applied uniformly over time. To appreciate a person publicly on Monday and then openly and harshly criticize the person on Tuesday is to negate all the good that Monday yielded.

What happens between a manager and an employee outside the workplace is sometimes a far greater indicator of dignity than what happens within the work environment.

**An Encounter in a Supermarket Aisle**

Give yourself the supermarket aisle test.

You, as a manager, are with your family in a supermarket. As you turn down an aisle, you realize that coming toward you from the other end of the aisle is an employee who reports to you.

What do you do?

Perhaps the height of indignity would be to turn the other way quickly to avoid a meeting or conversation. Only slightly higher on the scale of indignity-dignity would be to drop your eyes and avoid conversation as you pass.

Do you greet the person politely and move on quickly? Do you wait for the other person to greet you before responding?

Or do you stop and introduce your employee to your spouse and children, and show delight in meeting the employee's spouse and children?

Do you say something positive and uplifting about your worker to his family, showing your appreciation for him and the work he does? Do you say something that builds up your employee's value in the eyes of her children? You could say, "Your dad is one of our experts. When we run into a problem, he's one of the first people we turn to for help." Or "Your mother is one of the finest engineers we've ever had in our company." Or "I know you must be very proud of the work that your parent does."

You can always find something to compliment about a person. Your goal as a manager is to find the things worthy of compliments and then to give the compliments. Again, the expression of appreciation must be genuine. It must be rooted in a reality that both you and the employee recognize.

## Putting Appreciation into the File

Not only should the statement of appreciation be spoken readily and repeatedly to fellow coworkers, but those who are in management positions should be quick to put notes of appreciation into a person's employment file.

Most of what goes into a person's file are negative comments. Many managers are quick to document failures, errors, or inadequacies—from absenteeism to costly mistakes. The manager who upholds the dignity of the employees will also put positive comments into a worker's file. Cite the things that are done well, the helpful acts, the second-mile behaviors, the morale-boosting involvement.

Don't just say, "I value you," to the employee and the current peers. Say it to the person's future boss!

We heard about a manager who writes an annual letter of recommendation for each employee she supervises. She isn't doing this to suggest to her employees that they seek other jobs. Far from it! Her intent is to keep these employees working for her.

In her letter, she cites all of the good qualities of the employee just as if she was recommending the person for a position elsewhere. "That way," she told me, "should I take another job or be promoted so that I am no longer directly responsible for these employees, I will have set them up for success with the person who follows me in the role of supervisor." (In the past five years, she's had only one employee out of twelve leave voluntarily, and the person took a higher-paying position in another state.)

## Indignities That Must Be Eliminated from the Workplace

There are ten things that yield absolutely no benefit to the workplace. All of them relate to a person's dignity.

1. ***Emotional abuse.*** Continually criticizing the lack of effort or productivity, the failures and mistakes, or personal hab-

its can become emotional abuse if there is no attempt made to remediate the person's mistakes or to provide a way out of a failure cycle.

2. **Public humiliation.** No employee deserves to be reprimanded or made fun of in front of peers. No person deserves to be held up as an object lesson or as a focus for ridicule.

3. **Racial slurs.** No employee deserves to hear any comments related to race.

4. **Ethnic name-calling.** No employee deserves to be stereotyped by nationality or cultural origin.

5. **Sexual harassment.** No employee deserves to be regarded as a sexual object or treated in a way that is sexually demeaning. This includes all remarks about a person's sexuality, sexual orientation, or sexual behavior off the job. It definitely includes any remarks that may be construed as correlating work performance with sexual favors. If you suspect that a fellow employee is embarrassed or repulsed by something you consider a compliment, ask the person if what you said was considered offensive. If you have offended the person—even if you feel yourself in the right—apologize.

6. **Personal criticism.** No employee should ever hear comments made about appearance, friends, home life, age, tradition, religion, or any other aspect of personal life.

7. **Blatant exclusion.** No employee deserves to be consistently and obviously excluded from group functions to which all others are included.

8. **Invisibility.** No employee should be made to feel invisible. Greet your employees. Look them in the eye. Shake their hands. Recognize their presence.

9. **Personality conflicts.** No employee should be singled out and denied access to training, opportunity, or promotion on the basis of a personality conflict or personal dislike. If you don't get along with a person or seem always to be in conflict with the person, find out why. Talk to the person. Get to the bottom of the trouble, and resolve it the best you can. Nearly every personality conflict can be resolved if both parties will make the effort.

10. **Old grudges.** If you are holding something against an employee—an attitude, a past action or statement, a consistent behavior—let that person know what is bothering

you. Clear the air. Find a means of reconciling and moving on in life.

Some Theory X managers hold to the position that these behaviors are a part of being a tough manager. Not so! It *is* possible to be a successful manager without ever resorting to humiliation, abuse, name-calling, or criticism. If you have ever been guilty of these behaviors as a manager, we encourage you to admit your mistakes and to make amends!

Denial of dignity results in hopes being frustrated. Frustrated hopes result in disappointment. Disappointment yields anger. And anger brings hostility.

Dignity, on the other hand, brightens hope. Hope yields enthusiasm. Enthusiasm brings about a more positive outlook on tasks. A positive outlook brings about an extra effort that yields positive results in productivity, quality, and morale.

## Indignity Is in the Ears of the Recipient

Perhaps at no time in a manager-employee relationship is dignity more important to uphold than at a time of discipline or termination.

Theory R requires, first of all, that you as a manager have done everything within your power to avert the need for discipline or termination. Even so, there are occasions when discipline or termination is required.

Keep in mind always that indignity is in the ears of the recipient. What a person means by a statement isn't always what is perceived by the person to whom the statement is directed. You and a fellow employee may have highly different definitions for a term. Even your tone of voice may convey a meaning you didn't intend. If at any time you suspect that you have insulted an employee, apologize.

## Twelve Ways to Uphold Dignity

If you find yourself in a situation where disciplinary action is necessary, here are just a few suggestions for upholding the dignity of an employee. We know we are only reminding you of their wisdom.

1. *Always reprimand employees in private.*
2. *If changes in policy need to be made, make them and announce them to the group as a whole without reference*

to any incident that may have caused you to change the
policy.

3. Say "please" and "thank you" to employees.
4. Share responsibility for mistakes.
5. Don't dwell on past mistakes.
6. Find a way of channeling your anger about a situation
   into a positive act.
7. Give employees equal access to rewards and to the possibility of upward mobility.
8. Avoid labeling an employee in your mind and definitely in
   your encounters with the employee.
9. Never egg on an employee to challenge you, rebuke you,
   rebuff you, or fight with you.
10. Never laugh at an employee's mistakes.
11. If you do wound the dignity of a person in front of peers,
    make your apology to that person in front of peers.
12. Look your employee in the eye.

## Upgrade Rather than Degrade

The key in showing dignity to others is this: upgrade them rather than degrade them.

Give them a high-esteem profile to shoot for. Let them know that you believe in them, appreciate them, and want them to be a part of your group.

Don't downplay a person's importance, contribution, or life in any way. To do so is to downgrade the overall quality of your entire workforce and to set in motion the behaviors that will cause all of your employees to feel less secure and less motivated to contribute to your company's overall good.

No matter what a person's job may be, never demean the person for having that job. Uphold the fact that the person is working, and encourage the person to give the job the best effort.

Our colleague and friend Lefty Scumaci once said to a busboy in the dining room of a hotel we frequently use for Value of the Person—Theory R Seminars: "Curtis, you have the most important job in this restaurant. If you didn't clear off the tables so quickly and cleanly, nobody could sit down to eat! Customers would have to wait, or they'd go someplace else. You've got an important position!" Curtis really heard Lefty, and in all our travels, we've yet to come across a busboy as good as Curtis.

**Employees
Expect
Discipline—
They Don't
Expect
Indignity**

Employees know they aren't perfect. They know they make mistakes. They fully expect their mistakes to be called to their attention.

Employees also know that people who make mistakes repeatedly and willfully are subject to discipline. They expect discipline in those cases.

But employees do *not* want a manager to demand perfection (which isn't possible), to call attention to mistakes with a dose of ridicule, or to trample their dignity in exacting discipline.

An employee related this instance to us as an example of a worker's dignity being trampled: "The manager asked this guy named Ben in the photo lab to order some special paper for a shoot we were doing in a few weeks. Ben placed the order, and when the box of paper came in, he checked his order against the packing sheet and then put the paper on the shelf in its sealed box. Ben had ordered paper from this company before without any problem, but this time, when the time came for the paper to be used, he discovered that the paper in the box didn't match the box lid. We had a delay of several days while replacement paper was ordered and delivered. The agency was really ticked at us.

"The lab manager chewed Ben out in front of all his coworkers for not inspecting the paper thoroughly before shelving it."

We asked this employee, "What should the manager have done?"

He said, "He could have done lots of things. In the first place, Ben felt that he had followed company policy. The policy in the past had been for boxes to remain sealed so that nothing could get misplaced or used before the time it was needed. The manager could have said, 'Ben, I should have told you to check the paper. In the future, please do so.' Or he could have said, 'Ben, I think we need to establish a new policy about checking paper when it arrives.'

"At the very least," the employee continued, "the manager could have called Ben into his office and talked to him about it privately. There was no reason that we all had to hear Ben get chewed out. It wasn't our job. It just made us uncomfortable for Ben. And we probably lost a little respect for our manager, too. At least I know I did."

Another employee told us this story: "One of our employees was burned when a temporary supervisor told her to soak a gasket in a certain chemical—one that she shouldn't have used because she hadn't been trained in safety for that chemical. Management blamed the employee for the accident, and she was forced to sign a paper stating that if she was injured again on the job, she would be terminated. Word of her discipline spread through our unit like wildfire. Morale has been bad ever since."

We asked this employee what should have been done instead. She said, "In the first place, the regular supervisor should have stood up for her worker. If there was any blame, it should have been placed on the temporary supervisor who gave the directive. In the second place, this employee should have been asked, 'Are you trained to use this chemical wash?' When the supervisor didn't ask, the worker should have said, 'I'm not trained to do that. Please show me how.'"

The conclusion: Blaming an employee unfairly for an incident that isn't solely that employee's fault is regarded as denting that person's dignity. Punishing a person beyond what is viewed as reasonable by other workers is also a blow to dignity. Any blows to an employee's dignity are demoralizing—to the employee primarily but also to fellow workers.

We noticed in these stories that neither of these employees balked at the discipline or denied the fact that the employee was partly to blame. They weren't concerned with the fact of discipline, but they were very upset about the way in which the discipline was carried out.

## What About Terminations?

A number of people have asked through the years, "Did you ever fire a manager at Pittron?"

Yes.

The vast majority of the administrators and managers with whom I worked at Pittron came to see the value of valuing. They got on board with the new approach to management and to true leadership within the company. But the one or two who didn't were let go.

You may ask, "Well, how can a manager who values people fire people?" My response is this: "How can an administrator who values the employees *not* fire a manager who refused to value them?"

If you realize that a manager under your supervision opposes Theory R and chooses to remain opposed to Value of the Person concepts and to maintain a confrontational style, isolate that person.

- Purge the exploiters and the oppressors. Every operation has exploiters or oppressors—people who continually seek to create adversarial relationships. They may be able to perform a task well, but they also can infect morale to the point that they keep others from performing their tasks well. Move such people into positions where they do not supervise others. And then remove them if your first move is unsuccessful—in other words, move them again. If those efforts fail, terminate them. Select people who are for reconciliation. Make them accountable for Value of the Person behaviors, just as you hold them accountable for bottom-line results, safety, or production quotas.

- Don't delay in taking action to isolate people with a confrontational style. Neutralize their influence as quickly as possible. You'll be able to implement Theory R much faster and on a much wider scale.

- Give people a chance to change, but if they refuse to change, grow, or learn a new skill, procedure, or style of leadership, release them. Valuing people means giving them opportunity to change, to grow, and to learn a new skill, procedure, or style of leadership. Valuing people means going a second mile and sometimes a third and fourth mile. But ultimately, valuing people means putting an end to willful, purposeful failure.

---

I've fired very few people in my life, but each time, I've done so only after exhausting every other avenue I knew, and I've done so reluctantly. I've also done so with the perspective that I am probably doing the person a favor. The present job is very likely too difficult, too stressful, or too demanding—and the person is better off getting a fresh start elsewhere in a position more suited to skills, temperament, or circumstances. Sometimes firing a person is the kindest and most loving thing you can do.

In letting a person go, I've always tried to do so with the thought that the person still has great value. Just because someone has failed in this job does not mean that the person is a failure or that the person will fail at the next job. The opposite is likely to be true. The next job has the potential for being the person's greatest success.

We believe in fair severance packages, in helping a person relocate, in doing whatever is possible to help the person land on the feet and move forward in life.

The way a company's managers fire a person usually indicates the way they care for their current employees. Are they as kind and considerate of the person's feelings as possible? Does the company do its best to help the person find a replacement job? Is the decision to fire kept private? If so, there's a good likelihood that the company places a high value on caring and on confidentiality in matters pertaining to the ongoing workforce.

We're strongly opposed to managers who fire people in a burst of temper solely because they believe their power is being challenged. We're opposed to managers who fire people simply to prove they can. We're opposed to terminations that are rooted in emotional reasons rather than in performance facts.

## Upholding Dignity in Times of Downsizing

Sometimes the reason for termination rests not with employee behavior but with a company decision to close an operation or to downsize.

In those times, a manager will find it even more critical to show love, dignity, and respect to the employees who remain in order to pull them into a cohesive work unit and reinstill morale, which takes a severe hit during downsizing.

A major corporation polled its employees last year in the wake of a downsizing announcement. The people expressed these reactions:

- Uncertainty
- Paralysis
- Betrayal
- Mistrust
- Disrespect
- Unequal, unfair treatment
- Lack of clear direction
- Meanness
- Work overload
- Not listened to
- Not involved
- Powerless
- Anger

All of these are very normal reactions. What surprised us, however, was the response of the managers to the poll:

- "They shouldn't feel this way."
- "This is the real world."

- "People need to be more responsible for themselves."
- "Their perceptions are wrong."

The last statement, in particular, caught our attention. Perception is reality in human relations. Managers should never hold to a position that they are right and everything is OK if the employees perceive otherwise. They can try to change employees' perceptions—take action perhaps to inform, convince, or persuade them to see things differently. But perceptions, however inaccurate, must never be dismissed as being unimportant.

**THEORY R SAYS,**

*An employee's dignity is vitally linked to work and to the appreciation shown for the work. A wise manager appreciates employees, includes them in the group, and avoids behaviors that are demeaning to employees.*

Notice, too, the overall attitude of these management opinions: "Well, tough luck. That's life." Downsizing means job loss, change, uneasiness, and sadness. The managers should have recognized the basic human reactions, and they should have compassionately asked,

- "How can we provide more help?"
- "How can we express more concern?"
- "How can we provide more encouragement to those who are leaving and to those who remain?"

Here are some suggestions for ways in which a manager might employ Theory R during a period of downsizing or layoff:

1. *Keep employees informed about company downsizing plans.*
2. *Talk directly with each employee who is being let go.*
3. *Do your best to help the person find other employment.*
4. *Help the person envision a bright future.*
5. *Negotiate a fair severance package on behalf of each employee to the best of your ability.*
6. *Do not speak ill of a terminated employee.*
7. *Plan events and activities that can bind remaining employees together.*
8. *Let employees whose positions are being eliminated know clearly that they personally have done nothing to warrant dismissal.*

Upholding a person's dignity brings about reconciliation and relationship. It is always the right thing to do.

## THEORY R AT WORK

Think about a recent incident in which your dignity was trampled upon.

What should have happened instead?

What insight did the incident give you into how you should treat employees who report to you?

# 9

# Treating Others with Respect

**T**hink about your organization or, for that matter, your life. How do you feel when you know that you are treating others with respect? How do you feel when you are treated with respect?

In Theory R management, a third key element in conveying value to a person—in addition to demonstrating love and dignity—is to show respect. *The message of respect is this: "I recognize you."*

In recognizing a person, you are calling attention to that person's contributions, performance, and accomplishments. You are saying, "You count. Your efforts and achievements are worth noting. They're important!"

So much of who we are as people is related to what we do and the successes we enjoy. Praise and recognition build up a person. They convey, "I notice you. I see you. You are someone important."

A person who enjoys the respect and recognition of others

- feels self-esteem and confidence blossom.
- has more enthusiasm for the job.
- takes greater pride in the work.
- becomes an active participant.

All of these elements have a positive impact on the workplace and home, and all are the qualities every manager desires to see in employees and colleagues.

## Respect Acknowledges Personal Accomplishments

A prime way to show respect for another person—perhaps *the* prime way—is to call attention to that person's accomplishments and positive behaviors.

We say to one another, "I respect you for . . . ," and the way we complete that sentence is nearly always in behavioral terms:

- Your achievements
- Your performance
- Your ability to communicate
- Your fair treatment of others
- Your perseverance
- Your confidence
- Your ability to survive the storm

We tend to respect people for what they do. In the workplace, respect is shown in two major ways: (1) by frequent, genuine verbal praise; and (2) by positive public reports.

Praise is best given person-to-person. It goes well with a clasp on the shoulder or a firm handshake. "You did a great job" is all that needs to be said. What is most important is that your fellow employee knows that you know.

Periodically, you may want to announce the accomplishments of those you work with to group meetings or all-department gatherings. Sometimes an accomplishment may be worth a ten-minute celebration. The accomplishment need not be work related. It may be related to the person's family or an off-the-job performance: "Great solo at church last Sunday," or "Your daughter did a great job in last week's game," or "I see where your wife earned a promotion." Seek out the good deeds, successes, and winning moments of people you work for and with and people you supervise. Report them!

We heard about a school that allows its students to ticket good behavior. The students write out citations for other students to acknowledge what they do that depicts positive, helpful, courteous, uplifting behavior. Some students who are cited are given all-school recognition at a daily assembly hour. What a great way for building community spirit and school morale!

Praise is especially effective when it is for something that is not known or recognized by everyone. Find an opportunity to praise the small deed that an employee tends to feel is invisible or that tends to go unnoticed. Does an employee consistently hold doors open for others? Point out to the person that you have noticed and that you approve.

## Respect Begins with Meeting Basic Needs

In the workplace, the beginning of respect lies in meeting an employee's basic needs for supplies, safety, and health.

There's no integrity in saying, "I have high regard for you," and then refusing to give that person the raw materials (equipment, training, work breaks) needed to do the work.

There's no integrity in saying, "I respect you," and then failing to provide for that person's safety (with equipment, protective clothing, and training).

There's no integrity in saying, "I recognize your value," and then demeaning that person with filthy rest room and lunchroom facilities.

## Fixing the Environment in Department 32

A desire to reconcile and to build relationships opens the eyes of a person. When you deeply desire to do the right thing, very often you find yourself more and more aware of things that are wrong and need to be fixed. You begin to see areas that need reconciliation as never before.

That happened to me at Pittron. In taking the risk to walk the floor of the foundry, I knew I was putting myself into a position to hear about more problems. That is always the risk a manager faces in becoming vulnerable to the employees as never before. Certain workers will always take advantage of that vulnerability and voice their dislikes, express their problems, or call attention to things they'd like to see fixed.

As a manager, you'll also see things that need fixing that you never knew existed. My suggestion to you is that you go into an area looking for problems, not trying to avoid them. Keep your eyes wide open. What can you identify and resolve *before* it is brought to your attention? What problem can you isolate and attack *before* an employee has an opportunity to tell you about it?

At Pittron, Department 32 was the chipping department. The area was filthy and hot because the work was dirty and hot. Department 32 was also an area within the foundry that had experienced a great deal of racial unrest. I knew walking into that department the first time I was going to find things that needed to be fixed.

I ask myself several questions each time I walk into a manufacturing operation of any kind. I first asked those questions about Department 32:

---

- "Where are the employees eating?" I want to see what kind of facility they have for buying food, eating the lunches they've brought from home, or even just relaxing a little away from the line or away from their desks.
- "Where's the nearest drinking fountain?" Is it clean? Is it working? Is the water cold?
- "What are the rest room facilities like?" Are they clean? Are they working? Are soap and towels provided?
- "What about locker rooms?" Many operations provide lockers where workers can store their clothing, shoes, protective clothing (such as hard hats and goggles), and even tools. Do these areas have showers?

---

Looking at these facilities can tell you a great deal about how an organization values its people.

When I walked into Department 32, I was appalled.

The men had *no* place to eat. They were eating on the line where they were working—as previously stated, a filthy place.

Most of the toilets were clogged and virtually unusable. The men had no lockers. Showers were provided, but most of the shower heads had been stripped away. One was dripping. Mold was everywhere.

It didn't take any ingenuity at all to see that things weren't right and needed to be fixed.

I called the director of engineering and the superintendent of maintenance, and I painted a mental picture for them of what I envisioned for the area: a large air-conditioned lunchroom with lots of light, a telephone, an expanded rest room, and an area with lockers and showers that worked. They went away, and over time, we came up with a blueprint.

Meanwhile, I had established a policy that if employees wanted to call a meeting with me, they could. I let everyone know that I'd show up ready to meet—not reluctantly or grudgingly but positive about reaching agreement.

I think this is a critically important policy for a manager to have. If a manager calls a meeting, everybody jumps to attention. Everybody shows up. It's only fair that if employees feel a need to meet with a manager, they have an opportunity to do so. Assumed, of course, is that the need for a meeting is real (in both cases). A meeting must have an agenda and a purpose.

As word got around to my palace guards that I was planning some changes in Department 32, they called a meeting with me. I recognized at the outset that it was a political meeting. (Managers are quick to tell whether a meeting is about a real problem or whether the agenda is an attempt to realign power.)

One of those who had called the meeting was Jim—a very knowledgeable person with a great deal of manufacturing experience. I had a lot of respect for him. In fact, when I left Pittron, I recommended Jim as a person for my job.

Jim said, "The others have asked me to be their spokesman for this meeting. We'd like to go on record that we oppose what you are proposing in Department 32. You shouldn't be doing this." (To "go on record" meant that the men were serious. It meant literally that their comments were going to be recorded and made a part of our regular operations report to corporate headquarters.)

I said, "Why shouldn't we be doing this?"

Jim responded, "It's obvious, Wayne, that you just don't know people."

If he had said anything other than that—such as "Wayne, you obviously don't know operations," or "Wayne, you obviously don't know what this will do to productivity"—I might have been more open to what he was saying because I was new to operations. But when he said that I didn't know people, I felt a red flag go up.

I said, "Why don't you tell me what I don't know about people?"

Jim said, "The fundamental thing you need to realize is that in a union operation, you never give anything away. If you want to provide the union members with this unbelievable new facility down there in Department 32, you need to get something in return. You need to negotiate this. We as a company need a lot of concessions from the union. You need to trade off these new facilities for the things we need. If you don't do that, we want to go on record that we oppose this for the reasons I just stated."

I thought over what Jim had said. It made a little sense. Perhaps we should be getting something in return. And then something rose up inside me that I can't really explain. I just knew that I knew: that was the wrong motivation.

I said to the men in that meeting, "No. We're not going to negotiate this new facility. We're going to take this step in Department 32 because it's the right thing for our company to do for its workers. Our workers should never have had such deplorable conditions in the first place. We should never have allowed the facility to degenerate to the point that it became an item for negotiation. I've got more respect for the men than that."

The employees in Department 32 got their new facility. Pittron got much more in return than ever could have been negotiated. It got a group of workers who felt better about themselves as workers. The better they felt about themselves, the more they were willing to communicate with others. The racial tensions eased. Cooperation improved. Morale rose. And employees reflected greater pride in their work and showed a greater desire to produce perfect quality.

## Preventive Human Relations

Opportunities to enhance respect exist in any organization. Your particular work environment may not require lockers, showers, safety goggles, or an in-house cafeteria. You can always be on the alert, however, for opportunities to enhance an employee's sense of well-being and the ability to work to the best of the ability. Seeing these opportunities requires sensitivity. Ask,

- "What will help this person?"
- "What can I do to make the workplace (or home or neighborhood) a more pleasant place?"
- "What more can I do to bolster this person's self-respect?"

Too often managers dismiss a perceived need by thinking, *That's such a small thing. It doesn't matter.* The little things can loom large over time. Ultimately, they may even be at the heart of a formal labor grievance.

Finding ways to show respect amounts to preventive human relations, not unlike preventive medicine in principle. Create the physically, emotionally, and relationally healthful environment, and you prevent problems from arising—problems that will otherwise slow down your organization and sap the time, energy, and material resources of your employees and managers.

Finding innovative ways of building up respect is a means of proactive management rather than reactionary management marked by crises, disagreements, and sometimes strikes. Proactive Theory R management is not only much more efficient and productive but much more rewarding and fun!

**How Employees View Acts of Dignity and Respect**

Employees frequently see respect in company policies. For example, in a seminar, a group of employees labeled these as examples of ways in which their company extended dignity and respect to them:

- Giving free meals
- Offering stock purchase options
- Providing improved benefits
- Handing out elevator keys
- Granting light duty if needed
- Honoring an employee's request for a change of shift
- Extending the opportunity for voluntary overtime
- Implementing regular crew or staff meetings
- Giving discounts
- Making service awards
- Issuing paychecks that don't bounce
- Arranging for personal development seminars
- Providing in-house day care
- Holding safety meetings (in which workers were advised about safe procedures and the proper way to handle new equipment and chemicals)

At least half of these items are ones that most managers would take for granted as good business policies, economic in nature. The employees, however, viewed them as examples of management looking out for their best interests and respecting them as individuals.

And what about examples of disrespect? A few items made the list that the managers of the employees most likely would never have thought about:

- Not telling employees what happens to their suggestions, or not telling workers why a suggestion hasn't been implemented
- Instituting automatic shift rotations (which employees perceived as continually causing shifts in their personal and family routines, creating a lack of home stability)
- Giving managers one type of bonus party and employees another (apparently at different restaurants with different menus)
- Posting new regulations without discussing them face-to-face with employees
- Cutting back benefits without a thorough explanation
- Inserting new policy directives in paycheck envelopes rather than having a meeting about them

As with love and dignity, respect must be what is perceived by the employees. As a manager, listen to what your employees wish for. In our experience, we've found that many of the wishes are areas in which you can act to show respect.

One day a worker said to his manager, "Hey, why don't you get us a yogurt machine in the cafeteria?"

"Yeah," another employee piped up, "there's too much junk food and not enough healthy food in the cafeteria."

Deciding what was made available in the cafeteria wasn't part of the manager's responsibilities, but at the next meeting he had with his manager, he passed along the idea. He, in turn, passed it one step farther. The idea was adopted, and within a month, a new salad bar and a yogurt machine had been added to the cafeteria's offerings. Before the quarter was out, the menus in the cafeteria had been revised to include at least one low-calorie, low-fat entree at lunch. (Sales in the cafeteria increased significantly over the next six months, with fewer employees bringing their lunch from home and more executives eating in the regular company cafeteria—which in turn provided more communication opportunities between employees and executives.)

For the most part, you aren't going to find the wishes of your employees to be unreasonable, extravagant, or absurd. Employees have a good sense about what a company can and cannot do, and what should and shouldn't happen in the workplace. They know a pipe dream from a realistic request.

**THEORY R SAYS,**

*Respect an employee's needs.*

*Respect an employee's desires.*

*Respect an employee's potential.*

*Respect an employee's family.*

If you ever doubt what more might be done to show respect to your employees, ask them sincerely, "What more can we do to make your work environment a safer, healthier, more productive place?" Your asking alone will be a sign of respect. Your meeting the needs that are voiced will be respect in action.

## Respect My Family, Respect Me

Finally, one of the foremost ways for an organization to show respect for its employees is to recognize and respect each employee's family.

An employee is nearly always connected to others—a spouse, parents, children, roommates. Just by recognizing the importance of the relationship to the employee, an organization extends respect.

An organization might convey respect to the family in several ways:

- Hold open houses of the facility or plant. Let the children of employees see where Daddy or Mommy works. You can't imagine the pride built in a family when a young son is allowed to sit in the seat of Dad's forklift or sit behind the desk in Mom's office.
- Invite spouses to holiday parties.
- Recognize spouses and family members at awards banquets.
- Hold companywide picnics to which families are invited.
- Periodically pay for a spouse to accompany an employee who must attend an out-of-town personal development seminar.
- Feature family accomplishments in the corporate newsletter.
- Have bring-your-teen-to-work days to introduce them to their parents' workplace.
- Send letters of recognition or appreciation for the employee to the employee's spouse. Whenever possible, recognize the spouse's role in the accomplishment.

Extend value to an employee's family and a cyclic effect begins. Family members place greater value on the workplace and the working parent or spouse. Employees feel more pride in their work and feel more appreciation at home. A community spirit is developed that ultimately spills over into the neighborhood and city.

Showing respect is always a win-win proposition.

In so doing, you'll be extending value to your employee!

## THEORY R AT WORK

What more might you do to help meet the basic needs of employees in your area with regard to their

- safety?
- health?
- general well-being?

What more might you do to help a fellow employee reach more of personal potential?

# 10  Theory R Management Requires Tough Personal Discipline

**T**heory R, with Value of the Person principles, is not an easy, weak, sentimental, or lax approach to problems and decisions managers face every day. It is a tough, disciplined, exacting management style.

**What Theory R Management Is Not**

As we move toward discussing some of the practical means of implementing these principles, let's explore at the outset what Theory R management is *not*.

**Theory R Is Not Intended to Replace Current Management Programs**

Theory R management is not a replacement for programs that are already in place and seem to be working. (If a program is not successful, however, a manager would do well to eliminate it and consider alternatives.) Rather, it is intended to be a foundation—a way of thinking and responding, a leadership style—that gives support to all other programs.

One day, I brought home a bouquet of flowers to my wife, Nancy. For several days, the flowers brightened our home and gave her pleasure. But then, they wilted. They had no root to give them ongoing nourishment or to sustain their vibrant colors. I saw in those flowers a strong analogy to many human resource programs.

Many management programs come and go like bouquets of cut flowers because they have no root—no foundation. Programs bear results, but they do not produce ongoing results unless they are firmly grounded in something basic to human nature: the value of the person. Conversely, if a program is built upon a strong foundation of affirmation, appreciating acts of recognition and respect, the chance that such a program will enjoy long-term success is greatly enhanced.

The wise manager will recognize that acts of love, dignity, and respect are not substitutes for raises, promotions, or improved benefits. Rather, a desire to show love, dignity, and respect will compel a manager to seek the best possible good for employees or coworkers. That best possible good will include concrete rewards.

*Valuing People Is Not a Substitute for Giving Tangible Work-Related Rewards*

Love, dignity, and respect don't cost a manager anything. At the same time, they cost a manager everything because that manager will do the utmost to get employees everything they need and everything that is possible to attain. The manager who shows love for employees, has respect for them, and upholds their dignity will want to see them rewarded and will put the job on the line for their advancement and benefit.

The wise manager will recognize that relationships marked by love, dignity, and respect are not established overnight. Such relationships take time to establish. They are long-term endeavors.

*Theory R Is Not a Quick Fix or a Short-Term Solution for an Employee-Management Problem*

Love, dignity, and respect are not Band-Aids for serious economic mismanagement or employee-employer disagreements. Loving and respectful actions can set the stage for better understanding and improved communication, but they are not quick fixes in and of themselves.

Some of the toughest decisions a Theory R manager will ever make will spring from love for a fellow worker. Showing love, dignity, and respect to employees means showing love, dignity, and respect to all employees with impartiality and with an eye toward greater excellence for all involved. Sometimes that means enacting disciplinary measures or requiring an employee to enter a drug treatment program in order to maintain a position with the company or insisting

*Showing Love, Dignity, and Respect to Others Is Not a Weak, Sentimental Approach*

that a person take a leave of absence to work out stress-causing problems (rather than bring that stress to the workplace).

Loving others is hard work. It requires extra time, extra effort, and greater personal discipline. The same goes for upholding the dignity and respect of employees and colleagues. It means putting your reputation on the line and standing by people who may not always appreciate your support.

Traditional management styles require very little in the way of personal character on the part of managers. Theory R requires a great deal of personal integrity. Theory R managers can't fake concern. They must live it out in practical, specific, and action-oriented ways. Traditional managers can remain distant from employees and give lip-service support. Theory R managers must get close enough to employees to know their successes, hear their problems, get involved with their lives, and actually become their coworkers. Employees will see clearly if managers are genuine or fake. Theory R managers are vulnerable to such scrutiny.

Theory R doesn't create some type of pie-in-the-sky fantasy world. Theory R is practical and specific. It calls for a change in behaviors so that all employees are treated more fairly and more positively.

***Theory R Does Not Require That People Always Agree on Matters of Procedure***

Theory R calls for people to come into agreement as human beings and to agree to affirm, respect, and extend dignity to one another. It does not require that all persons agree initially on every fine point of every discussion.

People are always going to have their own opinions. The Theory R manager faces the challenge of ensuring that every person's opinion is valued and that meetings in which varied opinions are expressed are characterized by respect.

***Theory R Is Not a Club to Be Used by Employees Against Management***

Our experience has been that some employees invariably say, "This person is not a Theory R manager because she disciplines us," or "This manager isn't using Value of the Person concepts because he fails to give us everything we want." The intent of such employees is nearly always manipulative to try to cause the manager to give in on key areas of discipline. Theory R management is *not* a giveaway program.

Value of the Person principles have universal application. When these principles are implemented, the work environment changes—whether the environment has two people or two hundred in it. The results that flow from the change in relationships are possible in small offices and large corporations, factories and stores, school districts and universities, hospital and government agencies, union organizations and financial institutions.

*Value of the Person Concepts Do Not Vary According to the Size or Nature of an Organization*

When Kate was named vice president over the creative division of her small corporation, she inherited an area that was in vast disarray, an area that had been managed in a traditional way. She accepted her new position in a time of informal downsizing (i.e., unannounced, unscheduled, but necessary reduction in overhead and staff) and severe corporate cash-flow difficulties, which had resulted in no increase in salaries or benefits to the employees for the previous two years. The division had fifty-five blue-collar and white-collar workers in seven distinct areas—from print shop to public relations, marketing to photography.

Was Kate given a budget for implementing new worker involvement programs? No.

Did she have the opportunity to hire replacements for workers who resigned or were let go? No.

Could she anticipate a lessening of workload for the area? No.

She faced tough situations—ones demanding a leader who was tough, fair, and capable of dealing with highly creative people. She immediately implemented several changes:

1. A weekly staff meeting was held with all supervisors to better coordinate work flow and discuss employee concerns. That was augmented by a monthly staff meeting with all workers—a time of sharing information in both directions. In both meetings, all who attended were encouraged to voice their opinions freely.

2. Personally, she set a trend by showing up for work earlier and staying later. Although her door was always open unless she was in a meeting dealing with confidential matters, employees found the early-morning and late-afternoon times to be ideal opportunities for personal conversations related to corporate concerns.

3. She discovered that rooms with windows were being used to house file cabinets, and she implemented a restructuring of the physical environment so that the creative employees under her supervision might have offices with windows; the file cabinets were moved to interior office areas.

4. Unable to spend corporate money on a fresh coat of paint for their offices, she and the other employees pooled their money and artistic talent, and they met for two weekends to paint their office areas—a creative, team-building exercise that was perceived more as a party than as work.

5. When employees resigned, she fought hard to have a significant portion of their salaries made available for increases to those who remained and were required to take on the extra workload.

6. She restructured one area to remove an obnoxious supervisor from direct contact with employees. The supervisor, a whiz at statistics, was made her personal statistician in analyzing marketing trends and department workload. In restructuring another area, she eliminated two part-time positions and, in so doing, eliminated two problem employees.

7. She frequently posted congratulatory notes and copies of complimentary memos on bulletin boards to share good news with those she supervised.

8. She worked diligently with employees to find more cost-cutting measures and a better way of using networked computers to save time, energy, and money.

9. She implemented an in-house education program so that creative workers in one area might help train workers in other areas who were interested in learning new skills. Lacking a personnel development budget, the department literally chose to develop itself!

A general feeling of goodwill took hold in the area. With it came an outflow of creative and physical energy.

Within a period of two years, Kate had reduced the staff from fifty-five to thirty-five full-time employees, cut the division's budget from $5.3 million annually to $2.7 million, and *doubled* the department's productivity, picking up several awards for outstanding creative effort in the process.

Kate did *not* institute a new program, seek a quick fix, or require that everyone under her supervision agree with her. She was perceived by her employees as anything but weak or sentimental! She provided tangible rewards, whenever possible, in creative ways.

---

**What Theory R Management Does**

In addition to recognizing all that Theory R does *not* do, we need to recognize all that it *does*.

Theory R establishes a relational base for improving all interpersonal relationships—whether at work, at home, or in the community. It can and should operate wherever two or more people are working together toward a common goal, whether that goal is manufacturing a widget, building a marriage, or solving a city's traffic problems.

Theory R encourages reconciliation, not confrontation. When a person does what is right by and for other people, reconciliation is the result. And reconciliation requires effort.

**THEORY R SAYS,**

*Relationships matter most in any corporate setting, whenever two or more people are working toward the same goal or at the same task.*

We can fight day and night over our differences. Arguments are easy to come by. Consider your family life. Isn't it easier to fight about things than to get along? In nearly all situations, it's easier to have confrontation than to experience harmony. Yet virtually everyone agrees that harmony is more productive and more enjoyable.

Theory R provides a basis for agreement, not disagreement. When managers and employees alike mutually agree to give love, uphold dignity, and respect their rightful place in the company, an attitude of cooperation is established. Cooperation yields communication. Communication yields understanding. Understanding brings about agreement and reconciliation.

The organization that comes into agreement about goals, policies, procedures, and rewards is poised for forward motion and positive growth. Nothing stands in its way of working toward excellence.

Finally, Theory R calls for mutual recognition among employees that our value as human beings transcends our places on an organizational chart, the nature of the tasks we perform, or the rewards we may be given by a company. Our value is rooted in our humanity, not in our job descriptions.

**THEORY R SAYS,**

*Reconciliation is more productive than continual confrontation.*

In all, Theory R presents a way of life. It is not limited to the workplace, although that is the focus of this book. At the same time, Theory R is *for* the workplace. It is a sound business theory in that it provides a means of improving the work environment so that more work is done more efficiently with the highest standards of quality for maximum profit.

These principles of Theory R directly challenge the way most managers in our nation have been trained to think.

In many ways, our Japanese competitors have locked on to the human factors much better than we Americans. Read what Dennis Laurie says in his best-seller, *Yankee Samurai:*

*The cornerstone of the Japanese firm is the employee. The company nurtures that resource with an entire body of policies, practices, and traditions, all directed toward making the workplace an environment where the employee can reach his full potential . . . become a "whole man." The Japanese firms, in Japan, largely succeed.*

**THEORY R SAYS,**

**When you love others, uphold their dignity, and respect them, you'll be compelled to find a way to make peace with them and to get along with them.**

*The elements that have been described here combine to form an almost seamless system that treats the individual as an economic, social, and psychological entity. The worker experiences spiritual fulfillment. Socially, and spiritually, the employee is fused to the firm and becomes an integral part of it. It is this approach that is the unique—and arguably the most important—feature of the Japanese management style; it is fundamental to the firm's success.*

*The value placed upon the employee in Japan is reflected in the policies that have been discussed which are constantly reinforced by senior Japanese managers. There are thousands of examples of this reinforcement, but here are two.*

**THEORY R SAYS,**

**Every human being deserves to be valued highly, both within and outside the organization.**

*Mr. Shige Yoshida, an executive vice president of Honda who has been instrumental in that firm's American success, told me: "We believe that the most important asset of the company is people. It is not the production equipment or computers; it is the human resources which make the organization competitive. Of fundamental importance is how the company treats people. If people are satisfied with management, they will perform well. The issue is not pay alone but overall management. If people feel that they are treated well, they will stay with the company."*

*And here are the words of Matsushita's almost mythic founder, Konosuke Matsushita: "The company builds people before it builds things. It is a fundamental tenet of Matsushita to develop extraordinary qualities in ordinary men."*

Theory R asks, Are you willing to place such high regard on the humanity of your organization?

A traditional management philosophy—perhaps not always that spelled out in college textbooks but certainly one that we have seen repeated hundreds and hundreds of times in corporations and organizations across our nation—tends to be marked by several practices.

**The Theory R Challenge to Traditional Management Philosophy**

Buildings and machinery are usually considered not expendable and, therefore, are valuable. People are considered expendable and, therefore, are less valuable than the machines they operate or the job descriptions they fill. Indeed, machines and buildings are called fixed assets, and the labor force is usually called variable cost, fluid, flexible, and malleable.

Dollar for dollar, more is spent each year on the upkeep and maintenance of machines than on the upkeep and maintenance of employees.

Consider the hospital that chooses to spend $1.4 million on an additional magnetic resonance imager (MRI) rather than to give its nurses a raise, the university that would rather add a microfiche system than hire needed librarians, or the media studio that upgrades a sound board without providing for an additional sound engineer in the same budget.

The first solution to which most managers turn when faced with a need for improved productivity or growth is either an economic or a material solution. Some favor an infusion of cash into an operation in order to turn things around. Others attempt to get more or updated equipment to make things better. Rarely do managers turn first to their people resources and ask themselves, "What more can we do for our people?"

Theory R challenges this approach and says, "Spend as much on people as on things."

*First, Traditional Managers Are More Prone to Invest in Material and Economic Resources Than in People Resources*

A great deal of meeting time and memo paper is spent manipulating and fine-tuning the organizational chart. Who reports to whom. How departments and divisions compare. Where weaknesses need to be bolstered. The concern is frequently focused more on procedures and flow charts than on the well-being of the individuals who fill the slots on the chart.

A human resource manager once said to us, "I *love* my programs. I just don't like the people. They mess up my programs!"

*Second, Traditional Managers Regard the Organization as More Important Than the People in It*

Theory R challenges this and says, "Do what is right for the person first."

**Third, Most Managers Have Learned the Right Words Associated with Management, But They Frequently Have Lost Sight of Doing the Right Things**

They talk about quality, but so often, the quality to which they are referring is the quality of the product, the quality of the performance, or the quality of the workplace. They rarely think in terms of the quality of a fellow employee's life.

Managers know the importance of the bottom line, and they value good bottom-line figures. Usually, they value them more than the employee who is at the end of the line. They ask, "Are we in the black or the red?" rather than, "Are the employees well fed—emotionally, physically, and mentally?"

Theory R challenges this and says, "Be concerned first about the quality of your employee's life and the quality of your workplace relationships."

**Fourth, Most Traditional Managers Are Held Accountable for Profit, Productivity, Return on Investment, Safety, and Quality Factors But Rarely for the Relationships Among the People They Supervise**

For Value of the Person principles truly to be implemented, they must become a priority. Managers must be held accountable for the way they treat people and the way employees treat one another.

No executive would allow her managers to come in on Monday morning and say, "This week, I'm not going to be at all concerned about our profitability," or "Today, I don't care about quality." Yet many traditional executives never blink twice about a manager who holds this attitude: "I don't care about the employees—only that the work gets done."

For Theory R to become a priority, means of accountability must be established. Ask yourself,

- "What's the penalty for having poor human relationships?"
- "What happens to the manager who is not affirming employees or respecting them?"
- "What are the consequences for failing to uphold employee dignity?"

Theory R management calls for managers to be evaluated by the way they implement Value of the Person actions—love, dignity, and respect. A manager should not have the prerogative to pick and choose what is important. Either Value of the Person behavior is important—and on par with other vital business concerns—or it is not.

Many organizations have their priorities structured as in figure 10.1.

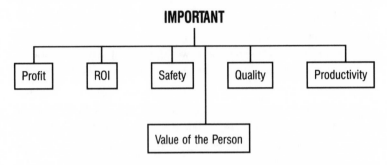

FIGURE 10.1. Traditional organizational priority structure

Theory R challenges the traditional approach and says, "Value of the Person behavior is a must-do aspect of the corporate culture." The new bottom line of what's important to an organization for meeting the challenges of a global economy must look like figure 10.2.

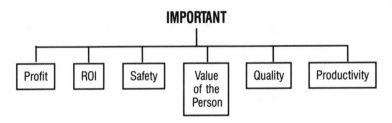

FIGURE 10.2. Theory R organizational priority structure

Stand back a hundred yards and look at most management structures, discussions, and decisions, and you'll find managers far more concerned with the structure of their organizations, their material and economic resources, and their ability to use buzzwords and fad philosophies to manipulate the bottom line and the output of their workforces than they are with the people they manage.

The fact of the matter is, however, that businesses—large or small, profit or nonprofit, union or nonunion—operate only because of people. No factory manufactures a product without people involved in the process; no service organization renders a service without people involved in the process; no sales entity makes a sale without people involved in marketing and merchandising activities. Businesses are first and foremost people. Without people, you can have as much money and equipment as you can imagine, the finest organizational chart, and the best-intentioned corporate philosophy, but absolutely nothing will happen.

On the other hand, show me a workforce that has high morale, good training, and an opportunity to create and produce—employees who truly enjoy coming to work—and almost in spite of economic conditions, equipment breakdowns and inadequacies, and less-than-formal organizational charts, I'll show you a workforce that's poised for turning a profit and producing a top-quality product or rendering a top-notch service.

People are the pivotal factor of any enterprise. They are the most important asset. They are the most important product.

American managers need to recognize these facts.

## Reversing Traditional Misconceptions

In broad general terms, traditional management seems to advocate several postures:

1. Rule your employees with an iron hand, but pay close attention to what customers need and want.
2. Distance yourself from employees. Stay an enigma to them.
3. Be especially tough when it comes to exacting discipline and setting disciplinary policy.

*In the next several pages we present the Theory R management alternatives to these positions.*

## Alternative #1: Treat Your Employees as Well as You Treat Your Customers

Theory R calls upon managers to begin to treat employees as well as they treat customers.

Over the years, we have spent considerable time studying how companies deal with customer complaints. Anytime a customer complaint is filed, a company takes it seriously and acts on it—usually on a highly individual basis. That's good business. No company can afford to alienate its customers.

When an employee has a complaint, however, most companies dismiss the complaint as being relatively unimportant. They fail to give an employee's criticism the same due they would give a customer complaint.

If employees come to you with problems, treat them as you would customers. Hear them out with the same degree of courtesy. Work to solve the problems to their satisfaction.

Bear in mind that some employees don't know how to make suggestions in a form other than complaints. They are far more likely to come to you and say, "Why don't you do something about _____?" or "Why don't you fix _____?" than to write a note and stick it in the suggestion box saying, "Wouldn't it be a good idea if we _____?" or "How about changing _____?"

If you close your door on complaints—refuse to allow them, dismiss employees out of hand, pay only the slightest attention to them—you are going to miss some wonderful opportunities to fix some legitimate flaws or failures within your operation.

Theory R challenges managers to get to know their employees as they never have before.

We saw this sign posted in a laboratory:

*Alternative #2: Get to Know Your Employees, and Let Them Get to Know You*

> *We who are willing*
> *led by the unknowing*
> *to do the impossible*
> *for the ungrateful*
> *have done so much*
> *for so long*
> *with so little*
> *that we now are qualified*
> *to do anything*
> *with nothing.*

Two key words that Theory R managers must consider in getting to know employees are these:

- **PROXIMITY.** Managers can't possibly become more familiar with workers if they remain aloof from them physically. They need to see them, face-to-face and eye-to-eye. Managers frequently tend to literally look down on their employees. They observe assembly line operations from overhead offices and catwalks rather than walk the line where the employees are gathered. Others may work in locked-off executive floors, inaccessible to those immediately beneath them, both literally and figuratively. Wise managers get down on the floor where the action is.

- *AVAILABILITY.* Can any employee make an appointment to see you? How much of your time do you make available to your employees? Does your secretary give lip service to employee availability but in actuality close the gate on employees seeking a meeting with you?

## How Open Is Your Door?

When we ask a group of managers, "Who among this group has an open-door policy?" nearly every hand in the room goes up.

But when we ask a group of employees, "Who among you has a supervisor with an open-door policy?" very few hands go up.

It's not possible to have it both ways. We've concluded that managers very often think they have open-door policies when they don't.

An open-door policy is one in which employees can walk into your office at any time and be made to feel welcome. Furthermore, both the worker and the manager feel comfortable.

If you have a procedure of having someone screen all of your appointments and all of your calls, you don't truly have an open-door policy. Consider why calls and appointments are screened in the first place—generally, to weed out problems.

## Becoming Familiar with a New Group

A manager sometimes is put into a supervisory role over people about whom the manager knows very little, if anything. Perhaps the manager has been hired in to take over the position; perhaps the manager has been transferred from another department.

*There are several ways a manager can get a running start on getting to know the people.*

*PHOTOS.* Insist that all personnel files have photos in them. If they don't presently, send someone out into the workplace with a camera, and avail yourself of one-hour photo processing. Put names with faces.

Many medical schools make it a standard practice to take photos of all the incoming students and then to distribute the photos (with name labels) to every basic science professor so that professors can learn the names of their students more quickly. Students are made to feel like colleagues from their first day.

**PERSONNEL FILES.** Read the person's application for employment. You may or may not want to read all the other documents in the person's file. If you note that the file is filled only with negative reports, make a decision that you are going to find some positive information about the person to add to the file! Or purge the files. You might even ask employees to fill out new forms—ones that call for information you'd like to have—and start a new set of files with those forms.

**NAME LISTS.** Become familiar with the names of the people you supervise. Be sure you know how to pronounce each person's name correctly. If you have doubts about how to pronounce a name or which name a worker prefers to go by, ask. Look for your employees' names in the newspaper.

**MINGLE WITH THE TROOPS.** Periodically join the employees for lunch, or order in pizza for everybody and have a spontaneous celebration party. (You may be celebrating your fifty-fifth month as a manager or a secretary's one hundredth day without absenteeism.) Ask your employees how things are going with their family members.

If a manager under you is handing out awards in a special meeting, or if a department under you is having a Christmas party or a going-away party, make an appearance. Say a few words of thanks to those being honored. Be sure to speak to them personally and directly if at all possible.

It's difficult, if not impossible, for a manager to really get to know employees unless some time is spent with them off the clock. You don't need to show up at every event in every employee's life—that would be physically impossible and probably an unwise practice to start—but you can show up periodically and spontaneously at certain events and send a very strong signal to your employees that you care about what happens in their lives.

The event might be the championship game in which an employee's child is playing, the local variety show in which some workers are performing, or a high-school play in which an employee's child has a starring role. We're not at all suggesting that you crash a private party. Find public events in which your employees are participating, and attend as a member of the public.

## Getting in Touch with the Front Line

The frontline supervisors function where the real work happens. They are the prime enforcers of administrative policy, and they put up with the most grief. Those above them are coming down on their heads continually to exact more productivity, higher quality, and better employee performance. The employees below them are constantly kicking them for improvements in the workplace, better treatment of themselves, and more rewards. The frontline supervisors generally hear about equipment breakdowns, grievances, confrontations between employees, and other types of problems before anyone above them. At the same time, they are often blamed or called upon to justify problems with the bottom line by those to whom they report.

What are the words frequently heard from frontline supervisors? "I've seen 'em come, and I've seen 'em go." Frontline supervisors tend to see it all—and to get the heat from all directions.

In our opinion, managers and executives need to view their frontline supervisors in a new light.

---

- Make this group your first priority. They, perhaps more than any other segment of an organization, need to experience your affirmation and acts of care and respect. They need to know that you understand the pressures they are under and that you will work with them to alleviate as much of the stress as possible.
- Make a special effort to provide training for this group in Value of the Person principles and behaviors.
- Support your frontline supervisors' attempts to enact a Theory R leadership style.

---

We have never seen Theory R implemented successfully in an organization without the support of the frontline supervisors. They are the ones who are with the people. They, above all others, need to develop people-relating skills. Too often they are ignored.

## Letting Yourself Be Known, Too

Theory R challenges managers not only to get to know their employees better but also to allow themselves to be known by them.

In traditional management philosophy, managers are encouraged to remain essentially unknown to people they manage. It is against good manager protocol to express personal weakness, doubt, hurt, frustration, or failure. Needless to say, managers experience these things—and they eventually do express them through temper tantrums, outbursts, ridicule, and sometimes ulcers and heart attacks—but it is against traditional management teaching for managers to give expression to any sign of weakness or error before employees.

The result is often one of self-justification or scapegoating on the part of managers. When managers must always be right, the pressure builds to maintain at least the illusion of perfection. The result is that employees tend to be criticized unfairly or extremely or to be blamed for anything that goes wrong in the workplace.

Employees, of course, see through this and resent it. They know managers aren't perfect, and therefore, employees usually come to regard them suspiciously and even to label them as hypocrites.

Theory R calls for managers to recognize their humanity and admit it to others. This vulnerability requires authenticity on the part of managers. The more leaders make themselves available to their followers, the more followers will have an opportunity to appraise the integrity of the leaders:

- Do actions match up with words?
- Is there consistency in what they believe, say, and do?
- Is there stability in their lives and in their ability to relate to others?
- Do they say what they mean and mean what they say?

All of these are character issues. Theory R managers are willing to put character on the line.

## It Takes Two to Reconcile

Theory R challenges managers to reconcile differences with least favorite employees.

One of the most courageous things a manager can ever do is to target the least likely to be won over person in the group as the person to value. We dare you to do it.

This is not to say that the archenemies must be a manager and an employee. Any two people who come into agreement about Value of the Person concepts and who begin to exhibit affirming, appreciating, and recognizing behaviors will be witnesses to others.

John and Gary once had been engineers, working side by side. They had been friends. Something happened between them, and neither man was able to let it go. John had gone on to be a supervisor. His former friend, Gary, was still in the lab and under his supervision. Their conversations through the years had been monologs. Gary might have said, "I need this." John might have said, "I want you to do that." No conversation. No rapport. No friendliness.

The next day after attending a Value of the Person—Theory R Seminar, Gary got off the elevator with a fellow engineer, and he spotted John talking with another supervisor. As he walked by the two men, he said, "Good morning, John."

John responded in a friendly way, "Good morning, Gary." That doesn't sound like an earth-shattering exchange, but the engineer who was with Gary nearly dropped his teeth. He knew of the long-standing animosity between the two men, and he stopped in his tracks and said in disbelief, "What is going on here?"

Within the hour, news had spread through an entire division of the company that John and Gary were back on speaking terms. Everybody who heard the news left work that day a little happier.

Wherever reconciliation needs to take place, it should.

## A Maintenance Check for People!

Just as machines need maintenance to keep them in good working order, so do people. The manager who understands people will adopt a maintenance check for employees.

Take the temperature of your organization:

---

- How is morale?
- Are the employees happy?
- Is the atmosphere characterized by uplifting attitudes and by a sense of fun at working hard and working well?

---

If you have answered no to any of these questions, it is time to put Theory R into practice. Theory R management calls for employees' human needs to be maintained on a daily basis. Value of the Person principles in action put the grease on the wheel and the break in the day.

The traditional manager generally understands the need for a physical break in the course of a day. The Theory R manager, however, goes beyond physical breaks and gives employees a psychological or emotional break.

Occasionally, lubrication needs are applied to human relationships; a new tone is set for the entire organization. Interpersonal "grease" can sometimes be as simple as a smile in passing or an office picnic or an unexpected half day off or a spontaneous birthday celebration during a coffee break or a genuine hearty handshake and "thank you."

The human touch gives a person a break that may be only five seconds long. Nevertheless, it can be a touch that reaches the heart and keeps workplace relationships humming.

## Never Laxness

Theory R has no sympathy for laxness. There's no profitability in laxness. The most unkind thing managers can do for employees is to encourage them to be lazy or to allow them to continue to under-achieve. If managers promoted that attitude, the company would soon go broke.

Many people, we've discovered, seem to equate the toughness required in making business decisions with a tough demeanor or a tough manner of speaking. The two don't have to go together! Never do we advocate soft, weak-kneed, or sentimental business decisions. Never do we maintain that a manager should go easy on demanding excellence. But always, we hold out that love, dignity, and respect must be shown.

---

- A manager who gives genuine love must be available to receive that type of love.
- A manager who extends dignity must maintain personal dignity.
- A manager who shows respect must earn respect.

---

Managers must exact discipline and require certain behaviors. That is not contradictory to showing respect and love to employees.

For example, if you are talking with a person who has an absentee problem, you do not say, "I'm sorry you're absent so much. It really doesn't matter." No! You say to that employee, "Is there a problem here? Is there a reason you are absent so much?"

The employee might respond, "My child is sick all the time."

"Well," you might ask, "what can we do to help you find proper sick-child care?" The overall position of the manager is that absen-

*Alternative #3: Toughness Is Not the Opposite of Valuing*

teeism cannot continue—a position not voiced with threats or coercion—but a position that is maintained even as the manager seeks to find a way of solving the underlying problem for the absenteeism.

As a Theory R manager, your goal is to find a way to help your employee resolve problems and not only get to work but have a desire to get to work. Absenteeism isn't the core problem. The difficulty or situation causing the absenteeism is the core problem. Ultimately, the core problem is the one that must be solved.

Consider, for example, an employee who is making repeated errors that involve a certain computer program. The goal of the Theory R manager is not to dismiss that person's errors out of compassion but to find the reason for the errors and fix them. Perhaps the person needs more training. Perhaps the person needs more practice before tackling real tasks. The manager is entirely correct in requiring improved performance. But along the way, it takes no extra effort, time, or money to say to that employee, "I want you to be the best computer operator we've ever had. I believe you have it in you to do that. Let's see how we can eliminate this error rate."

Theory R requires that you respect employees enough to challenge them and then you help them to be everything they can be. Managers nearly always want their employees to be more and do more. Few, however, are willing to help them get to that higher performance level.

Some of the toughest people I've met—and in the steel industry you encounter tough men at every turn—also had the softest hearts. There was nothing weak about men who could handle machines pouring metal at 2800 degrees Fahrenheit when they tenderly held little children or lovingly cared for their elderly parents.

Truly tough people, who are secure in their strengths and abilities, generally have what it takes to show kindness to those in genuine need.

**THEORY R SAYS,**

*Treat your employees as well as you treat your customers. Listen to them.*

*Work with them to alleviate their problems.*

*Get to know your employees, and let them get to know you.*

*Create an atmosphere of reconciliation—even in times of discipline and the establishment of strict standards and high goals.*

- To be sensitive to an employee's pain, weariness, or frustration is not a sign of weakness; it's a sign of confident caring.
- To be sensitive to the reasons behind an employee's absenteeism or absentmindedness is not a sign of weakness; it's a sign of concern.
- To be sensitive to the toll that stress is taking on an employee—whether work-based or home-based stress—is not a sign of weakness; it's a sign of compassion.

In sum, Theory R takes a distinctly different approach to the way a traditional manager relates to an employee. Value of the Person concepts call for manager behaviors that are grounded in concern, caring, and compassion. The difference is not related to results, goals, or standards of excellence; rather, it is related primarily to the tone, style, and content of a manager's interactions with others.

Looking back over the things we've discussed in this chapter, we hope you'll conclude with us that there's nothing cheap, sentimental, or easy about Theory R.

**Tough Personal Discipline**

Theory R requires an inner toughness and a very deep commitment to doing the right thing for other people.

- Confrontation is easy. It's simple to hold grudges, trample on the feelings of others, be disrespectful, resort to indignities, or fall into hate.
- Reconciliation is hard work and never-ending work.

Theory R requires leadership.

## THEORY R AT WORK

Have you ever experienced reconciliation with a person? How did you feel? What was the outcome of that reconciliation? What changes in attitude or behavior did you see?

What Theory R leadership qualities do you need to adopt and implement?

If you are in a management position, what more of your material resources might be channeled to your most important resource of all, your people?

# 11     Theory R Challenges Managers to Become Leaders

**A**person is a manager only within the confines of an organizational structure. A manager is a manager only if something and someone are available to manage.

Theory R leadership is an inner quality and a personal characteristic. Leaders can exist in any role; leadership can be manifest in any circumstance, at any rung of an organizational chart, or behind any title.

Theory R calls on executives and managers to be leaders. It also issues that challenge to rank-and-file employees.

In the last chapter, we cited qualities, characteristics, and actions that set Theory R managers apart from their traditional peers. But we did not address two issues that permeate traditional management practices. We call them the trappings of traditional management.

## The Trappings of Traditional Management

By traditional management, we refer to the way things have become, intentionally or unintentionally. Traditional management exists in most work environments. It has evolved over the years into what it is, and the style is primarily marked by two overriding issues: (1) the trappings of power; and (2) the trappings of greed.

Power is the stance that says, "I dictate; you obey." No questions asked. No involvement in the process. And if questions and involvement are formally requested, the managers generally want to give the illusion of inclusion, not true participation. *Power* and *control* are virtually interchangeable words in the workplace.

In the traditional workplace, power is held at a premium. It is guarded at all costs by managers. Power and control, however, are not the same as leadership.

Any organization must have leadership. Someone must take charge of situations and be responsible for them. The buck has to stop somewhere. And managers *should* be the ones who say, "This is the way we're going." That does not mean managers need issue such a directive in a style that demeans or is backed up by devaluing threats to those being led.

***Unfortunately, power is often substituted for leadership:***

*#1: The Trappings of Power*

Power rules by threat. Leadership leads by example.

Power insists on having its own way. Leadership seeks the best way for all involved.

Power runs according to an I-win-you-lose philosophy. Leadership strives for a way in which everybody wins.

Power says that only one person can have an opinion that counts. Leadership says that all opinions are valid, but some are more workable and beneficial than others.

Power says, "I'm more valuable than you are because I have control." Leadership says, "Each of us is valuable. In this circumstance, I have authority for the outcome and responsibility for your welfare."

Power says, "I can treat you any way I want because I'm in charge." Leadership says, "I must treat you with respect because I'm the leader."

Power says, "You must serve me." Leadership says, "The greatest leader is the servant of all. I must serve you."

The difference between power and leadership is not one of rank or position. It is one of attitude and interpersonal behavior. *Leadership seeks to engage people, not enrage people.*

*Power vs. Leadership*

The type of power we're referring to here might also be called *positional power*. It is not power rooted in the inner person. Posi-

*Positional Power*

tional power is external, generally granted by someone else. Personal power, on the other hand, flows from within.

Positional power depends on job descriptions and titles. Very often, positional power provides no room for personal growth or creativity. Managers find themselves doing what the last manager did to fulfill the role. All in all, positional power is a poor substitute for true leadership.

*Personal Inner Power*

Personal inner power, on the other hand, recognizes that individuals can mobilize and be mobilized. Personal inner power says that individuals have leadership capacities that can be exerted, and that the power of the person can extend far beyond a job description or title in influencing positive attitudes and behaviors.

Supervisors who embody personal inner power aren't likely to allow themselves to get locked into a series of tasks (positional power). Instead, they are challenged to be leaders among men and women. They dream dreams for their people that are beyond quotas. They envision the way things can be for everybody—with win-win situations all around. They see that people make the difference in an organization, not slots on a company chart.

Personal inner power is very much associated with leadership. Positional power is not.

The foremost indicators of positional power tend to be economic. Traditional managers almost always turn first to economic factors to validate, bolster, garner, or acquire power. Managers who have the best performance are those who have the best bottom line. Promotions are almost always geared toward those who manipulate and take credit for economic success.

It follows, then, that those who fill the upper slots of an organizational chart are those who control the greatest amount of economic and material resources and who, not surprisingly, receive the greatest economic and material rewards.

When you reward a person with money and position—or with the trappings of power—you send a strong signal that these are the two greatest hallmarks of good corporate performance.

Think for a moment, however, about what we all tend to value most in life. We do not value money or position. In fact, we would gladly trade all of our money or position for the things we truly value: health, family, love, fulfillment, peace of mind and soul, and an hour more of life.

One of our colleagues, Tony Campolo, often shares with our seminar participants his observations after years of sitting at the bedsides of persons facing death. Never, he says, does he hear, "If only I had made one last sale," "If only I had spent more time researching that new computer program," or "If only I had opened one more store." The "if only's" are far different. They are about people and relationships: "If only I had spent more time getting to know my little girl," "If only I had loved my wife more," or "If only I had taken time to throw a baseball with my little boy." Strip life to its basics and the values that really matter are concerned with relationships.

All of these true values come from and are verified not by economic factors or corporate status but by quality relationships. At the heart of leadership is the ability to relate to others. People who do not value relationships severely limit their ability to become true leaders. This applies not only to the workplace but to personal and family relationships as well. True leaders take responsibility for the tenor and quality of all relationships in which they are involved. An arrogant attitude drawn from positional power tends to create negative relationships. An affirming attitude arising from leadership tends to create positive ones.

Nevertheless, in the workplace traditional managers strive to guard not true values but their position—their turf, their power base, their ability to control information or resources. And they exercise that power primarily through economic means, from control of a budget to bribes to threats that hit the pocketbook.

Personal inner power, by contrast, is power that is derived, in part, from an inner satisfaction that the person's relationships are in order. Personal inner power allows a leader to look in the mirror and say, "I'm at peace with my family and my coworkers." It does not need to rely on economics for its existence.

**#2: The Trappings of Greed**

Greed is a natural offshoot of power. Greed is the desire to have more and more at the expense of others. Greed assumes that those in power should have more than those without power—on the basis of position, not necessarily accomplishment or degree of effort.

Greed says, "I deserve more than you because I'm better than you are." The opposite is an approach that says, "What I earn and you earn is based on the work we perform, not our character or our value as individuals."

In a traditional management structure, both power and wealth rise to the top, usually in disproportionate measures. Furthermore, traditional management style dictates that only a few have power and wealth, and that the primary reason for workers is to create power and wealth for those at the top.

In 1992, the average chief executive officer received in total compensation 160 times more than the average worker in the corporation!* Don't tell us that greed isn't rampant in corporate America.

**THEORY R SAYS,**

*People come before economic and organizational concerns. They are the most important asset and the most important product of any organization.*

We are not suggesting that we adopt some type of utopian everybody-earns-the-same-amount philosophy for the American workplace. That is the opposite of capitalism and free enterprise, the opposite of rewarding a person based on the quality of performance. We do suggest, however, that workers are not slaves. Their value to the workplace is not disposable. Neither is it for the sole purpose of creating a fat bonus for the person at the top of the organizational chart. Their purpose is to be part of a corporate effort that is profitable, and the corporation will remain profitable only if some of the profits are returned to employees in the form of pay, benefits, and recognition.

In all, in a traditional management environment the economics and structure of the organization come first—not the people. Traditional managers overlook this key fact: without people, a business does not have economics or structure.

*Our people in American business are our number one resource.* They are the source of all creativity, ingenuity, ideas, skill, and effort. The quality of a company's employees makes or breaks a company. When a company loses good people, it loses economically and organizationally.

**Theory R Calls for Inner Motivation**

What does it take for people in top-management positions to divest themselves of the trappings of power—to give up "because I say so" control, to deny the lure of greed, and to do so because absolute power and runaway greed are not parts of doing what is right?

It takes character of the highest order.

The motivation for Theory R is internal. It is motivation that is self-imposed, not dictated or demanded from someone higher up the

*According to *Business Week* (April 26, 1993), the average CEO received $3,842,247 in total compensation, compared to $24,411 for the average worker.

chart. It's a rare kind of motivation that calls upon a person to ask questions such as these:

- "What more can I be doing for my fellow employees (above me, below me, and laterally)?"
- "How can I show more concern for the welfare of people with whom I work on a daily basis?"
- "What more can I do to build up the dignity of people with whom I work?"
- "How can I better recognize the achievements of my employees?"
- "Am I showing enough respect for others?"
- "Do I really show love to my employees in practical, pragmatic ways that they can experience?"

If these sound like soul-searching questions, they are! Theory R asks a manager to look inside and ask, "Am I treating my employees the way I would like to be treated?"

It's rare motivation that will cause a person to want to extend value to others at all times—at home, at church, on the streets of the city, in the factory, in the office, at the mill, on the subways, in shops, at the family dinner table, in the company cafeteria, on the assembly line, and in the corporate conference room.

Value of the Person concepts are rooted in right behaviors across the entire spectrum of life. They work to better a friendship, a marriage, a family, and a community, and they work in corporations and organizations of all types.

There's nothing lax, easy, or sentimental about this motivation.

## Tough-Minded, Forward-Thinking

One of the most profound editorial commentaries we have read in recent years is that by Stanley Truskie. Truskie writes,

*With all the talk these days about empowerment, teamwork, and participative management, one may well get the impression that effective leaders are soft, easy-going, "warm and fuzzies" who lead by creating a club-like atmosphere where people can do their own thing, at their own pace. Nothing can be further from the truth.*

*My professional work and research with more than 200 executive leaders of the nation's top companies reveals that the exceptional ones—those who build successful organizations—are focused, tough, demanding, and results-driven.*

*One of the key attributes I have found that contributes to exceptional leadership is the sincere desire to lead in the service of others. Those lacking this attribute—the highly ambitious, self-serving executives with narcissistic tendencies—are the ones who are brutally tough and wear people down.*

*They are abrasive, destructive, and vindictive. In the long run, they usually fail. The exceptional leaders, on the other hand, are the ones who build organizations that are consistently successful. They develop toughness in their people by challenging, inspiring, and demanding.*

*It's the kind of toughness that results in the desire to do the very best one can. It's the kind of toughness that is mirrored by the exceptional leader. . . .*

*You cannot instill honesty and openness if you lack integrity and conviction; you cannot inspire an intense desire to succeed if you lack persistence and determination; and you cannot evoke high standards of performance if you lack a passion for achieving excellence.*

*Proclamations, written messages extolling the virtues of being the best or attaining world-class status, are nice-sounding, provocative words found in many corporate-mission and vision statements. But these end up being nothing more than wish lists if the spirit of the message is not embodied in the character and displayed by the behavior of leaders who sponsor them.*

We couldn't agree more.

---

**Theory R Doesn't Deny a Manager's Style**    Some managers question whether Value of the Person concepts diminish or replace a person's management style.

Value of the Person behavior doesn't negate a manager's right to personal style. Every person is different. Each will express the self in highly personalized ways. Each will set distinctive goals and have a unique way of communicating.

That's OK.

Neither does Theory R do away with personal ambition. There's nothing within Theory R that compels managers to stunt personal growth or curtail their careers. In fact, the opposite is more likely. Theory R compels people to become fully who they are, including a full recognition and acceptance of their human needs, frailties, and weaknesses.

A manager can still wear a suit and tie. Most workers expect it of a manager and respect him more for it. His ties can continue to be a little old-fashioned.

A manager can still write memos in place of holding meetings. Her memos will undoubtedly be a little more personal and a little less dictatorial in tone.

A manager can still be shy. He'll work, however, toward looking his workers in the eye, and he'll become willing to enter his workers' world rather than retreat behind a desk and a closed door.

A manager can still be quiet in personality. There's nothing in Theory R that requires a gung ho, rah-rah, overly enthusiastic personality.

Neither does Theory R keep a person from aiming at the top of the corporation. Her ambition will not be stunted by valuing others, although her personal ambition is likely to be enlarged to include ambitious dreams for everybody she supervises. She'll also aim for the top through hard work, honest results, and superior performance rather than attempt to get there on the backs of others.

Neither does Theory R ask a manager to give up any managerial tasks or business skills. Theory R does *not* take away the right of a manager to manage the operation. It calls for a manager to receive input from employees, but it *never* takes away the right to manage.

My World War II experiences showed me clearly that all persons in combat—which means killing—want a leader they can respect, a leader they trust to be a tough, disciplined person of integrity, a leader who says what he means and means what he says.

In many ways, the corporate world is no less a battlefield. Competitors are enemies. Job losses are casualties. New product innovations are just as potent as new weaponry. And those who engage in the day-to-day struggle to survive—to keep profits flowing from quarter to quarter, to keep the line running smoothly, to keep the inventory moving—want leaders who lead.

Theory R never asks managers to give up their ability to make sound business decisions or to engage in the tasks of management: writing memos, preparing reports, analyzing data, researching, handling necessary paperwork, bringing problems to the attention of superiors, reading or studying ways of improving an operation.

Theory R does call for managers, however, to move beyond a task-only orientation and to regard people and relationships as prime ingredients in making an operation more effective—both in the workplace and at home.

Theory R challenges managers to be more than technicians who hide behind their expertise, their experience, or their longevity and who give directives based on numbers and probability.

Again, it takes courage and discipline. It requires leadership.

---

**Leading or Managing?**     Here are a dozen questions to ask yourself if you are questioning whether you are leading with Theory R skills or just managing:

---

1. "Am I so busy combating the urgent that I have forgotten to do what is important?"
2. "Do my attitudes communicate to employees, 'I'm for you' or 'I'm against you'?"
3. "Do I respect employees' suggestions and input?"
4. "Am I visible and available?"
5. "Do I take employees' suggestions and problems seriously?"
6. "Are my decisions mostly short-term or long-term?"
7. "Is what I *do* consistent with what I *say*?"
8. "Are my decisions influenced by the 90 percent or the 10 percent of the workforce?"
9. "Am I more interested in playing the political game or in doing what is right?"
10. "Am I being effective or merely efficient?"
11. "Am I making decisions that are cowardly or courageous?"
12. "Am I paying attention to all relationships or just some of them?"

---

There are three more things that Theory R leadership requires that a traditional management style does not.

**Leadership Requires More Than Management**

Leaders must know where the pack is going. They must be privy to information about company goals and direction. They must be willing to convey that information to the troops in an inspiring, nonthreatening, or nonoverwhelming way, and they must be enthusiastic about going toward the stated goal.

*First, Leaders Know and Give Direction*

It's easier for managers to demand blind loyalty than to build informed loyalty. Leadership requires that people give clear, precise, and thorough information so that all workers will know where they are going and where they fit into the overall direction of the organization.

Leaders must present an example to workers that is appealing, not one that repels. It's easier for many managers to be mean and exacting supervisors than to find ways to be models worth emulating and following.

*Second, Leaders Must Find Ways of Encouraging Others to Follow Them Rather Than Demanding That They Do*

As author Warren Bennis states, "Leaders take people to a new place. Leaders don't push others, they pull. They energize those around them with a vision and bring them to identify with the organization's tasks and goals."

They are called upon to find new ways of challenging, motivating, and inspiring those who follow. From-behind managers, on the other hand, need only to enforce the prescribed rules, which are usually set in concrete. From-behind management requires no flexibility and very little innovation.

*Third, Leaders Are Called Upon to Be Innovative and Creative*

Lloyd Dobyns and Clare Crawford-Mason point out an interesting fact in their book, *Quality or Else: The Revolution in World Business:*

> At the turn of the century, no high jumper could hope to be a world-class competitor unless he used the scissors

*method, the style still used in some secondary schools to get young athletes started. Then, a few years later, someone developed the roll-over method, in eastern and western versions, and if you couldn't do one of the two, you could forget a gold medal. Roll-over was king until a high school senior named Dick Fosbury found he could get a lot higher if he went over the bar backward; now, if you can't master the Fosbury Flop, you can just as well get off the field and avoid embarrassment.*

The question Theory R asks a person is this: Are you willing to adopt a new perspective in the way you treat those around you—an innovative and creative perspective that truly has the potential to take your company or organization higher?

**Take a Step Beyond**

A Theory R leader who truly begins to live out Value of the Person principles finds that life gets a little more complicated. It's no longer a matter of what the contract says or the union fights for or the company mandates. It's going beyond what is formalized and in writing to explore what is motivating workers and, in some cases, keeping them from being all that they can be (and all that the company needs them to be).

A Theory R leader cannot and willfully chooses not to hide behind layers and layers of bureaucratic indifference.

Are you a leader? Evaluate this list of qualities.

**Qualities of a Theory R Leader**

1. Spirit of Initiative
   - Do you reach your own decisions?
   - Do you have the courage to act?
   - Do you cooperate with others?
2. Willing to Risk
   - Do you act in the face of need?
   - Are you willing to stand alone?
   - Are you willing to lose face, be vulnerable to others?
3. Sense of Responsibility
   - Do you respond with ability (response plus ability)?
   - Do you accept challenges?
   - Do you hold yourself accountable for actions?

4. Authenticity
   - Are you truthful with self and others?
   - Have you developed your own style?
   - Do you have integrity—walks the talk?
5. Generosity
   - Do you give of self?
   - Do you give of possessions?
   - Do you give of personal potential?
6. Patience
   - Do you go the second mile?
   - Do you err on the side of giving someone a break?
   - Do you give relationships time to build?
7. Perseverance
   - Do you stay committed to the long haul?
   - Do you stay in relationship?
   - Do you continue to work for reconciliation?

Many managers don't want to learn the skills or take the risks that leadership requires—especially leadership that compels them to value their employees rather than demand that employees value them. The fact remains, however, that leaders promote greatness and excellence in themselves and in others. Managers only maintain the status quo.

Leaders take a company forward. They are the ones who pave the way with double-digit productivity, perfect quality, and maximum profits. They are the ones with highly loyal, highly enthusiastic, and creative workforces. They are the ones who bring a company to life and then to the fullness of its potential.

Leaders lead.

From-behind managers tend to keep a company marching in place.

## People Skills Require Training

One reason that managers often resort to a confrontational management style is that they have never been trained in people skills. Most managers are promoted to their supervisory positions not because of their ability to deal with people but because they are bright, have certain technical skills, have seniority, or have a forceful personality that stands out in a crowd.

If you are in an upper-level management position, one of the smartest things you can do is to include people-relating skills and valuing skills as part of your criteria for promoting people into supervisory positions. They should probably be the foremost factors you consider in naming a person to a management role.

Managers can fire or discipline employees for failing to perform their tasks well, for failing to show up for work consistently, for not producing fast enough, or for being insubordinate. Perhaps it's time that managers can be disciplined or fired for not treating their people with love, dignity, and respect.

If you are a manager, choose to become a leader and then avail yourself of people-skills training. Find someone who can help you communicate more effectively and relate more easily to others. Have the courage to enact and to practice what communication specialists advise you to do.

**Two Sets of Qualities**
This chart outlines five distinct differences between a manager and a Theory R leader.

| Manager | Theory R Leader |
|---|---|
| Seeks short-term profits at the expense of long-term profits and relationships | Committed to long-term profits as a by-product of long-term relationships |
| Satisfied with the status quo—reacts to changes | Initiates positive changes |
| Uses the big stick approach | Uses personal influence |
| Instinct for survival | Instinct for accomplishments |
| Stresses efficiency—doing things right | Stresses effectiveness—doing the right things |

Again, in Theory R we regard every person as being capable of being a leader. While some may hold that leaders are made and others that leaders are born, we contend that leadership is latent within every person and must be brought forth.

Our friend and colleague Reid Carpenter cites *five basic traits of Theory R leadership that need to be developed:*

*1. VISION.* The Theory R leader has a vision for employees, co-workers, and family members that extends beyond personal desires and limitations. The Theory R leader helps people gain a greater vision for their lives, then helps them turn the visions into reality.

2. *WILLINGNESS TO ENGAGE.* The Theory R leader is willing to engage in the lives, joys, hurts, hopes, and aspirations of employees, coworkers, and family members. A degree of vulnerability is a prerequisite to experience growth in any relationships, at work or at home.

3. *CHANGE.* The Theory R leader accepts change and sees it as an opportunity for growth and development. The leader encourages employees, coworkers, and family members to embrace change as a possibility for growth.

4. *SERVANT.* The Theory R leader takes on the garb of a servant and understands that by giving the self to serve employees, coworkers, and family members, power is not lost but gained. Ultimately, the goal of Theory R management is service. It's a manager's job to *help* people do their work rather than crack a whip or exact obedience. Think of your life. There's not one long-term relationship that you have that is not based on mutual servanthood.

5. *BELIEF.* The Theory R leader develops a fundamental belief and value structure that acknowledges love, dignity, and respect as the rights of everyone.

Every person has the capacity to lead the self, first and foremost. A person has the ability to take charge and exert the will over feelings, attitudes, values, beliefs, behavior and, ultimately, performance. A person has the ability to turn potentiality into capability, and that is a matter of taking charge, making decisions, exerting influence, and moving from past performance to a better future performance—in other words, leadership!

Don't limit yourself to being a manager. We challenge you to become a leader, an innovator, part of a new breed of American businessmen and businesswomen!

## THEORY **R** SAYS,

*Choose to be a leader.*

*Leadership is tough. It takes discipline, courage, and an ability to deny the trappings of traditional management: power and greed.*

*Leadership is rooted in service.*

*Leadership cannot be separated from the quality of a person's relationships.*

*Leadership is what America sorely needs.*

## THEORY **R** AT WORK

Are you a leader or a manager?

Have you felt trapped by traditional approaches toward power and greed? How?

What can you do to become a more effective leader?

# 12    The Choice to Walk and Talk Together

**M**ost formal communication in a traditional management structure flows top-down with lots of informal lateral communication among peers.

The trouble with top-down communication is that it is nearly always one-sided and nearly always dictatorial—"I say, you do" in tone.

If questioned, traditional managers frequently respond,

- "It's worked this way in the past. We'll continue to do things this way."
- "The numbers show that this is the most productive, useful way to proceed."
- "The years of experience give me the authority to tell you what to do."

Such managers are rarely innovative. They follow the company line and do what they are told to do. Most such managers are comfortable being governed by numbers, just as they are comfortable governing by them.

Theory R calls for a new approach: talking *with* employees rather than always talking *to* them.

In talking with employees, managers need to find something to talk about other than the facts of policies and procedures. Many times, jokes can be shared in a way that upholds the respect of both parties, funny anecdotes can be recalled without damaging the dignity of any person, or mishaps occur that can be laughed about (without laughing *at* any party involved). As our friend and colleague Tony Campolo says, "Make the workplace a fun place." When all joking, teasing, and laughing is prohibited, who wants to be there? We certainly don't.

## But What Do You Think?

Positive communication between managers and employees can also be enhanced if managers will go beyond the facts of announcements to share opinions, thoughts, and feelings.

What happens when managers give only top-down pronouncements or instruction? They are perceived as being messengers from on high. Or they are perceived as *thinking* they are on high! Employees know that the latter isn't true. Managers aren't gods. And they hope against hope that the former is also not true. Employees want managers who are more than gofers for upper levels of administration. They want managers who think and feel, and who are willing to express those thoughts and feelings.

After all, if managers are unwilling to tell employees how they think or feel, they are also likely to be unwilling to tell superiors what they think or feel, much less convey upward what the employees think or feel!

How much should be told? That will vary from person to person, given the comfort level in entering into and sustaining healthy relationships. At minimum, Theory R calls for managers to give thoughtful explanations about *why* certain policies and procedures are being implemented, at least to the best of their knowledge.

Theory R calls for managers to ask their supervisors—all the way to the top—for such reasons. It is not a matter of insubordination but a matter of realistic communication. The decision with a rationale undergirding it will be more respected by those at the end of the manufacturing line or at the bottom of the organizational chart.

Managers should also be willing to express their thoughts and feelings about matters outside the work environment. How do they feel about the local high-school team's latest victory? About an employee's announced engagement to be married? About the impending arrival of a baby? About the latest layoffs at a competitor's factory? By giving voice to feelings, managers do two things:

- First, they recognize that employees also have feelings and opinions—very human things to have. They validate the right of employees to have opinions and feelings. To a great extent, this is recognizing the dignity of the other persons as individuals.
- Second, they are in a stronger position to say, "We will stay the course and proceed toward excellence, even given contrary thoughts and feelings." This is a critical matter to consider.

If managers hold to the position that they cannot or will not give expression to their thoughts and feelings, they are perceived by employees to be in such complete agreement with everything being touted as the company line that employees will soon regard them as little more than robots. On the other hand, if managers can and will say, "There are a few things about this that probably need adjustment; I'm going to work for those changes with my superiors, and I ask your support in the meantime in following the new procedures as they've been given," employees tend to say, "Ah, we at least have managers who see this with some degree of realism and who are going to be open to suggestions."

At all times, expressions of thoughts and feelings should be couched in positive terms for the sake of all involved.

## Staying Positive—with Room for Improvement

It's one thing for a manager to say, "I think this is 100 percent law and 100 percent good, and I'm feeling 100 percent fine about it."

Workers suspect such a stance because they know it can't possibly be true. Nobody is *for* virtually anything 100 percent of the time with 100 percent positive feelings. Furthermore, nothing ever stays exactly the same forever. Most procedures and policies are subject to modification, and deservedly so. Most reaction to new procedures is usually less than 100 percent, to a great extent because people don't like change.

It's another thing for a manager to say, "This is the law, but I think it's an entirely bad one and I'm extremely upset about it."

Such a manager is likely to face anarchy from both above and below! Furthermore, such a statement is rarely true. Most things aren't 100 percent bad or worth such a severe reaction. Employees are likely to perceive such a statement by a manager as equally ingenuous as a statement of 100 percent support.

It's yet another thing for a manager to say, "I think there are some things about this that can and will be improved over time. I feel sure we'll be able to work for those improvements. I'm positive about the direction we're taking as a company, and I hope you'll join me in supporting this decision."

Such a manager is perceived as being a real, live, thinking and feeling human being—one who is committed to being a leader and working for the improvement of the company, one who is simultaneously loyal to the organization and holds faith in the organization's potential. Not only can employees respect such a statement, but the manager can respect the self more. (And there's little about such a statement that can be criticized by superiors.)

In expressing thoughts and feelings, a manager is sending a signal to employees: you have the freedom to express thoughts and feelings, too. Theory R advocates that because an individual has inherent value—and thus, dignity—opinions and feelings should be expressed.

All cards on the table. Without punishment. In Theory R, all opinions and feelings are considered valid—in other words, they have a right to exist within a human being. They are a big part of what makes us human beings.

## The Value of Venting and Communicating

A Theory R manager should create opportunities in which employees can vent. We know of one manager of a 3M rock-crushing plant who has become very intentional about doing this. At least once a quarter, he schedules a time when he meets with each shift (of a twenty-four-hour-a-day operation) in the employees' break room. He makes himself available for an informal discussion of problems, questions, and ideas. For his part, he comes to the meeting with updated information about the status of the company.

The tone of the meeting is relaxed. Value of the Person behaviors are discussed. A key question asked at each meeting is, "How are we doing as a plant in conveying love, dignity, and respect to one another?" These meetings have had a very positive impact on the company.

Two key principles are embodied in this manager's actions:

- Opportunities for venting emotions and communicating ideas are periodic.
- Opportunities for venting emotions and communicating ideas are informal.

One of the most valuable aspects of expressing opinions and feelings is that it allows a person to vent what is inside. Opinions and feelings are there. Without venting, the opinions and feelings can quickly boil into a rage or extreme frustration or drag the person down into discouragement and despair. A slavery mind-set takes over. An internal downward spiral begins to occur.

Without venting, an employee can become completely absorbed by thoughts and feelings. Then the employee plays them over and over again mentally. The more mental rehearsal, the more the employee tends to move toward an entrenched—and more extreme—position about them. Things that were "some bad" or "sometimes" tend to become fixed in the mind as "all bad" and "all the time." Ultimately, a worker's complete and fixed preoccupation with thoughts and feelings will affect performance in the workplace.

When that happens, you can look for less productivity, lower morale, more accidents on the line or more errors in the office and, ultimately, an explosive tension that may erupt in violence (at its worst) or resignation (at its best). With an unhealthy attitude, malignancy begins to take root in the organization. Rarely does that type of tension in a person go unnoticed by others. It more frequently spreads like wildfire.

There's another major benefit to encouraging the communication of emotions and opinions: increased awareness.

All managers have blind spots. They usually cannot see themselves with accurate objectivity. They frequently don't see problems, even if they are right under their noses.

This isn't necessarily a fault limited to managers. Workers at all levels are usually blind to certain aspects of their work and the general work environment. Theory R calls for improved bottom-up communication as well as better top-down messages. Employees at all levels need to be honest with one another in an affirming, respectful way.

The expression of thoughts and feelings sends a signal to managers that something is amiss. Or in the cases of the expression of positive thoughts and feelings, the message is that things are all right and on target.

Either way, managers get valuable feedback.

We know of a restaurant entrepreneur named Pat who, in the first year of managing a restaurant for a major corporation, was told by a kitchen manager: "You think you're cool. Do you realize no one around here likes you? You've got major problems." It took a lot of courage for that kitchen manager to make such a statement. It also took a lot of courage for Pat to hear it.

Up to that point, Pat thought of himself as a superb manager. He was getting the job done. He was running a tight ship. He was seeing an improvement in the operation's bottom line. Pat wasn't at all prepared for that hour when the kitchen manager said, "I've got something to say to you."

In looking back, Pat considers that kitchen manager's comments to be a major factor in his success today. He took the man's suggestions to heart and reevaluated who he was and how he was acting toward his waiters, cooks, and kitchen staff. He realized that his people skills were sorely lacking, and he made major changes in the way he related to the people he worked with.

Almost immediately, he began to see even better results than he had previously imagined. His upward climb began until finally he set out on his own. Today, he has several successful restaurant franchises with more than two thousand employees. He runs his business as a Theory R leader.

If a sailor sees a leak in the ship and doesn't say so or cry out in alarm, the captain may not be able to make a decision that will save the ship from sinking.

On the other hand, if employees are free to say, "Things are better now," or "I'm really enjoying work more," the manager can take satisfaction in knowing that the changes made are having a positive impact and are appreciated.

Finally, we need to underscore the point made earlier that thoughts and feelings do give rise to behavior. ***How we think and feel about something invariably and inevitably affects what we do.***

Another way of saying this is: thoughts and feelings will ultimately be expressed, even if their expression isn't encouraged or desired. And the tendency is for negative thoughts and feelings to be expressed with far greater frequency and volume than positive thoughts and feelings. Discouraged, angry, or frustrated workers are going to be the most vocal ones. They are the most likely to behave in a way that will sabotage or undermine the overall operation through such common behaviors as increased absenteeism, carelessness, rudeness to customers, or efforts to instill mutiny among the ranks.

In encouraging the venting of feelings and communication of ideas, a manager not only lowers the emotional temperature of the workplace but gains valuable information to make changes before employees reach the point of burnout or boil over.

## Thoughts and Feelings vs. Behavior

There's a critical difference, however, between encouraging the expression of thoughts and feelings and encouraging workers that their behavior be based on them.

People—managers or workers—can and should feel free to say, "I don't like this." They still may be required to do what they don't like. While communication is ideally a two-way street, the flow of authority in an organization is always top-down—which is a fact of life from birth to death. Most of us don't like everything that Mom and Dad tell us to do as children. Nonetheless, we obey or face consequences. We don't know anyone who relishes taxes or changes, and yet we are all required to pay them, endure them, overcome them, and flow with them!

Managers always have the prerogative to require adherence to given policies and procedures. Otherwise, an organization becomes frayed and fails to move with one purpose toward a commonly agreed-upon goal.

The Bible includes a very good story about this: "A man had two sons, and he came to the first and said, 'Son, go, work today in my vineyard.' He answered and said, 'I will not,' but afterward he regretted it and went. Then he came to the second and said likewise. And he answered and said, 'I go, sir,' but he did not go. Which of the two did the will of his father?" (Matt. 21:28–31). The Bible answers the question: the first.

No matter how employees may feel about something or what they may think about it, performance is based on what they do.

This is a point worth elaborating. Many traditional-style managers tend to reward their employees on the basis of expressions of loyalty more than on true performance or constructive ideas. The employee who says, "Yes, sir," without qualification tends to move up the organizational ladder faster in a traditional-style management structure.

A Theory R manager recognizes that behavior is the foremost criterion of success. And a Theory R manager encourages idea offering as a form of behavior to be rewarded.

In the end, the employee who says, "Yes, sir," but fails to perform well is far less valuable than the employee who performs well and says, "Yes, sir, and I hope you'll consider . . ."

## What Happens When All Suggestions Go Unheeded?

When a manager consistently refuses or refutes all ideas given by workers, employees will revolt, cower, or say to themselves, "What's the use?" None of which are good results for an organization.

The same holds true when employees perceive that they are being asked for ideas as a ploy of manipulation or appeasement, which often happens in traditional-style management organizations that claim to desire employee input but actually have little regard for suggestions coming from the lower reaches of the organizational chart. "Lip service" is a polite way of labeling what such managers give to the ideas they find in employee suggestion boxes.

The question ultimately arises: Why allow a person to express thoughts and feelings if the ideas and opinions aren't going to make a difference?

In the first place, any leader of worth will recognize that some opinions of employees are valuable and should make a difference. The percentage of worthy ideas is probably directly related to the quality and quantity of information given to the employees, the skill and creativity of the employees, and the degree to which a manager solicits ideas. A good manager has substantial control over factors one and three, and can do a great deal to enhance skill and creativity.

The Theory R leader, therefore, does three things in communicating with employees and in encouraging their communication:

1. The leader gives employees as much information as possible without compromising productivity and the need for privacy and confidentiality.

2. The leader helps employees grow in their abilities to perform and communicate. Communication, of course, is a skill—just as much a skill as tightening bolts, assembling components, or pouring hot metal. The good manager encourages opportunities that build communication skills.

3. The leader asks workers questions:

- "How are you?"
- "What can I do to make your job better?"
- "What can we do to increase our department (or unit, line, division, or corporation) morale, productivity, or work environment?"

If a manager does not create an environment in which employees are not only free to but encouraged to express their opinions, that manager is going to lose out on some excellent ideas. A good manager hears out employees, sifts through the ideas, and adopts and rewards the ones that can truly better the institution.

The manager who does not create such an environment also loses out on quality relationships with coworkers.

And ultimately, the manager who does not create an environment rich in the flow of communication will not grow as a manager. The manager will cease to improve, cease to have new and fresh ideas to suggest upward, and cease to advance within an organization.

Positive, free-flowing communication is a tremendous asset to a manager on all accounts. It is a win-win situation, one to be encouraged, continually monitored, and enjoyed.

These same principles of communication, of course, are vital to a successful husband-wife or parent-child relationship. Conveying information, helping others grow in their abilities, and being open to improvement are behaviors that can make a marked difference in family relationships.

**Channeling Opinions and Feelings into Ideas**

What might a manager do to encourage a greater percentage of good ideas from workers? Good ideas tend to flow upward if a manager will do the following four things.

***1. Encourage Ideas as a Product of Opinion and Feeling***

In other words, the good manager continually channels opinions and feelings into ideas and holds out ideas as the best end product of opinions and emotions.

Feelings—emotions—are not the best agents of change. Their expression can lessen tension or boost morale, but feelings in and of themselves do little to move an organization forward. Opinions are statements of like and dislike. They tend to promote feelings. If I voice my dislike for a new procedure, I tend to feel negatively about it; if I voice my approval, I tend to feel positive. The better alternatives to thoughts and feelings are ideas.

Ideas arise as the result of answers to the questions "What if?" and "How about?"

A traditional-management-style manager says to employees, "Here's the new procedure. Follow it."

A Theory R manager says to employees, "Here's the new procedure. If you can think of ways to make this even better for the company as a whole, let me know."

A traditional-management-style manager says, "I don't care how you feel about this. If you're upset about it, tough. Learn to live with it."

A Theory R manager says, "I can sense that you may not approve of this. If you have a problem with it, help me come up with a better solution, procedure, or policy."

A traditional-management-style manager says, "Your opinion is only your opinion. Keep it to yourself."

A Theory R manager says, "Your opinions are important. Channel them into an idea about how we might improve our operation."

## 2. Encourage Ideas That Are Concrete

Don't accept vagueness. The best ideas are specific, directed, and focused, and they result in behavior that can be measured. They are concrete rather than abstract.

The abstract suggestion might be, "Improve the work environment." The concrete idea might be, "Reposition the work stations," or "Add more shelves for storing supplies."

The abstract suggestion might be, "Communicate better." The concrete alternative might be, "Have a meeting with us once a week about this matter."

Encourage ideas that can be put into effect in practical, behavioral ways so that you and your employees know they have been implemented.

Ask your employees, "How can this be implemented? What specific changes need to be made? When should the changes be made? How should we communicate the changes to everyone involved?"

**3. Encourage Ideas Aimed at the Improvement of the Overall Company or Operation**

The wise manager encourages ideas that are not personality based or personality directed but are aimed at the improvement of the overall work environment and the product manufactured or service rendered. Keep the company and the product in a primary position, not the administration or the organizational chart.

Most employees need help in seeing beyond their immediate niche in an organization—no matter where they are on the organizational chart. Foster a concern for the whole. Help employees see the big picture. Point toward factors that employees may not know about or be aware of that may have led to the new policy or procedure. Cite overall trends within the organization, within the industry, and within the international marketplace.

Employees at all levels are usually quick to offer positive suggestions, but often suggestions reflect their immediate concerns and are very limited. That, perhaps, is the number one reason so many suggestions aren't adopted. Help employees see how the pieces of an operation fit together and how a decision or policy in one area can affect the whole.

The traditional-management-style manager will say, "This is how we are going to do things."

The Theory R manager will say, "This is how this procedure affects us and the company as a whole. Here are a few reasons *why* this action has been taken. In coming up with ideas that might provide a better way, think about how the entire company will be affected. Think about what can be done to improve things for all of us."

**4. Encourage Ideas That Are Customer-Oriented**

We've all had the experience of standing in line only to have a bank teller close a window in our faces, of arriving at the store just as the "Closed" sign is put in the window, or of having a clerk hurry us out of a dressing room because the department store is preparing to close. Five extra minutes were all we needed!

We heard the story of a man who arrived at a Boston Chicken rotisserie fifteen minutes after the business had closed. Rather than turn the customer away, the store manager welcomed him in, and as he prepared the man's order, he conversed in a friendly manner with the customer. The customer responded by expressing interest in the operation, so the store manager showed him the kitchen area.

As he prepared to ring up the man's order, he said, "I'm sorry the food isn't as fresh as it normally would be so I'm only going to charge you half the normal price." The customer left the restaurant that night not only grateful that he had dinners to take home but very pleased at the way he had been treated.

The store manager didn't know that his customer was a friend of the owner and an investor of the Boston Chicken franchise. A few days later, the customer phoned his friend and said, "I went to Boston Chicken initially because of you, but I'll be going back to Boston Chicken because of the way I was treated there tonight."

The owner of the franchise later applauded the store manager and his district manager publicly, giving a major boost to both men.

Ultimately, all services and products must have consumer or customer satisfaction, or they will not succeed in the marketplace.

Encourage your workers to think like a consumer, not a producer.

## It's Not Enough That You've Thought of It

During one Value of the Person—Theory R Seminar, employees were asked to identify what their company could do to improve the ways in which it showed love, dignity, and respect to them. Knowing full well that their managers were present, several employees had the courage to say, "We don't like the new policy regarding shift rotation." The key manager present responded—kindly and with genuine concern, by the way—like this: "We've thought about that. We took the very concerns you've expressed into consideration before we made the decision, but we still felt it was the best way for the company to go."

What happens when a manager says, "I thought about that"? In most cases, employees don't believe it, at least not with 100 percent enthusiasm. Furthermore, employees tend to conclude, *The door is closed*. A manager who has already thought about the complaint apparently has already drawn a conclusion that has taken that complaint into consideration; therefore, there's little likelihood that the issue can be reconsidered.

A Theory R manager will do two things to circumvent this "I've already thought about it" syndrome. First, the wise manager won't say that to the employee but will say instead, "I hear what you are saying. We'll reconsider our decision." (This is a wise path to take because if the employee's complaint is strongly held and widely spread, management will eventually need to reconsider the position. Sooner is better than later in most cases.)

Second, the wise manager will say, "Help me come up with a better alternative."

## Criticism Hurts and Is Rarely Positive

**THEORY R SAYS,**

*All opinions and feelings are valid and worthy of expression.*

*People of diverse opinions and feelings can still treat one another with love, dignity, and respect.*

*Opinions and feelings benefit the company and the individual most if they are turned into constructive, concrete ideas.*

*A flow of positive ideas is valuable to any organization; constructive ideas should be solicited, evaluated, and used to move the organization forward.*

*The good manager will help employees develop good communication skills, will ask idea-generating questions, and will reward employees for good ideas.*

All my life I've heard the phrase "constructive criticism." I'm still not sure I know what it means. It seems to me—in my personal experience and from what I've observed in business over the last several decades—that criticism has a much greater potential for wounding than for building up.

When I was a boy, one of my teachers told me, "You'll never amount to anything." That teacher probably doesn't even remember making that remark, and it may have been made in passing or in anger. I don't recall. All I know is that those words stuck with me, and I've never forgotten them. They hurt me far more than they ever helped me become who I am today.

When my classmates voted in school for the boy "most likely to succeed," I was sure I didn't receive a single vote. I was just happy there wasn't a vote for "most likely to fail."

Through the years of consulting and conducting Value of the Person—Theory R Seminars at our nation's leading companies, we've met literally hundreds of people who have told us,

- "I've spent my entire life trying to overcome my father's (or mother's) criticism."
- "I never had a teacher who encouraged me."
- "I can still hear that person's criticism ringing in my ears—even after all these years."

For years, we did an exercise in our seminars in which we asked people to list the ten most critical comments ever made to them, and then the ten most affirming comments. We then asked the participants to reflect on their lives. We asked, "Did you develop more in the area of the criticism or the praises?" Invariably, audience members told us that they became what they were praised to become, not what they were admonished against or told they'd never be.

When I, Nancy, was in elementary school, a teacher criticized me severely in math class. I developed a block against math because I perceived that my teacher believed I'd never be able to master the subject. As I prepared for college, I seriously thought about entering the field of medicine. I shied away from it for one reason: I didn't think I could do the math. Even today, I panic when someone asks me to answer a math-based question. I've often wondered what would have been the outcome if that teacher had helped me believe in my potential to understand mathematics rather than criticize my lack of ability at that time.

In calling for Theory R managers to praise their employees, we are not saying that managers should never point out an area of weakness or error to an employee. Rather, we are calling for managers to introduce such corrective measures by saying, "Let me show you how to do this," or "This is the way I've found to be most effective in doing this task," or "Have you considered trying . . . ?"

## Moving Beyond Your Comfort Zone

One of the greatest challenges a Theory R leader will face is the risk of moving beyond the personal comfort zone. We all tend to respond more positively to certain individuals or to certain personality types than to others. Each of us has preferences.

The challenge in Theory R is to recognize the individuality of each person and to be willing to explore the individual's uniqueness.

- Don't allow yourself to draw conclusions too quickly about a person.
- Keep searching for something that you have in common.
- Keep asking questions and attempting to understand the person's motivations.

As stated earlier, you as a manager aren't required to become friends with every person you work with. You aren't being asked by Theory R to move into the neighborhood of your employees, begin to attend their community social functions, or even to participate in their home lives on a regular basis. You are, however, being challenged to communicate better with every one of your employees and every one of your peers and superiors.

Good communication flows from having some sense of mutuality and commonality. The more you can do to understand your coworkers and find ways of relating to their feelings, needs, and ideas, the better you will be able to express yourself to them.

People in upper levels of management have to overcome the feeling that they might lose control if they make themselves vulnerable to those beneath them on the organizational chart. To a certain extent, Theory R managers do lose control but in this way:

- If you as a manager mingle with the group, you must be willing to be touched and talked to.
- If you're willing to be touched and talked to, you must be willing to listen.
- If you listen, you're going to hear all kinds of problems and expressions of need.
- If you hear expressions of need, you're going to feel compelled to do something about them.

The needs of the workers are ultimately going to exert some control over you—over your priorities as a manager, over your daily agenda—and that shift of control is frightening to many managers.

It takes a true Theory R leader who is a big person—not just a big cheese—to risk involvement with employees.

## Avoid Absolutes

Phrases such as "You are required," "You must," and "You are mandated" should be deleted from your memos. Also remove the coupling of new directives with heavy-handed threats of the "if you don't do this, we'll do that" nature. Employees rarely respond positively to threats, and in our opinion, they are counterproductive to the performance of the vast majority of employees who will never find themselves in a position of needing reprimands or censure.

Don't threaten employees with statements such as, "If we don't achieve this goal, they'll shut our department down," or say "If we don't show more enthusiasm, we might be cut in the next round of downsizing." Don't draw conclusions that may never happen. Don't anticipate the worst. Instead, as a Theory R leader, motivate people toward success and toward attitudes and behaviors that will create success.

## Be Consistent in Your Communication in All Directions

Consistency in communication includes the way managers treat their fellow managers, not only their subordinates or superiors.

We heard of an instance in which a manager got on board with Value of the Person leadership principles very quickly. He did some very positive symbolic things with his employees—moving his office closer to them, adopting an open-door policy, hosting a lunch for the company to thank them for their contributions, and so forth. His relationship improved with his workers, and their respect for him rose. We believe, along with his vice president, that his behavior toward them was genuine.

His ongoing behavior with his fellow managers, however, remained dismal, and if anything, it grew progressively worse. He showed genuine compassion for those he perceived as being lesser in rank, but he ripped his peers to shreds at every opportunity. He showed absolutely no concern for the overall well-being of his colleagues, and he did his utmost to undermine them and force them into positions where he could degrade them and display one-upmanship.

He was a good father to his workers but a lousy brother to his peers.

Is it possible to be that way? Yes, it's possible. It's not an advantageous position to take, however. You see, he didn't have a problem being benevolent to persons he considered to be no threat. He could extend love, dignity, and respect to persons he viewed as weaklings and of no threat to his position as a manager.

Rather, he had difficulty with extending love, dignity, and respect to those with whom he felt himself to be in direct competition for a promotion. He thought that the only way to succeed was to steamroll over them.

What happens in cases like these? Often, a person even higher on the organizational chart takes notice and certainly isn't going to favor the promotion of that person to a level where he can challenge, undermine, and disregard him. He's going to reap negative results from his negative behavior from a source entirely unanticipated.

Furthermore, if his behavior remains negative toward his fellow managers as a group, they're likely to join forces to do him in. All in all, not showing his peers that he genuinely values them is going to have a detrimental result.

**Go for Excellence!**

We all have a tendency to compare ourselves with others. Theory R calls for persons to evaluate honestly where they are and then to set goals for where they want to be, not in comparison to others but in comparison to where they believe they can go.

The point is, we can always figure out better ways to communicate with and to live in harmony with others. Relationships can always be strengthened:

- If your communication is poor with your workers or peers at present, work to make it better.
- If your communication is good at present, it can be better.
- When communication gets better, recognize that it still isn't the best it can be.

Never think that where you are is secure. There's a tendency for every business or corporation that is at the top of its field to see itself as always being number one. If that happens, complacency and laxness quickly set in. And if that happens, a rapid decline may be just around the corner.

Never think you've arrived.

Eastern Airlines was once rated the number one airline in the nation. It no longer exists.

Continental Can was a Fortune 500 company. It no longer exists.

Bucyrus-Erie was once a major manufacturing conglomerate. It no longer exists.

Keep striving for excellence on all fronts! Capture a good, better, best vision. Focus on what you want to become and then go for it!

Seeking to improve communication is a prime way you will improve relationships within your organization. It's the key to reconciliation. Good communication is always a right thing to do—at work, at home, in your neighborhood, and in every group to which you belong.

**THEORY R SAYS,**

*Communication can always be improved.*

*Communication is worthy to be improved.*

## THEORY R AT WORK

What more can you do to improve your communication skills?

How willing are you to share your thoughts, feelings, and ideas

- with your coworkers?
- with your peers?
- with people you supervise?
- with your superiors?

How willing are you to let others vent their feelings, ideas, and opinions?

Can you recall an instance in which you felt soundly criticized or reprimanded? How did you feel? What happened to your sense of value?

How are you feeling and thinking about something in your workplace right now? Can you channel those thoughts and feelings into a good idea?

# 13

# Theory R's Policy-Making Rule: Lead the 90 Percent

**T**raditional managers are often so intimidated by the idea of stepping outside the boundaries or of making an exception that they become paralyzed. Theory R leaders are flexible and open to possibilities—especially when they see that something is right to do.

A worker named Big Cooper walked into my open-door office at Pittron one day and said, "Mr. Wayne, I have a problem."

"What is it?" I asked.

"I need an advance in pay."

Cooper's request the day after payday was clearly against company policy, and he knew it. I heard myself responding, however, "That's not a problem. What's the real problem?"

Cooper went on to explain that his wife had left him and he needed an advance in pay—and also a few days off—to go to her where she was staying out of state and see if he could reconcile their relationship.

Cooper was a hard, mean man at that time. He had a severe absenteeism problem, and one more absence would have given the company sufficient reason to fire him. As far as my palace guards were concerned, Cooper was in the exact position they wanted him. They knew he was going to take the time off whether it was granted to him or not; therefore, the company could fire him and not have any trouble if the dismissal resulted in a grievance. For a number of good reasons, in the opinion of the palace guards, I should not have even considered giving Cooper time off.

I chose to take a risk, however, in an attempt to help the man and possibly help save his marriage. I gave Cooper the time off and the amount of money he needed.

My palace guards were irate. They felt certain that I was setting into motion a policy that was going to bring the company to its knees. If word got around that one employee received money the day after payday and was able to sidestep the absenteeism policy, they argued, everybody would soon be lined up to do the same. They foresaw nothing but chaos and doom in the simple gesture of helping.

I didn't believe anything the palace guards said would happen, and it didn't. Cooper was the only employee who ever came to me requesting such an advance. Furthermore, he and his wife, Mildred, were able to reconcile their differences. He returned to the workplace more eager than ever to do a good job. His loyalty toward the foundry increased 1,000 percent. He never made another request for an advance. His absenteeism stopped.

Employees who make a request that they know is against company policy are in desperate need or are attempting to manipulate or use management for their own purposes. A manager can usually tell the difference.

In the first place, people who attempt to manipulate the system are likely to make repeated requests that buck company policy. They aren't likely to abuse the system once and then let the matter rest. In the second place, people who attempt to circumvent or manipulate company policy usually take great pride in the accomplishment (if successful). They tend to spread the news widely that they have succeeded in outfoxing or outmaneuvering management. A manager may be fooled once by such persons but rarely twice. Most employees know that, too.

And what about employees who are desperate? The last thing on their minds is job performance. What would have happened if I said no to Cooper when he requested an advance in pay and a few days off? I would have lost a worker who had years with the company, was well trained, and did good work. The company would have spent a lot more money in hiring and training his replacement than in giving him the advance.

Had the employee opted to stay at work, he certainly wouldn't have been happy. He would have been emotionally away—consumed by his problem. He would no doubt have spent part of his energy on solving it rather than giving 100 percent to the work at hand. He would also have been resentful of the fact that he was forced to stay at work. That frustration certainly wouldn't have had a positive impact on productivity, the quality of his work, or team morale.

## The Exception Doesn't Necessarily Become the Rule

Many times a manager will make a decision that is right for the company without any direct relationship between the decision and an individual worker. In some cases, the decision benefits the employees. In some cases, it doesn't.

In our experience, however, we've found that when a company makes a decision that is right for an individual employee, that decision is also right for the company.

A secretary named Carol went to her immediate supervisor one day with an unusual request. Carol worked in a university history department. She asked the department head if he could arrange for her daughter to be given a series of psychometric tests that were sometimes offered by the education department to help diagnose learning difficulties in students at a nearby school.

The department head made a two-minute phone call to the professor who regularly conducted the testing, and the next week, Carol brought her daughter with her to work so the tests could be administered. Indeed, her daughter was diagnosed with attention deficit disorder, and she subsequently was prescribed medicine by a pediatrician, which greatly increased her ability to concentrate in school and complete tasks.

A few weeks after the testing, the head of the education department came to the head of the history department. She was quite upset, insisting that the history department head had neglected necessary paperwork and bypassed standard procedures. She lamented, "We can't possibly test every university employee's child!"

The history department head said to her, "You are right. That would be impossible. But in all my years here at the university, I've never had a teacher or staff member ask this of me. I've made one referral to your department in twenty-one years. I doubt if I will ever be asked to do this again. And just think what valuable assistance your department has provided this one time."

The education department head went away in a huff but later apologized and admitted that she had overreacted. To the history department head's surprise, the next semester the education department announced a special "Saturday of Testing" just for the children of university employees! In addition to psychometric tests, aptitude, intelligence, and standard grade-level achievement tests were going to be offered. The education department had found a new way to serve its constituency and conduct an interesting research project at the same time!

## The Precedent May Never Be Cited!

Very often traditional managers say, "I can't do this for one person because then I'll have set a precedent, and I'll have to do it for everybody." Chances are, you won't.

The opposite approach is to deal with a specific problem in a specific way when you see the problem or it is brought to your attention. Your choice to address the specific problem before you, and to solve it to the best of your ability, is a choice you make because it's the right thing to do—not because you are setting a precedent or a policy. People have *individual* needs. You need to deal with them as such.

## Set Policy for the 90 Percent Majority

Traditional managers frequently set policy based on the behaviors of only about 10 percent of their employees and, in effect, penalize the remaining 90 percent.

A good manager must recognize that in any average workforce, about 10 percent of the people are always going to rip you off. They're going to be the rule breakers (and rule benders). They're going to be the prime causes of unrest, error, and grievance. They're also likely to be the ones who are absent the most and who cry the loudest if reprimanded or fired.

About 90 percent of the people are faithful, loyal, steadfast employees who do a good job. And unless they experience an accident or unusual circumstance, they aren't ever going to make a "mess up" list.

Most policy manuals seem to be written for the 10 percent that is the problem segment. And the majority of traditional managers we've met tend to fall into the rut of managing the workers who create the problems. Policies are established and rules are made in direct response to the relatively small percentage of troublemakers, goof-offs, and perpetual rule breakers in any group. This applies not only to manufacturing corporations but to hospitals, schools, banks, restaurants, and virtually all service organizations.

Take a look around you. Take a look at other companies with which you may have some experience or familiarity. From what we have seen through the years, we conclude boldly that *most* management decisions about workers are made *not* with keeping the vast majority of honest, hardworking, trustworthy employees in mind but with closing loopholes and tightening down the screws to eliminate or provide a means of handling problem workers.

Consider, for example, the policy that a major airline instituted a couple of years ago requiring good grooming for its baggage handlers. Now ask yourself, "Who sees baggage handlers? Do customers really care whether the person who handles their luggage in the underbelly of airports is cleanly shaven and has short hair?" What no doubt triggered the policy was a manager's concern about the grooming of one or two people. Rather than talk to those people and attempt to convince them to engage in better grooming practices, the company instituted a policy that upset hundreds of baggage handlers!

In another instance, we received news of a company that was experiencing a vandalism problem in one of its rest rooms. Finding out who the person was should have been a fairly easy task. It doesn't take a lot of detective work to discover who in a certain area or department is consistently trashing a rest room. Rather than deal with that one individual, however, the company installed video bathroom monitors that operated during certain hours of every workday. What a demeaning action for those who needed to use the facilities!

The fact is,

---

- most quality control programs are aimed at the workers who produce the most errors, not the vast majority of employees who have perfect or near-perfect quality records.
- most productivity incentive programs are geared toward improving the productivity of employees who are the least productive, not the most productive.

---

Why not spend as much time, energy, and resources on ways to create an environment in which people want to come to work—indeed, can't wait to get to work and are eager to be at work—as on programs to document, eliminate, and alleviate absenteeism? Why not show more concern for the 90 percent of the workers who are doing it right than for the 10 percent who aren't? Why not spend the money and resources for rewarding people who produce the most rather than spend the resources attempting to cajole performance out of those who produce the least?

We strongly recommend that you review your organizational policy manuals with these overriding thoughts in mind:

## THEORY R SAYS,

*Make rules and policies that serve the majority.*

*Don't punish the majority by gearing company policies toward the few who are always going to break company rules, no matter how lenient or flexible the rules may be.*

- "Are these policies for the 90 percent or the 10 percent?"
- "How can we change our policies to reflect more accurately what we desire to see as majority behavior?"
- "What more can be done to recognize and uplift model employees?"
- "Do our policies truly reflect the Theory R management style?"

## Your Company's Absenteeism Policy

Every organization we've ever encountered has a policy regarding employee absenteeism. These policies are nearly always examples of managing the exception.

What percentage of employees tends to show up late consistently or willfully abuses absenteeism policies? Usually, 10 percent or less. Our initial 25 percent absenteeism rate at Pittron in 1972 was an indicator of major trouble and was one of the telling signs as to how close the company was to going under.

Even with an absenteeism rate of under 5 percent, a company is likely to spend a great deal of time monitoring and documenting absenteeism, fiddling with absenteeism policies, and executing disciplinary measures for excessive absenteeism. Entire file cabinets are filled with absentee reports. Entire management meetings are spent discussing the problem and how to lower the percentage a notch or two.

Why aren't all these resources and time spent creating a workplace that benefits the 90 percent who want to work and who are rarely absent?

We're not saying that the 10 percent who are consistently and willfully absent should go undisciplined. They should be. In most cases, managers need to go beyond the fact of their absenteeism to ask why they are absent and what can be done about the underlying causes of their consistent tardiness or absenteeism. In some cases, the employees should probably be terminated. These workers, however, need to be dealt with on an individual basis.

In the first place, there's no main cause for a person to be chronically tardy or absent. If there's one reason that employees don't show up for work regularly and on time, it's probably because they don't enjoy their jobs enough.

In the second place, strict absenteeism policies have a negative effect on good employees—perhaps even more of an effect than on problem employees. Good employees tend to fear what might happen if they slip up. That fear is not the deterrent that most managers think it is. Rather, it is a fear that demoralizes and erodes trust (more than most managers think).

## Absenteeism Programs Don't Control Absenteeism

Threatening employees with punishment for absenteeism doesn't make them want to come to work. Punishing employees with an absentee problem doesn't usually solve their root problem.

At the root of absenteeism is the desire of an employee to stay at home rather than come to work. We're not talking about absenteeism that stems from a major illness or injury. We're talking about willful absenteeism—missing the bus, sleeping in, having lots of minor emergencies that take precedence over getting to work. Tardiness is the close cousin of such absenteeism.

Why be concerned about absenteeism? Every manager knows that absenteeism is the number one factor that affects productivity and quality. It is to the workforce what a breakdown is to equipment. Without people, work doesn't get done, no matter how fine the facility or upgraded the tools.

Furthermore, absenteeism tends to become infectious. It can spread quickly throughout any workforce—be it hospital, school, TV station, bank, insurance company, or agricultural processing plant. If unstemmed, it becomes a tide that can swamp a company.

Over the years at Pittron, I encountered very few lazy people. Workers at a foundry are usually men with physical strength and ability who need the jobs. If given jobs they find satisfying, they take personal pride in their ability to work and take home a paycheck.

Absenteeism results when employees no longer want to come to work, when they find the work environment to be more unpleasant than the unemployment line. The best cure for absenteeism, therefore, is to create an environment in which workers want to come to work.

What kind of environment is that? It's an environment in which they are praised for the quality work they do, respected for putting in a full day for a full day's wages, regarded with dignity, and shown some appreciation and care. It's an environment in which employees are called by name and, perhaps most important, they know they will be genuinely missed if they are absent.

At Pittron, we went from 25 percent absenteeism (which meant that one out of every four workers was absent on any given day!) to an absenteeism rate of 0.5 percent (which meant that only one out of every two hundred workers was absent).

If a quarter of your workforce is missing, a quarter of the work you are scheduled to do can't get done, and people remaining on the job are going to feel even more frustrated and stressed when asked to do more than they can do in meeting quotas and filling customer orders.

On the other hand, when all employees are present and working at full steam, the workload becomes easier for everyone. Quotas are not only filled but exceeded. Meeting and exceeding quotas build team pride in work accomplished. Pride in one's work is a surefire motivator for getting out of bed and making it to the job site on time.

## Change or Grease the Noisy Wheel?

We're not kidding ourselves and we certainly won't kid you about employees who are lazy or malcontent. They do spell trouble to an organization. And they do exist. We don't know of an organization of any kind that develops without their presence.

The fact is, no matter how much you shield yourself with policies, rules, and procedures, you are always going to have the 10 percent who break them, try their best to circumvent them, or take no notice of them.

As our colleague Lefty Scumaci says, "While it's true that the noisy wheel gets the grease, sometimes the wheel needs to be *replaced* rather than greased!"

Sometimes it's the work environment that needs to be changed.
Sometimes it's the employee.
Sometimes it's the manager or frontline supervisor.
Again, the focus in Theory R is kept on the problem employee as the exception, and problem employees are never held out to be a good reason for policy making.

## What About the Stray Dogies?

Do you remember the old Westerns that depicted the great cattle drives? The primary purpose of the cowboys was to set the herd in motion toward a direction and then to deal with any strays as they strayed.

We've noticed something in those movies. The faster the herds moved toward a goal—for example, toward a river when they were thirsty—the fewer the strays.

A company that has rapid forward motion—with sure direction, momentum built up, great desire to achieve new goals, great morale—has very few strays. Those who are chronically absent or who chronically buck company policy stand out like sore thumbs. They are obvious not only to managers but also to fellow workers. And in most cases, a highly motivated workforce has even less regard for the rebellious, uncooperative stray coworker than a manager has (or can express because of lengthy, drawn-out procedures that must be followed).

## THEORY R SAYS,

*Make policy decisions for the benefit of the 90 percent of the employees who comprise the willing and loyal majority rather than make policy decisions to the detriment of the rebellious, disgruntled, or willfully uncooperative 10 percent minority.*

On the other hand, let a herd of cattle stand and graze in a pasture or on a mountainside awhile and you'll have more strays than you can round up! The cowboy's work is twice as hard and not nearly as effective.

In a company that is stagnant, more and more employees are going to find reasons to stray. Employees want to be where the action is. They want to go where things are happening. If the company has no direction, no new products, no new challenges or goals, no new growth, employees slack off and wander off.

The point is this: Keep them dogies movin'. A manager must become a leader. If the company hasn't set goals that are motivating, it's up to the manager to set some. It's up to the manager to say, "Let's see how good we can be. Let's see what all we can accomplish."

All the goals in a group don't need to be task goals. A manager obviously can't say, "Let's produce a thousand more widgets," if the company as a whole can't sell a thousand more or purchase the raw materials to make a thousand more. Some of the goals can be interpersonal: "Let's see how much more we can love and affirm one another. What else might we do as a group to better our community or to show our respect and appreciation for other departments in our corporation?"

Lead. Don't prod. In the long run, leadership of the 90 percent—rather than control of the 10 percent—produces vastly superior results, is more cost effective, and takes less time and energy.

It's a matter of perspective.

The minority will never thank you, no matter which way you manage. The majority will thank you, however, when you show Theory R leadership.

## THEORY R AT WORK

What is your company's present perspective on absentee employees?

Look through your policy manual. Do you sense that decisions have been made with the 90 percent or the 10 percent in mind?

How might you rethink or rewrite company policy to reflect the benefit of the majority rather than punishment of the minority?

# 14    Resolving the Past: Getting Rid of the Baggage and Starting Fresh

**M**arty and Bull were both part of the maintenance operation of a plant in Illinois. They had been there for sixteen years. They had hired in at the same time, they had become friends, and then something had happened between them during their first year of working together that had put them at odds with each other. Marty had gone on to become the supervisor of the maintenance area. Bull remained a mechanic. And for fifteen years, Marty and Bull hadn't communicated.

Not communicate? We asked how that was possible, and we received this answer: "They just grunted at each other and avoided each other as much as possible."

Both Marty and Bull attended one of our Value of the Person—Theory R Seminars. After the seminar Bob, Bull's friend, said to me, "Why don't you do something, Wayne, to get Marty and Bull together?" I said, "Hey, we've done the seminar. That's all we can do. It's up to them now." I knew even as I spoke those words that they were a cop-out. I wasn't doing the loving thing by either of them to be so disinterested in their long-standing feud. Bob persisted, "I don't think I'm going to let you get away with that. I think you should at least try." He was right, and I agreed.

Very often in our culture, and especially in the culture of our workplaces, we find a "don't get involved" syndrome. The very opposite needs to happen if we are truly going to begin to pull together as work units, as companies, and as a nation in winning the economic war facing us. We need more people like Bob who will say, "I won't let you get off so easy. You've got to get involved. At least give it your best shot."

I went to Bull and Marty and asked if they would meet with me. I suggested to them that Bob be present as Bull's friend, and that Marty bring along his manager. Both Bull and Marty agreed to the meeting.

We met in a diner about five o'clock in the morning—a place and time they suggested.

If I was going to get up to be at a meeting that early in the morning, I felt there was no reason to play games. Everybody knew why we were there so I said straightaway, "If you're going to have the Value of the Person concepts in operation at your plant, you guys are going to have to drop your baggage, come together, and set a model for the rest of your fellow employees." Then I turned directly to Marty and Bull and asked each of them, "Will you? Will you drop your baggage and reconcile?"

My questions met only silence.

Bull—a very big man—stood up, and as he did, he knocked his chair over (unintentionally, I realized later). He reached over toward Marty— a short little guy—and I thought, *He's going to punch him out!*

Instead, Bull stuck out his hand toward Marty and said, "OK, Marty, why don't we try it?" Marty stood and reached out his hand toward Bull and said, "Yeah. We need to do that." Then Bull said to Marty, "Why is it that we don't like each other? Why don't we speak to each other?"

Marty responded, "I don't know." He paused for a moment and said, "Do you know why, Bull?" And Bull said, "No. I forgot, too."

For fifteen years the men hadn't spoken to each other, and they didn't even remember why!

If you're holding a grudge against someone and you can't even remember what started it, isn't it time you put down that baggage and walked away from it?

I recently talked to Marty and Bull, and I asked them, "How are you guys doing?" They said, "We're doing better than anybody else in the plant. We support each other. We're in relationship. We still wear our Value of the Person pins after all these years!"

**THEORY R SAYS,**

*Choose to get involved. Don't sit on the sidelines. Be an initiator and a participant in valuing others and extending affirmation, appreciation, and recognition.*

**Starting Over—
Leaving the
Excess Baggage
Behind**

Most people show up at work every morning with excess baggage. They bring with them far more than a lunch pail or briefcase.

This excess baggage sometimes takes the form of feelings and attitudes brought from home into the workplace. If an employee has left home after a loud and angry argument with a spouse, that employee is likely to spend much of the workday rehearsing that argument and continuing to fight it mentally. That means less concentration for the tasks at hand but also an attitude that is likely to be much more edgy and confrontational toward fellow employees.

Another type of excess baggage is what an employee carries historically in the workplace. Old grudges. Hurt feelings that have never healed. Breakdowns in communication. The baggage includes a long list of emotional hurts, bitterness, anger, and disappointment. The result is usually nonexistent or poor communication. Feelings of alienation keep the employee from fully participating in the team process. All joy about work evaporates over time.

Just as too much baggage can slow down a traveler, so these emotional burdens slow down an employee. They keep the employee preoccupied with human relationships rather than the tasks at hand or the customers who need attention and service. They cloud an employee's creativity, stunt personal growth, and stifle the willingness to offer suggestions or participate in group activities.

Isolation can result. A greater percentage of the communication becomes non-work-related. The emotional baggage becomes a drag on the productivity of the company.

The Theory R leader recognizes that all employees bring a certain amount of baggage with them. It simply isn't possible for people to separate themselves completely from the outside world upon entering the factory or office building. The Theory R manager needs to

- take steps to help that separation process between work and home.
- help create an environment at work that is at least as positive, and perhaps more positive, than the employee's home environment.
- give employees an opportunity to start over with one another.

In our Value of the Person—Theory R Seminars, we encourage managers to create opportunities for a fresh start.

One of the most dramatic examples of a manager doing this happened at a Fortune 500 plant. The head of the division declared an incinerator day for all personnel files. Employees were given their own personnel files to peruse. And then they were given the privilege of purging those files of any information that they didn't want in them.

On the way out of the plant that day, workers were invited to burn the past by tossing any unwanted documents from their files into an incinerator that had been placed in the courtyard.

That same day, all records about absenteeism were erased, and a new program of presenteeism—with rewards for good attendance records—was implemented.

The division head simultaneously announced that from that day forward, management would make a concerted effort to add positive information to personnel folders so that a personnel folder would reflect a more complete profile of an individual's performance.

The event sent a powerful signal through the company that a new day had dawned! It gave workers an opportunity to start anew with the company, just as a new hire-in might, and to build a new record for promotion, recognition, and advancement.

Another company implemented a policy of good notes in the wake of a Value of the Person—Theory R Seminar. These notes—set up as forms and distributed widely—could be used by any employee to call attention to personal success or the achievement of a fellow worker. The forms were to be turned in to supervisors for inclusion in a worker's personnel file. A cynical person might conclude that such a system would result in employees padding their work records in a false way. However, employees were very honest and straightforward about their successes. In most cases, they reported achievements that had gone unnoticed by their managers: "I've doubled my output on this machine in the last two years," or "Jim had fifteen no-error days on the line this month, a personal high for him."

The reports boosted morale among the workers and helped balance out the workers' personnel files. They gave managers new insight into the performance levels of persons they supervised.

**Giving Your Employees a Fresh Start**

## Don't Let Hurts Fester—Move On in Forgiveness

An employee is never more vulnerable and in need of love than during a time of death. Several years ago, Lefty Scumaci's mother died. Over the years, Lefty has become a prominent person in Pittsburgh, and he experienced a tremendous outpouring of love. The mayor, senators, congressmen, city councilwomen, friends, and even enemies came to the funeral home. His former colleagues, however—international union officials who were located just about a mile and a half from the funeral home—didn't show up. Nothing hurt Lefty more. The last place he wanted to go was to a union gathering.

Lefty let that hurt become baggage to him. He often said to our Value of the Person—Theory R Seminar audiences, "You may think it doesn't matter who shows up at a funeral home until you experience a death in your family."

Bob Hudgins, director of plant engineering operations, corporate engineering, from Owens-Corning, was attending a seminar in which Lefty made that statement. He stood and said to Lefty, "Don't you need to drop your baggage and forgive?"

Lefty was silent, feeling as though he had just been hit with a two-by-four right between his eyes. The truth, the accountability, and the insightful candor of the seminar participant had a dramatic effect on Lefty. He responded with equal candor and a great deal of vulnerability, "You're absolutely right. It's time to drop my baggage for good."

Not long after that incident, an international union conference was scheduled in Pittsburgh. Lefty initially had no intention of going, but as an act of choosing to drop his excess baggage, he went to the meeting.

In the quiet of his thoughts, Lefty forgave his colleagues for the hurt and disappointment they caused him. He wore his union badge with pride that day and greeted in a loving, generous manner the very people who had failed him in his time of need.

It takes a big person to forgive another person's failures. There's nothing soft or easy about it.

## Find a Way to Start Over

We usually hold a debriefing and implementation session the morning after we've conducted a Value of the Person—Theory R Seminar.

In one particular case, our seminar had been attended by a frontline supervisor named Jim, who happened to be in conflict with just about all of the operators who worked under him. During the debriefing session, one operator who had experienced a number of confrontations with Jim spoke up and said, "I just packed my car this morning to drive back home." (The group had driven quite a distance to attend the seminar and had stayed overnight.)

The operator continued, "I want you to know that the only baggage I'm taking home is my dirty clothes packed in my suitcase. I'm leaving all of my other baggage here." He turned to Jim and said, "What about you, Jim? Are you leaving your baggage here, too?" Jim nodded, and the two of them rose and shook hands. They had an opportunity to start fresh in their working relationship.

Starting over may require

- admitting past failures.
- acknowledging a breakdown in relationship.
- making amends.
- calling for a new direction.
- apologizing.
- asking for forgiveness.
- making adjustments.

The goal, however, is to reach a new mutual commitment to do the right thing.

Once baggage is set aside, people find that they face an ongoing challenge of resolving problems and overcoming differences. Theory R calls for coworkers not only to make it right but to keep it right. Employees must adopt an awareness that they are accountable to one another.

Employees and managers alike are challenged to keep from picking up again the baggage they have just set down. It takes a concerted, intentional effort to keep things right.

**Keeping a Relationship at the Right Setting**

No matter what your position in an organization, twelve areas need to be adjusted continually to a right setting. The following guidelines can help you make the necessary adjustments in your life, both at home and at work.

1. ***The right problem.*** Be sure you know what the real problem is before trying to resolve it. Have you gotten to the

core of the matter? Are you dealing with a symptom or the root of the problem? Listen closely. Ask probing questions in a positive tone of voice. Try to get to the heart of the matter.

2. **The right solution.** Recognize that any solution must be win-win. Ask yourself, "Will everybody benefit? What will bring the most good for everybody involved?"

3. **The right focus.** Keep your conversations positive and constructive. Always keep them aimed at solutions, answers, a forward direction, and the issue at hand. If you come out fighting, you'll probably lose your focus quickly. Arguments rarely stay focused on an issue; they usually become personal. And personal comments are derogatory, demeaning and, ultimately, destructive.

4. **The right attitude.** View problems as opportunities to improve existing situations. Stay upbeat about the potential of yourself, those around you, and your organization.

5. **The right motive.** Put yourself in the other person's shoes; show empathy for the situation, the life, the needs, and the constraints. Do what is right for that person because it is right and for no other reason. Do not expect anything from the person in return.

6. **The right range.** Envision long-range effects rather than a short-term fix. Think about the long haul of a relationship. Ask yourself, "How will my behavior in the next five years help me develop a twenty-year relationship with this person?" If the behavior won't build, reconcile, or bring growth to a relationship, don't do it, no matter how effective your behavior may be in bringing about a short-term result.

7. **The right relationships.** Your overriding concern should be how to solve the problem and still maintain the relationship.

8. **The right respect.** Show respect for another person's feelings and opinions even if they differ from your own. Recognize that the person has a right to ideas, viewpoints, and feelings. Respect a person's heritage, culture, race, and age. Respect the person's skills, abilities, talents, and knowledge. Every person on earth knows something that you don't know and can do something that you can't do. Keep in mind that you can and should find something to respect in every person.

**THEORY R SAYS,**

*Resolving the past is critically important to moving forward.*

*Relationships need to be made right, and they need to be kept right.*

9. ***The right goal.*** Be determined to create a victory for all involved. The result you seek should be growth for the individual, for your department, and for the company. In seeking the right goal for others, you'll reap the very goal you want in your life.

10. ***The right creativity.*** Be open to new ideas. Give others the opportunity to express their ideas. Not only will you create a feeling of partnership, but the expression of creative ideas usually spawns further creativity in everybody who hears them. Invite workers to suggest and explore with you new options, alternatives to proposed solutions, and better ways of doing things.

11. ***The right commitment.*** Solving problems, building relationships, and bringing about reconciliation take an ongoing commitment to doing the right thing. Be willing to pay the price of walking the talk. Determine within yourself that you are going to stay committed to your workers, your company, your marriage, and your family.

12. ***The right role of leadership.*** View yourself as a leader, regardless of your position on a corporate chart. Every person can be a leader in valuing others and in making a positive difference in an organization.

If you face a problem at work, try devising a solution and then checking it against this checklist. Ask yourself, "Is my attitude right? Am I really dealing with the right problem? Is my commitment level right?" If you have any doubts, reappraise your position. You may want to ask others for their input.

## THEORY R AT WORK

Is there someone with whom you need to make amends and start fresh?

How can you establish a new beginning in your department at work?

What new start might you make as a family?

# 15 Theory R's Law of Reciprocity and the Spiral Effect

**H**e got what he deserved."

"She's paid what she's worth."

"He gets only what he works for."

How many times have you heard those kinds of statements in today's workplace? The law of reciprocity in traditional management structures says, "The company rewards what workers give."


Theory R takes a decidedly different approach to reciprocity—the view from the employee's perspective.

We believe 90 percent of all people give back what they receive. If they receive love, dignity, and respect, they will give back love, dignity, and respect.

When an employer takes as a motto, "Ask not what your people can do for you; ask what you can do for your people," employees nearly always respond with a like motto, "Ask not what your company can do for you; ask what you can do for your company."

**THEORY R SAYS,**

*Employees give back what they receive.*

---

- Hate an employee; you'll get back hate.
- Be disrespectful to an employee; you'll get no respect in return.

- Show an employee no appreciation; you'll find yourself not getting appreciation.
- Insult an employee; you'll be the object of insults.

The good news of this law of reciprocity is that the converse is also true:

- Give an employee love; you'll get back love.
- Uphold an employee's dignity; your dignity will be upheld.
- Show respect for an employee; you'll be respected.

## Theory R Generates Positive Vibes

Love, dignity, and respect are like magnets. They draw people toward them. And managers who demonstrate acts of affirmation, appreciation, and recognition to employees are also like magnets. Employees want to be around them and associate with them. Employees who have Theory R managers nearly always like their managers, uphold them, are loyal to them, and are frequently openly affectionate when they talk about them.

The reward of Theory R to a manager who lives out Value of the Person principles is a great one: enthusiastic support.

## Is Anyone Immune to Love, Dignity, and Respect?

We do not believe that anyone, over time, is immune to the effects of love, dignity, and respect when they are applied consistently and sincerely. Even the hardest cases seem to fold when they are given genuine, heartfelt love and respect.

A lawyer named Mike is a prime example. He never met a client he liked; he never had a good word to say about anything. Obviously, he treated his clients with respect *to their faces,* but behind their backs he had little positive to say. Much of what he felt he vented on his secretary, Judy.

Whatever Mike dished out, Judy took with a smile. She continually found ways of showing value to Mike and of speaking well of other people—even those Mike dismissed, diminished, or discredited.

We've been watching Mike slowly give in to her valuing behaviors. He doesn't say so to Judy, but he says to some of his peers, "You know, Judy's fair. I trust her. She always wants to do the right thing."

Perseverance is vital in your efforts to value others. It is over time that the valuing actions of love, dignity, and respect have their effect.

## THEORY R SAYS,

*The desire to do what is right is a part of human nature. Human beings want to treat others in a right way, and they want to have others treat them the same way.*

In many ways, Value of the Person principles have to be caught more than taught. Somebody has to model loving behavior to another person before that person is likely to exhibit loving behavior to another.

Most of us have a frame of reference for valuing long before we enter the workplace. We know what it means to be affirmed, cared for, and respected from someone—usually a parent. Sometimes another significant adult in our lives—perhaps a teacher, coach, spouse, mentor, aunt or uncle, grandparent, or godparent. Perhaps even from a child of our own. We know how it feels.

What needs to happen in the workplace is not teaching these behaviors as much as being reminded of them. We need to be reminded that it's the right thing to love others, uphold their dignity, and show respect for them. We know it's true. We've just forgotten it a little, especially in the workplace. And sometimes we need to be shown how these behaviors can be expressed in the workplace, and we need to feel permission to exhibit these behaviors.

Sam Shoemaker, an Episcopal priest, used to say with a twinkle in his eye, "There's a little bit of the Holy Spirit in all of us." What he meant was, "We all know that love, dignity, and respect are good things to extend to one another. Nobody had to drill that into us. It's a part of our fundamental, inherent humanity. We all understand the need to value the person, and we all believe it's a good idea. Why? Because it's a part of the nature that God has built into us."

Reid Carpenter, who frequently joins us in presenting Value of the Person—Theory R Seminars, says it this way: "We need to be awakened." We all have a frame of reference for knowing that love, dignity, and respect are right things. We've just let those behaviors go to sleep or be forgotten in our concern with winning life's competitive games.

## Bought or Valued?

Workers know when they are being bought instead of valued. Being bought is an act that is conditional, manipulative, demanding, and rooted in a control mentality. It's the exact opposite of being valued.

An effective illustration about being bought is one that Lefty Scumaci tells to our seminar audiences:

"I was on the road nearly all the time for twenty-one years, serving my international union. During those years, I would come home on weekends, and I'd try to spend as much time as I could with my young daughter, Francine. Nevertheless, I always had a feeling of guilt about being away so much.

"I fell into the routine that a lot of weekend fathers seem to fall into. I tried to 'buy' my daughter's love. Companies aren't all that different, you know. They try to 'buy' things from their workers. They try to motivate their workers with a variety of gimmicks to get them to do what they want. Workers know what's going on. So did my daughter.

"One weekend I came home, and Francine brought me her school papers to look at. I noticed that one of the papers had several stars on it—the kind that you can buy by the box and stick on items. I said, 'Great, Francine!'

"Then management mentality took hold of me. I said to my little girl, 'For every star you bring home, I'll give you a quarter.' I traded in love and praise for money.

"The next week I came home and found that Francine had a paper with three stars on it. Seventy-five cents. The following week, I came home to find fifteen papers with stars on them. I thought to myself, *I've created a genius!* Managers think the same thing. Workers produce a little faster and a little more after receiving a particular benefit, and managers think, *This is really working. I was brilliant to make that move.*

"And then I looked a little more closely at her papers. I asked myself, *Why would her teacher be giving her a star for all these mistakes?* Suddenly, it hit me what had happened. My daughter confessed to me that she had taken part of her seventy-five cents and had gone to the store and purchased her own box of stars. Then she had put one on every one of her papers the following week! Workers can find a way to manipulate any program intended to manipulate them!

"They can figure out ways to *look* like they're working eighty miles an hour when they're actually working two miles an hour. They can figure out ways to cover for one another, skate by, walk the fine line of bare minimums.

"I was glad I found out what was happening right away. I could easily have gone on for years thinking something about my daughter that wasn't true, and forcing her to be a cheat and a liar at the same time."

The advantage of most rewards is not the reward itself as much as it is the coupling of a tangible reward with an expression of genuine appreciation and recognition. The reward—the increased benefit, promotion, raise—means only as much as the heartfelt human-to-human value that undergirds it.

Think about your work experience. Think about the meaningless rewards that you've received in your life. The rewards were often quite nice—an extra half day off, an increase of fifty cents an hour, a new office. But what really made those rewards meaningful to you was that someone said to you sincerely, "We really value your contribution to this company."

Lefty sums it up, "If you pretend to care about employees, they'll pretend to work for you."

**The Spiral Effect**

The Theory R law of reciprocity is central to what we perceive as a spiral effect in every organization—a movement either upward or downward (see fig. 15.1).

The result of a philosophy in which people are regarded as less valuable than material, economic, or organizational factors— less recognized, less appreciated, less rewarded, less maintained, less affirmed—is a downward spiral.

The result of a philosophy in which people are regarded as the most valuable resource within an organization is an upward spiral.

In either case, a spiral effect is put into motion.

The nature of both spirals is fourfold.

**First, One Set of Factors Builds Upon Another, and Ultimately, All Factors Affect All Other Factors**

In other words, a factor such as low morale is nearly always related to absenteeism, and absenteeism can lead to confrontation, which can lead to more absenteeism, which tends to lower morale even further. The converse is equally true: High morale nearly always correlates with less absenteeism, which results in less confrontation. Less confrontation results in lower absenteeism, which affects morale in a positive way.

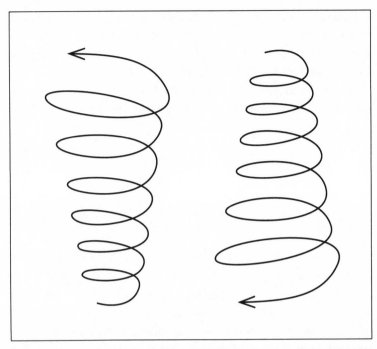

FIGURE 15.1. Graphic depiction of an upward spiral and a downward spiral within an organization

What may begin as a small confrontation—if it goes unchecked—can lead to a huge confrontation. What begins as low morale that stems from a lack of trust can quickly become no morale correlated with a complete lack of trust.

The more factors put into the spiral and the greater their growth, the more quickly things tend to fizzle, fray, or otherwise come apart at the seams. We all know this to be true in very practical ways in our lives. A little rip in a pocket—if left unmended—can lead to a bigger and bigger rip, which widens more and more rapidly. A little argument in a marriage—if unresolved—can lead to a hotter and hotter argument and, ultimately, to a complete meltdown of the relationship. On the other hand, a romantic dinner for two or a sincere apology may be the first step toward reconciliation, especially if followed by meaningful conversation and positive behavior.

When it comes to the value placed on employees, the spiraling effect doesn't look like a coiled spring. It looks like a tornado in motion!

*Second, the Spiral Tends to Accelerate in Motion, in Size, and in Consequences as It Grows in Any One Direction*

*Third, the
Spiral Effect
Is Always
Experienced by
the Employees
Involved, Even
if They May Not
Be Able to
Identify It or
Label It as Such*

Employees who are not valued know they are not being valued. And they don't let such expressions and behavior on the part of managers go unnoticed. They either react instinctively or respond consciously. Either way, the company suffers.

Conversely, employees who are valued know it. They also react or respond. Their companies benefit by their responses.

*Fourth, a
Spiraling Effect
Can Originate
at Any Point
on the
Organizational
Chart*

Not all devaluing behavior begins at the top of an organizational chart. Sometimes an employee can devalue a superior until a full-blown mutiny is in effect. Rather than display absenteeism, the upper levels of management become withdrawn, increasingly isolated, and more and more reactionary. They communicate less and in a more confrontational manner. Morale is destroyed, trust is bombed into oblivion, loyalty becomes a moot point, and the results of poor productivity and poor quality follow in due time, leading to poor profits and, eventually, economic failure.

At other times an employee might come into conflict with a fellow employee—the result being a malignant attitude that can infect an entire company and affect its quality and productivity.

**THEORY R SAYS,**

*When even one employee within an organization is not valued, the entire company achieves less than its full potential.*

*When the general tendency within an organization is to fail to value employees, the organization begins to experience a downward spiral, which if not reversed will ultimately lead to the demise of the organization.*

The contagious effects of devaluing move upward, downward, and outward with equally demoralizing, debilitating, and demolishing effects. On the other hand, we've seen a positive spiral begin with a janitor in one instance and a security guard in another. The positive messages generated by these employees infected their entire organizations with a hefty dose of high morale.

Every employee within an organization—no matter the position on an organizational chart—contributes effort and skill and a positive or negative attitude that affects morale. Diminishing any person's contribution diminishes the sum of the whole. Simple mathematics.

In the Northeast where we live, and where many of the rivers are broad and smooth flowing, the sport of crew is quite popular. Any crew team knows that a slack effort on the part of a team member, or the failure of a team member to synchronize his efforts with those of the others on the team, means a slower time at the finish line. The effort of each person must be maximal and coordinated.

In a company, the slackening of effort of one person on a manufacturing line means lower productivity for the entire line. A quality mistake made by one person at any point along the line, and the overall product has lower quality. Rudeness to one customer (in Theory R terms, devaluing that customer) in a restaurant, bank, or store means not only the probable loss of that customer but the likely loss of any other potential or current customer to whom that rebuffed customer talks!

When a manager fails to value one person, that failure is nearly always perceived by the workers immediately around that person. Workers know when the boss is ignoring, riding, downgrading, or otherwise devaluing a coworker. It is very difficult for a manager to fail to value one person without the behavior being perceived as a failure to value the whole.

This is a critical matter for managers to face. Very often, traditional-style managers don't care what one employee thinks (about them, the company, the process, or the product). The attitude is, "That's only one opinion." True enough. The corollary attitude is, "Workers come and workers go." A sometimes related attitude is, "I just have a personality conflict with that one person." Yet another common attitude is, "Anybody who doesn't like it here can leave." No matter the genesis of the attitude, the result is nearly always the same: a negative attitudinal virus invades the organization.

Epidemics begin with one sick person passing the sickness on to another person. Corporate failures can also begin with one devalued person, the closing of a family-owned business can begin with one disgruntled relative, or the demise of a retail store can begin with one dissatisfied customer.

The failure to validate that one opinion is generally perceived to be a failure on the part of the manager to value all employee opinions. The manager who makes derogatory statements about one person or singles out one worker for special ridicule is generally perceived as having little regard for the dignity of all employees assigned to that manager.

Therefore, snubbing, deriding, or demeaning one employee is going to be perceived as snubbing, deriding, or demeaning all employees in that immediate area of the company. And the perception of loss of value in that one area will tend to be generalized to other areas until the entire company has been infected and comes up sick. Again, perception is its own reality. It should never be diminished in importance or ignored.

We see this in our national economy at present. Workers in stable, forward-looking, progressive, profitable companies look around and see fellow citizens in their city being laid off, and their first thought is, *I might lose my job, too.* Even though that response may be emotional and irrational—which means that the workers haven't considered all factors—it is nonetheless real to them. The employees become demoralized. Entire cities and industries become demoralized. Hope diminishes. And a downward spiral begins.

**THEORY R SAYS,**

*Nothing good comes from devaluing another person.*

When we fail to show love, dignity, and respect for others—no matter who they are or our relationship with them—we enter into a lose-lose situation. It is impossible for both parties to win. In fact, we contend that it is impossible for even the devaluing party to win!

This goes against the grain of our competitive nature as human beings. We assume that when one loses, another must always win. This is *not* the case in human relationships. When one person refuses to love, show respect, or appreciate the dignity of another person, the person who refuses is also a loser:

- Speak ill of another person and you'll put yourself into a position to have others speak ill of you.
- Continually criticize another person and you'll soon find yourself being criticized.
- Express hate, derision, or any other negative emotion toward another person and you'll find yourself attracting those same expressions from others.

**At the Bottom of the Spiral**

As a downward spiral moves into the final stages of deterioration, employees no longer have a strong desire or commitment to work at all. Management has ceased to be effective. The downward spiral is marked by

- increased confrontation, including more formal grievances and generalized complaining.
- increased absenteeism.
- feelings of less trust and loyalty.
- low morale.

- less and less communication.
- poor productivity and quality.
- less company profit.

When poor productivity and quality result in less profit, the company begins to experience cutbacks and layoffs. Ultimately, if the spiral isn't reversed, the organization finds itself in economic failure—which means plant closings and "Out of Business" signs.

The downward spiral is a lose-lose situation. Employees lose. Managers lose. The company loses. Customers lose. Everybody involved loses.

By contrast, an upward spiral is marked by these characteristics:

**Hallmarks of an Upward Spiral**

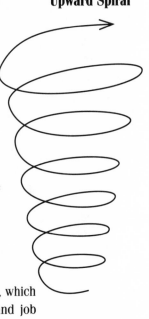

- Reconciliation
- Trust
- Loyalty
- High morale and enthusiasm
- Commitment (to one another and to the organization as a whole)
- Low absenteeism
- A low turnover rate
- Willing participation
- The flow of creative, positive, practical, and concrete ideas
- Increased productivity
- Excellent quality
- Good profits

All of these elements lead to economic growth and success, which in turn tend to lead to an increase in personal rewards and job satisfaction for the individual employee.

Where does one begin in reversing a downward spiral? *With reconciliation.*

The question arises, "If devaluing others always results in the same by-products, can you look at the by-products and work backward to say that devaluing is in effect?"

Much of the time, yes.

**Identifying the Spiral at Work**

## THEORY R SAYS,

*When looking at poor productivity and poor quality, two of the key questions to ask are these:*

- *"How are we treating one another as coworkers within this organization?"*
- *"What can we do to value one another more highly?"*

Not all companies fail as companies because they fail to value their people. Some companies fail to identify an appropriate market niche, fail to make wise investments of money, fail to calculate their expense-income margins correctly, and so forth.

What we can evaluate and attempt to identify is the percentage (or portion) of the overall problem that might be attributed to a failure to establish quality interpersonal relationships within the organization. Stated another way, we can ask, "Are we valuing our people highly enough? Has this failure contributed to the problem we are presently experiencing?"

In nearly all cases, wise top-level decision makers will conclude that a failure to value the people within the organization has played at least some part in the overall decline of the organization, and that placing higher value on the people in the company will play at least some part in bringing about a reversal of the situation.

## Spirals Can Be Reversed

A downward or upward spiral can be reversed in nearly all cases. A situation is never so good that it can never take a turn for the worse. A situation is rarely so bad that it can't be turned around.

When you find yourself in an upward spiral, continue to do the things that got you in that position. Don't stop doing the right things!

When you find yourself in a downward spiral, don't give up. Start doing the right things. Note that

- downward spirals are easiest to turn around if they are caught early.
- the turnaround nearly always requires an open recognition of the problem (and its possible consequences) by all parties involved.
- there must be a willingness on the part of someone in a leadership position to see the spiraling trend reversed.

## Six Key Questions to Ask in Evaluating a Spiral

As a manager, you can ask yourself very specific questions using the spiral manifestations as a guideline.

This is the area in which the direct correlation between Value of the Person principles and on-the-job behavior is probably the highest.

When people feel devalued or unappreciated, arguments, confrontations, complaints, and formal labor grievances rise. If a company begins to experience a significant number of negative encounters between workers or between workers and managers, the first thing to do in isolating the problem is to evaluate the tenor and quality of the interpersonal relationships within the organization.

Most workers do not argue, complain, or express grievances about a lack of promotion or raise, or even about the material quality of their workplace, nearly as often or as loudly as they complain about being treated poorly or unfairly. Managers are frequently surprised by this fact but rarely deny its validity.

(This is not to say, of course, that managers can cover poor work environments and low wages with a happy front of applause and a rah-rah attitude. Far from it. Managers who truly value workers will value them to the point of wanting to see the workers have a positive, clean, safe working environment and a wage that is fair compensation.)

*Question #1: "Are We Experiencing a Rise or Drop in Confrontations, Grievances, or Complaints?"*

Low morale manifests itself in various ways:

- Sullen and sluggish behavior
- Excuses
- A desire not to be involved in department, unit, or corporate activities
- An unresponsive attitude
- Downcast eyes when managers spontaneously encounter workers
- The tendency for an employee to keep one eye on the clock at all times
- Outbursts of anger or frustration between employees
- Outright sabotage of another person's work or position

*Question #2: "Are Employees Exhibiting Low or High Morale?"*

High morale, on the other hand, is marked by positive behaviors:

- Quickness of response
- Extra effort
- A flow of creative ideas
- A desire to be involved in everything the department does

- Spontaneous and natural communication
- A willingness to put in extra time if needed (and compensated) and extra effort to get the job done
- Mutual appreciation of one another
- Uplifting comments and smiles

If morale is low, turn first to an appraisal of the ways in which people are valuing or devaluing one another.

*Question #3: "Are Employees Quick to Offer Suggestions, or Does the Room Turn Silent When They're Asked for Opinions and Ideas?"*

When creativity ceases to flow in an organization, death of that organization is soon coming. If employees are silent, morose, negative in their comments, or unwilling to communicate quickly and without fear of punishment, ask, "What can I do to turn this around?"

Bear in mind that an insincere request for more input will not open up the channels of communication. The desire to communicate must be genuine and heartfelt.

*Question #4: "Do Employees Exhibit Trust and Loyalty?"*

These two qualities are often difficult to measure or evaluate. We suggest that managers take a look at body language. Ask yourself,

- "How do the employees express themselves in nonverbal ways during meetings or one-on-one conversations?"
- "Do employees look me in the eye or look away?"
- "Do employees cross their arms? Do they back away from me? Are they reluctant to shake my hand? Do they avoid contact with me physically or verbally?"
- "Are employees quick to respond to my questions or statements, or do they seem to weigh every word I say and they say—attempting always to say the right thing, the words they perceive I want to hear?"

If the stance, expressions, and behavior of a person seem to be closed or distant, assume that there is some degree of distrust at work. Distrust is a second cousin to disloyalty.

Ask yourself, "What can I do to engender trust?"

Trust is usually the product of people saying what they mean and meaning what they say, then acting in accordance with what they say (matching up the walk with the talk), and both saying and doing what is honest, fair and, as much as possible, generous.

An insincere compliment; an unnecessary reprimand; an idle comment about a person's appearance, race, age, or sex; a flippant question; an out-and-out insult—these are surefire ways to damage trust. Lying, behaving inconsistently, and showing partiality for one race, sex, or other unchangeable personal quality over another are all trust destroyers. Saying one thing and doing another are probably deathblows to trust.

On the other hand, employees respond to those who tell it like it is and mostly tell the good parts. People enjoy praise and generous encouragement to be all and achieve all that is humanly possible. People like for someone else to tell them about their potential, to compliment them sincerely, and to show genuine interest in their lives (including their families, their interests, their achievements outside work, and their troubles).

*Question #5: "Are Absenteeism and Tardiness on the Rise?"*

The wise manager asks this about the individual employee and the group as a whole. Apart from the rare occurrence of medically based epidemics or severe weather problems, a dramatic rise in absenteeism usually indicates that an employee or group of employees would rather be anyplace other than at work. And that's usually because work is a negative, frustrating place to be. Ask yourself, "Why?"

*Question #6: "Is Productivity Increasing or Decreasing, and Is the Quality of Work Improving or Suffering Decline?"*

Many factors contribute to productivity and quality. One factor most frequently ignored or discounted is the human factor. Face up to the possibility that you, or someone else in your organization, are consciously or subconsciously devaluing others. Look at other contributing factors, such as high absenteeism, low morale, stifled communication, and an increase in the number of grievances. Weigh the situation as a whole.

The fact is, employees who are valued highly as workers—who are affirmed, recognized, and rewarded for their work, and who are afforded courtesy, love, respect, and dignity—give their best effort with gung ho enthusiasm. Assuming that such employees are skilled at what they do, they usually are very productive and very concerned about the quality of their work.

We recently heard the story of Richey. When Richey began his new job at a restaurant, he was at a low ebb in his life. He had been laid off at the mill, and he was separated from his wife. He was quiet and withdrawn. The manager of the restaurant, however, began to encourage and affirm Richey, and to show an interest in him and his family. The more he reached out to Richey, the harder Richey tried at his job and the more he began to open up. The more the manager encouraged him, the more outgoing he became.

**THEORY R SAYS,**

*Always begin and end with the human factor.*

Today, Richey is working on a reconciliation with his wife. He has such an "up" attitude that customers ask to be seated in his section of the restaurant. And with his manager's blessing and help, he is pursuing an even better-paying position.

Richey is on an upward spiral, and so is the restaurant.

A devalued employee gives minimal effort and frequently demonstrates a "who cares?" attitude. Productivity and quality suffer.

Eliminate the value problems first, and you're much more likely to isolate any other factors that are leading to a decline in productivity and quality of performance.

## Each Worker Has a Personal Spiral, Too

When a new employee begins work with an organization, that employee begins a personal upward or downward spiral. Most of us start new jobs with a clean slate. Very few employees bring a negative record with them from a previous job. If anything, the manager's perception of a new employee is usually positive, or the person wouldn't have been hired.

Lefty Scumaci often says that from his viewpoint as a long-time union officer, many employees feel that shortly after they begin employment with a firm, that firm begins to make book on just how to get rid of them.

The reasoning is quite accurate in most places that operate with a traditional management style. Most of what goes into personnel folders is negative, not positive. Managers keep track of what goes wrong, not what goes right.

Even evaluation forms are frequently designed more to validate why employees are not being given a promotion or raise than to provide evidence for their being given one.

Employees begin to feel that they are on a downward spiral with the company with little hope of reversing the trend. When that happens, they experience a significant drop in morale. Communication lessens. Tensions mount. The work environment becomes a stressful, unenjoyable place to be.

The personal downward spiral makes employees less productive. They are also less likely to be concerned with quality.

A miserable situation is created, and for most workers, the only way out seems to be utter rebellion or increased absenteeism. The downward spiral on a personal level leads to personal economic failure, just as the downward spiral on the corporate level can lead to corporate economic failure.

## The Problem Goes Home

A personal downward spiral is rarely limited to the workplace. Downward spirals can also be experienced in a husband-wife relationship and parent-child relationships. Indeed, every relationship is subject to the spiraling effect.

When disappointments arise, they are followed generally by arguments. Both want from the other person what isn't there. A power play begins. And pretty soon, they quit showing to each other the basic courtesy and kindness that they showed each other earlier in the relationship.

They stop saying the high-value words that they once were so free in giving: "You're wonderful"; "You're so talented (or strong or beautiful or intelligent)"; "I admire you for your honesty (your character, your kindness, your special way with people)"; "I love you."

High-value phrases frequently are replaced with demeaning phrases: "You're just a . . . ," or "I don't like . . . ," or "Why can't you . . . ?"

And a downward spiral begins.

Positions become entrenched. Communication dries up. And eventually, if this trend isn't reversed, the marriage is doomed to separation or divorce. Even if the people continue to live together and call themselves married, they are living in a failed relationship.

That is one of the foremost reasons why Theory R and the Value of the Person concepts are not limited to the business arena. Theory R is not strictly a business theory or a management strategy. It is a philosophy toward all of life. The reason is simple: work is only part of life's whole.

All that happens outside the workplace affects what happens within it. All that happens within the workplace affects an individual's personal, family, and community life.

**Where Does the Organization's Responsibility Begin and End?**

The organization's responsibility for the personal downward or upward spiral in a worker's life begins in the workplace and is focused primarily there. But it isn't exclusively bound to the workplace.

The Theory R manager cares about fellow employees and is concerned about each fellow worker's total well-being. And care and concern don't begin and end when the factory whistle blows, the computer terminal is turned off, or the last dish is dried.

**THEORY R SAYS,**

*Valuing a person means valuing the whole of a person's life.*

As a manager or coworker, you are going to encounter fellow employees experiencing a spiral in one direction or another. Rarely can an employee psych the self out of the spiral that is already in effect. It is your responsibility—or your personal leadership opportunity—to attempt to pull that person out of the downward spiral through positive, genuine, meaningful words and actions.

Furthermore, we need to recognize that the downward spiral that begins at home can continue at work and, if unchecked at work, will continue at home. By tomorrow, the spiral will be just that much bigger, that much more entrenched, and that much more destructive—not only to the person but to the organization.

It isn't enough to say, "What matters at work is all that matters." What happens in an employee's life matters to all who are involved with that employee.

# THEORY R AT WORK

Consider your workplace. Are you experiencing a downward or an upward spiral?

- If the spiral is downward, what might you do to reverse it?
- If the spiral is upward, what might you do to ensure that it continues in an upward direction?

Think of a person in your organization or at home. Ask yourself,

- "Am I doing what is right for this person?"
- "Am I valuing this person highly enough?"
- "Am I finding ways to express the value I feel?"

# Theory R
# By-Products:
# An Impact on
# Productivity,
# Quality, and
# Profitability

16

**A** twelve-letter word has become paramount in industry: *p-r-o-d-u-c-t-i-v-i-t-y*. Nearly all managers view their operations in terms of productivity above all other factors. If a line or a division or a unit is not productive, it is subject to being eliminated. The most productive groups of people receive the most rewards and appreciation. That holds true regardless of what style of management is in place. Unless a company produces, it fails to thrive.

Productivity is the ratio of output to input. Output is what is produced. Input factors include labor, materials, energy, and capital. The desire, of course, is to have more output with less input—more product for less cost (in terms of wages and benefits, equipment maintenance costs, fuel, raw material costs, marketing costs, and so forth).

Every organization has its own volume of business and a measure for productivity. To the ad agency, it may be the number of jobs completed in a year. To the law firm, it may be the number of cases. To the hospital, it may be the number of patients served or beds filled. To the schools, student FTE (full-time equivalency) is generally the measurement. As you read this chapter, apply the concepts to your unique circumstance.

Improving productivity hinges on several elements.

**Factors That Affect Productivity**

What affects productivity? At least two sets of factors are at work.

*1. INVESTMENT FACTORS.* These factors include such tangible, concrete items as product design, machinery, equipment, process systems, and research and development. A manager can help improve productivity in this area generally through effective planning and organization.

*2. HUMAN FACTORS.* Employee attitude, trust, and relationships are among the more intangible, immeasurable human factors that have a direct impact on productivity. Although immeasurable in nature, these factors have measurable counterparts in the form of absenteeism, poor quality, and grievances and complaints.

Both sets of factors—investment and human—are ultimately c-o-n-t-r-o-l-l-a-b-l-e, another twelve-letter word. However, in most circumstances, a company will try to boost productivity by focusing on the investment factors. The more immeasurable human factors are frequently ignored.

Let's take a look at how the downward spiral works in declining productivity.

**Downward Spiral of Productivity**

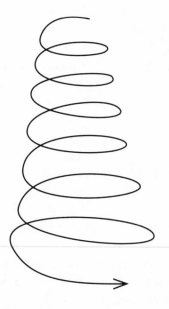

*Lack of trust*

*Broken relationships*

*Negative attitudes*

*Rise in absenteeism*

*Poor quality*

*Rise in grievances*

*Productivity stagnation*

*Investment stagnation*

*Collapse of company*

Too often, managers are late in identifying the downward spiral of productivity. They don't spot it until it hits the area of productivity stagnation. Rather than find and stop the seed problems at the top end of the spiral—where the immeasurable human factors can be controlled—the traditional manager will ignore the correlation between lack of trust, broken relationships, and negative attitudes on the bottom line. Instead, the traditional manager seeks to revise products, to invest in new machinery, facilities, system processes, or equipment, or to pour money into research and development (R&D).

What managers need to do is twofold:

- Realize the critical role of immeasurable human attitudes in the productivity equation.
- Recognize the pivotal role they play in influencing the human factors toward the positive end of the spiral (and creating a happy team and well-oiled operation) or toward the negative end of the spiral (where one finds an unhappy, grieving, noncaring workforce). Although the human factors initially may be immeasurable, their measurable counterparts directly affect the bottom line in terms of productivity and quality.

The impact of high morale—generally defined as positive widespread attitudes of trust, enthusiasm, and a prevailing sense of individual purpose—on productivity cannot be overstated. The importance of controlling these immeasurable human factors through Theory R management also cannot be overstated.

As a manager, you need to grasp that you have at your fingertips the power to unleash a dramatic productivity explosion—one that would force the development of positive (not crisis intervention) investment factors and give a boost to the productivity equation! Don't focus on the factors you can't control. Focus on what you can control. Be responsible for implementing Theory R on a daily basis, and let the people perform the quality work for you, in double-digit productivity style, as a natural by-product.

A company may be able to buy time, skills, and muscle. It cannot buy enthusiasm, loyalty, hearts, minds, or souls.

A young coal miner came to one of our Value of the Person—Theory R Seminars in Pittsburgh and eloquently made this same point to the group gathered there: "I have a message to all of you management people. Take a look at me. I'm a coal miner. I'm proud of my job and of what I do. You could pay me a thousand dollars a day for going down into those mines, and it would never be enough. You could double that salary and give me two thousand dollars, but it still wouldn't be enough. Sure, I'll take your money. But your money will never compensate for a lack of treating me with love, dignity, and respect. Your money will never be enough by itself. It will never satisfy my thirst as a worker to be treated as a person with value."

Show us a group of employees who are valued and we'll show you a group of employees with high morale. A group with high morale is a group that generally will find a way to work with machinery, even if it's held together by rubber bands, a group that will train itself in how to get a job done (through trial and error and grapevine sharing of information), a group that will figure out better procedures for simplifying the job and improving output, and a group that will be highly creative in finding raw materials or new sources of raw materials.

On the other hand, show us a group of employees with low morale and we'll show you a group that won't produce, no matter how state-of-the-art the equipment, thorough the training program, superior the raw materials, or streamlined the operational procedures.

Employees who are trusting, positive about the job, and loyal to their colleagues, managers, and company are going to show up for work, do their best, have no reason for grievances, and produce at a very high rate.

Employees who don't trust, have a lousy attitude toward the job, and feel no loyalty nearly always have a high rate of absenteeism, are more prone to filing grievances, and do slipshod work and precious little of it.

Theory R aims straight at the heart of productivity: the unseen, immeasurable, yet controllable factors related to attitude, trust, and relationships. It can make the difference in your business edging ahead of your competition and becoming a truly world-class operation capable of competing in the global market. The keys are these:

- Let productivity and quality become natural by-products of doing what is right for the people.
- Create an environment where people choose to be productive and do quality work—where high productivity and excellent quality become a state of mind in the people.

If you do so, you will find yourself scrambling to cope with the double-digit productivity improvement and quality excellence you will have as by-products. Theory R will do this for you—and much more.

**The Quality Cycle**

Employees who feel valued are ones who, in turn, value their jobs. They feel good about the work they do, the products they produce, the service they render, and their personal and group performance levels. They take pride in being winners and being part of a winning team.

This pride sets in motion a desire not only to produce more (or achieve more, sell more, generate more) but also to produce better quality. Employees who are proud of themselves and their work desire to produce quality products or give quality service. In both, a cycle is established that looks like figure 16.1.

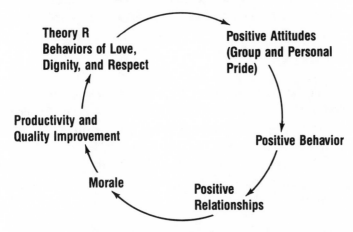

FIGURE 16.1. The quality cycle of self-motivated productivity and quality

The good news about productivity and quality is that they are self-motivating. When employees see that they are producing more and better, they become more motivated. Their sense of pride in their performance gives them more positive attitudes. The positive attitudes help them build relationships. (Everybody loves to be around persons with positive attitudes.) As the positive attitudes build, team morale builds, and each person's morale is affected in a positive way. The higher the morale, the greater the productivity and the higher the quality. And so the cycle continues.

In a period of downsizing and increased competition in the global marketplace, the importance of increased quality cannot be over-stated. James P. Womack, Daniel T. Jones, and Daniel Roose point clearly to this in their book, *The Machine that Changed the World: The Story of Lean Production:*

> *Perhaps the most striking difference between mass production and lean production lies in their ultimate objectives. Mass-producers set a limited goal for themselves—"good enough," which translates into an acceptable number of defects, a maximum acceptable level of inventories, a narrow range of standardized products. To do better, they argue, would cost too much or exceed inherent human capabilities.*

> *Lean producers, on the other hand, set their sights explicitly on perfection: continually declining costs, zero defects, zero inventories, and endless product variety. Of course, no lean producer has ever reached this promised land—and perhaps none ever will, but the endless quest for perfection continues to generate surprise twists.*

One of the twists that these three senior managers of the MIT International Motor Vehicle Program cite is that "lean production calls for learning far more professional skills and applying these creatively in a team setting rather than in a rigid hierarchy."

Theory R supplies the perspective and underlying foundation of appreciation and support that lead to the necessary creativity in a team setting.

**Nearly Overnight Results**

We experienced nearly overnight results at Pittron. Within sixty days we were showing a profit. Our quality improved to perfect. Productivity rose dramatically.

I was probably as surprised as anyone—not that valuing the person made a difference but that there was such a measurable amount of difference. The results were significant beyond anything we had imagined. In the twenty-one months that Operation Turnaround was in effect, Pittron had the results documented in figure 16.2.

With that dramatic increase in productivity and quality, it's obvious that we also showed a very high increase in the number of orders. We nearly quadrupled our workforce, up from about three hundred to nearly twelve hundred. Rather than fear or experience layoffs, workers had job stability.

| Before | After |
|---|---|
| Loss: $6 million | Profit: $6 million |
| Productivity: zero | Productivity improvement: up 64% |
| Quality: poor | Quality: perfect |
| Grievances: 1,200 | Grievances: 1 |
| Absenteeism: 25% | Absenteeism: 0.5% |
| Employees: 300 | Employees: 1,200 |

FIGURE 16.2. The results of Operation Turnaround at Pittron

Pittron is not alone in recording such dramatic results. Just a few months ago, a company president called us to say, "When I heard at the Value of the Person—Theory R Seminar about the increases in productivity and quality that some companies were experiencing, I discounted them somewhat. I readily admit that to you. I didn't expect those kinds of results in our company, certainly not in the short-term. We had a good productivity level, and we were a good operating company.

"In the last ten months, we've increased our net profits by 2 percent over last year. We've had no price increases, but we have been able to give all of our workers a wage increase. We've seen a significant increase in the bottom line that I didn't expect. We have seen a double-digit increase in productivity, and absenteeism has fallen to a level that it is almost immeasurable. We've had no grievances in over fifteen months. Our quality has improved dramatically."

Over and over again, in instances too numerous to recount, we've seen these by-products of Theory R in action:

- Double-digit productivity
- Increased profits
- Job stability
- Job satisfaction
- Improved quality
- Reduced absenteeism
- Decreased grievances
- Pride in workmanship
- Revitalization of the work ethic
- Cooperation and teamwork
- Open communication
- Innovative creativity
- Family stability

What great benefits, just from doing the right things to reconcile relationships!

And two more by-products are worth recognition. They cannot be measured, but they are very real nonetheless:

*1. **Reputation**.* A person, a department, or a company that implements Theory R gains a more positive reputation. Those who see Value of the Person concepts at work respond favorably to them ultimately.

*2. **Reformation**.* Theory R brings about a reformation in the workplace. Not a rebellion or a revolution but a reformation. A reformation is something that *re*forms the structures, protocol, and atmosphere of the workplace.

Both the reputation and the reformation associated with Theory R are positive. Theory R managers acquire a good reputation. Companies that are reformed by Theory R have a good public reputation, which is perhaps the best form of public relations a company can ever hope to have.

## Three Additional By-Products of Theory R

There are three additional by-products that companies have experienced as the result of implementing Theory R in their organizations.

## By-Product #1: When Employees Are Valued, They Give Extra Effort

Employees start spending more time at work. Not because they are required to do so. Not because they expect to be paid for the work they are doing. But simply because they want to be there. They enjoy their jobs to the degree that they like putting in the extra effort to do the best job possible.

A manager told us that he had to start telling some of his employees to go home. In one instance, the manager said to an employee, "I want you to go home. I don't want you working here this long. It's nearly six o'clock. That isn't fair to your family!"

The employee responded, "My wife doesn't expect me till seven."

The manager replied with surprise, "Until seven?"

"Yeah," the employee explained. "I used to go from here to the bar and drink for a couple of hours after work in order to relax. It took me about that long to unwind from the stress of the workday. Now I don't feel the need to unwind. I can get home by 6:30 and be more relaxed than I ever was in getting home at 7:00. Furthermore, I'm sober, and since I've started feeling so positive about my work, I'm in a lot better mood. At least that's what my wife tells me. She thinks she's got a great deal in my coming home at 6:30! It would never dawn on her to expect me any earlier."

Even though employees may not put in voluntary overtime or even be allowed to work overtime, there's a significantly higher probability under Theory R conditions that employees will put in a full day's work. Unhappy, frustrated, disgruntled employees rarely give maximum effort to the job. Happy, valued, respected employees tend to give 150 percent to the task. They'll get a lot more done even if they don't add extra hours.

Does extra effort affect productivity? You bet!

Various companies have reported these by-products after a Value of the Person—Theory R Seminar:

*By-Product #2: When Workers Are Valued, Waste Diminishes*

- Theft of goods and raw materials (from pencils to compressors) stopped.
- Graft in the filing of insurance claims and unnecessary medical tests and reports was reported.
- The number of large payments for workers' compensation dropped.
- Unemployment payments dropped (because fewer employees were terminated).
- Less redone work—which means less waste of materials (formerly required in the remanufacturing of faulty goods)—was needed.

Employees who value themselves because they are valued, and who in turn value the company, are not prone to theft or to any activity that will diminish the company's resources or profitability. Rather, they will do their utmost to build up the company.

Employees who are treated fairly are going to treat the company fairly and are not going to try to milk the company through false claims, lawsuits, or allegations.

In one company, after a Value of the Person—Theory R Seminar, employees became so concerned about theft in their midst that they found a way to put a stop to it. Their actions saved the company tens of thousands of dollars, and no doubt helped secure the viability of their plant and the security of their jobs.

Does a drop in waste affect the bottom line? Absolutely!

*By-Product #3: When Workers Are Valued, Racial Barriers Begin to Disappear*

Many workers in one particular plant where we conducted a two-day seminar were non-English-speaking Mexicans. They were very productive workers, but communication with them was difficult, both in the plant and at the seminar.

Mack, the senior employee in the plant, was a person with a hard-luck life. As the result of many personal tragedies, he had become a worker who wanted to come to work, put in his time, and be left alone. He didn't create problems for other people, and he didn't want or need for anybody else to create any more problems for him.

Mack felt that the Mexicans who worked with him were just what he didn't need—problem creators. Many of them used their inability to speak English as something of a crutch, and that made Mack's job more difficult. Through the years, he had developed a very strong dislike for the Mexican laborers.

Since 80 percent of the factory force was Mexican, Mack's problem was a big one. Furthermore, Mack wanted nothing to do with a seminar to which the Mexican workers were also invited. Spending two days cooped up with his enemy was more than he could take.

Mack was one of the first workers who met our seminar team as we toured the plant the day before the seminar. Lefty asked Mack if he was coming to the seminar—which the company was offering on an optional-attendance basis to the employees—and Mack vehemently replied that he wasn't coming.

Mack was a big guy—maybe six three and brawny—but that didn't deter Lefty. Lefty looked up at him and said, "You don't have any guts at all, Mack, if you won't even come to the seminar to find out what it's all about." Mack could easily have picked Lefty up and tossed him aside like a rag doll, but he didn't. Instead, he took Lefty up on his challenge.

At the end of the first day of the seminar, Lefty went over to Mack and said, "Are you going to come back tomorrow, Mack?" Mack had tears in his eyes as he replied, "Yes, I'll be here, Lefty."

The next day Mack was waiting for Lefty as he got off the elevator. He gave him a great big hug and leaned down and gave him a kiss on the top of his head. He said to Lefty after the seminar, "I believe in this. But what can I do?"

Lefty said, "Tomorrow, go into your plant and walk up to the worker that you hate the most, shake his hand, and have a cup of coffee with him." Mack just shook his head. He wasn't sure if he could do it.

| Theory R Management | Established Management |
|---|---|
| **P**eople first | **P**rofit |
| **R**espect for one another | **R**eturn on investment |
| **O**pportunity for everyone | **O**pposition |
| **D**ignity for all | **D**emands |
| **U**nity in all endeavors | **U**ncertainty |
| **C**ommunication at all levels | **C**apital |
| **T**eamwork everywhere | **T**actics |
| **I**ndividuality for the employee | **I**ntolerance |
| **V**alue of the person | **V**olume |
| **I**nterest in fellow employees | **I**mpasses |
| **T**rust in one another | **T**hreats |
| **Y**es to the right thing | **Y**ielding to power and control |

FIGURE 16.3. Summary comparison of Theory R management and established management

The next morning, however, Mack got to work early and stood by the time clock. He shook hands with every employee as he punched in for the morning. He sent a clear signal to the Mexican employees in that plant, "Let's let bygones be bygones." He dropped his baggage.

Mack is now a Value of the Person Point Person in the plant. It's his job within the company's Value of the Person procedures to tell top-level managers how his Mexican coworkers are feeling and what their needs are.

As part of the Point Team process (which will be explained in chapter 17), that company implemented a plan so the Mexican workers could learn to speak English. The English-speaking workers are learning a little Spanish, too.

Does an easing of racial tensions and improved communication result in a rise of productivity and quality? Of course!

**The Cost of Valuing Workers**

We've tried to buy productivity in this country.

We've tried to legislate it.

We've tried to negotiate it.

We've tried to arbitrate it.

And all four methods have failed miserably. The fact is, employees know when they are being used and when attempts are being made to reward them into working harder.

We have the greatest gimmicks going in our nation. All kinds of benefits are on the books. And what kind of increase do we see in the growth of the American economy? One percent? Two percent? That's pathetic.

Love, dignity, and respect are the most cost-efficient ingredients that can be added to the work environment. They produce vast rewards.

# THEORY R AT WORK

We challenge you:

Sincerely, genuinely, and wholeheartedly implement Theory R in your workplace.

Keep records.

At the end of twelve months, compare results related to productivity, labor grievances, absenteeism, quality, and profitability.

All other business factors in your organization remaining the same, we believe you'll be pleasantly surprised at the results.

Again, the motivation for implementing Theory R is not because achieving these results is most vital but because enacting Value of the Person behavior is the right thing to do. The by-products, nevertheless, flow in a positive way from an organization with healthy, reconciled relationships.

# Developing an 17
# Action Plan to
# Implement
# Theory R

**P**erhaps the greatest mistake a manager can make is to regard Theory R as a technique for improving bottom-line results. Theory R is a mind-set, a perspective, a way of thinking and living and acting. It is not a technique.

A technique is a gimmick. It's something you do in order to get other things done.

Managers who attempt to employ Value of the Person behaviors only as a technique, without the behaviors being truly heartfelt and genuine, are setting themselves up for a fall. When employees eventually discover that their managers are attempting to manipulate them, the managers will have all of their old faults heaped back upon their heads and added to them will be the despicable fault of hypocrisy.

If there was a lack of trust before, the managers will face a gulf of mistrust that is nearly impossible to bridge. If communication was poor before, it will be worse. If frustrations were kept just under a boiling point before, they are likely to erupt in anger and sometimes even violence. Managers who try to use Theory R to further bottom-line results, and have that as the sole motivation, will be sorely disappointed.

The implementation of Theory R into the workplace, therefore, is not the introduction of a new technique. It is the establishment of a new perspective about the value of people and relationships and the importance of reconciliation.

Theory R is not a new way of doing tasks.

Theory R is a new way of thinking and acting.

## Gaining the Competitive Edge

What kind of edge can a company realistically gain over its close competitors, those with like technology, similar access to investment capital, innovative research and development departments, and similar product features?

The one arena that holds the most potential is the human arena. The heart of the people is the greatest untapped resource available to most companies and organizations today.

Motivate the people, build up the people, affirm, appreciate, and recognize the people, truly value the people, and the people can and will give a company more return on its dollar, get more out of the available equipment, and maximize the use of existing facilities and supplies.

The company that realizes that how it treats people is directly related to how fast it grows will gain the edge needed for the next century.

Executives everywhere are looking to research and development departments, new machines and technologies, and new products to propel them forward. Executives with the same commitment to building relationships among employees—with the same fervency and capital investment—will lead the company to pull ahead of its competitors.

## Building an Action Plan

Theory R management challenges a leader to develop specific steps for implementing Value of the Person behaviors. A Theory R leader has essentially three goals:

1. Propel Value of the Person principles to the forefront of everybody's thinking. Raise the level of consciousness about the need to value others.
2. Review existing corporate documents in light of Value of the Person concepts.

3. Provide Value of the Person training where and when it's needed.

In the following pages, we'll explore each goal.

## Goal #1: Put Value of the Person at the Forefront

The foremost challenge a leader faces is in moving Value of the Person concepts to the forefront of employees' thinking.

*The goal of Theory R is that Value of the Person concepts become fixed within an organization. They must become the organization's mind-set.*

Theory R, and its Value of the Person emphasis, is not something that works on a short-term, quick-fix basis. Doing what is right must become a pervasive, ongoing way of thinking and relating within an organization. It is not something that a company should think about doing on a six-month trial basis. That isn't the right thing to do. If something is right, it is right all of the time and every time.

The same goes for an emphasis on relationships and reconciliation. Relationships can't be highly valued one month and then be put on the chopping block the next. Reconciliation can't be the tenor of one season and then be thrown away.

Furthermore, these Value of the Person concepts must become widespread within an organization. It isn't enough for one person to do the right thing or for one person to have relationships and reconciliation at the forefront of thinking. To be sure, each person can have an impact, and if only one person adopts this path, there will be some by-product (and perhaps even a great one in that individual's personal life and family).

For an organization to grow and to flourish, however, Theory R must have widespread acceptance. How does one achieve this acceptance?

### Awareness

People must be made aware of the need for doing the right thing, and they must be made aware that valuing the person is going to be given high priority.

A Value of the Person—Theory R Seminar is one of the best ways of presenting the concepts to your organization.

Take for example, Paul Vucish, lead engineer, Owens-Corning, Aiken, South Carolina, who as one man captured a vision for what

Value of the Person—Theory R could do to accelerate the growth pattern of Owens-Corning. His newfound "awareness" allowed him to present the principles to Dr. Sharell Mikesell, senior vice president, science and technology. Since that time, Owens-Corning has made great strides in adopting Value of the Person—Theory R as a way of doing business. And so a good company becomes better.

**Ongoing Reminders**

We can't be reminded too often to do or say the right things. We can't be reminded too often that relationships are valuable or that reconciliation is worth pursuing.

Visible reminders are important. Just consider what takes place when you are driving and the person in the next lane cuts in front of you, nearly causing an accident. Your inclination is to lash out—until you see the clerical collar the other driver is wearing. It's a visible reminder to control your temper and do the right thing.

So it can be in your organization. The concepts can be kept alive through the use of pins, stickers, bumper stickers, and posters. We invite you to use your imagination to raise the consciousness of the VOP in your organization.

**Leadership by Example**

Those at the top of the organization must exert leadership. Those with the greatest amount of authority within the organization must make doing the right thing a priority for themselves and for all persons for whom they are responsible.

In a very pragmatic way, the concern for human relations factors must find its way onto a manager's agenda and schedule. Following are some ways to do that. Bear in mind as you read through these suggestions that this is not a comprehensive list. It is only a starting point to help you begin to develop means that are geared toward your specific circumstances and people.

*VOP agenda items*. One of the best ways we know to keep love, dignity, and respect in the forefront of a company's mind-set is to put VOP—Value of the Person—on the agenda of every regularly scheduled meeting.

The plant manager of one 3M plant has required that Value of the Person be a part of the agenda of every crew meeting. At a quarterly meeting with the crew leaders, he specifically addresses Value of the Person concerns.

Ask people with whom you meet, "Are any of your employees experiencing any problems we need to address? Have any of your employees experienced a success? Has anyone in your area offered an idea or suggestion for us to consider?"

Here is an outline we recommend for the Value of the Person segment of a staff meeting:

**Value of the Person Action Log**

1. **Input**—Ask what concerns the people are registering, what needs they have, and what questions they are asking.

2. **Update**—Find out what's happening in the lives of the people and report positive VOP actions being demonstrated among them.

3. **Walk the Talk**—Discuss symbolic actions that need to be taken by management and those that are appropriate for employees to display.

4. **Communication**—Share ideas about how to improve communication related to VOP concepts and how to raise the consciousness of the people about VOP.

**VOP scheduling.** The manager who truly desires to extend love, dignity, and respect to workers will schedule time with the employees. Ask your secretary to help you remember to block out a half hour or hour every week just to mingle with the employees. Circulate among the employees without a business agenda in the back of your mind. One manager I know blocks off this time as MBWA (management by wandering around). Another manager said he calls this time floor cruising.

Make yourself visible to your workers. Let them see you coming and going from their workplace. Let them see you greeting other workers in a friendly, genuine manner. Let them see you stopping to chat for a few minutes with their immediate line supervisor. Even if you don't take time to talk to every employee you encounter, you can greet each one with a smile and hello. You can show your employees that you are accessible and, above all, that you are a human being. You will be sending a strong symbolic signal!

Occasionally order in pizza for an area or department, and share it with the employees there.

Bring in a dozen donuts to an area.

One plant manager orders in Popsicles for employees on every day the temperature tops 100 degrees. He helps distribute the Popsicles on occasion and usually stops to share one with a group of line workers. The break takes only a matter of minutes, and at the bulk rate he pays to a local vendor, the cost is about eight cents a person. But what a message of value is being sent!

*VOP people report.* Establish mechanisms for learning more about your employees, especially their successes and personal problems.

I personally found an easy way to gain information about crises in the lives of the employees at Pittron. When a worker's spouse or child was hospitalized or there was a death in a family, medical insurance forms and death benefit files were processed by our personnel department. I set up a routine procedure whereby I was notified of such family crises as part of the personnel department loop. Other companies have used this technique to good advantage.

Joyful events—such as births, weddings, graduations, a spouse's promotion or award, a winning game—should also be communicated to you.

One executive I know asked her personnel manager to read and clip the local newspapers for her on a regular basis (as part of a revised job description, I might add), so that she could be advised about any employee or member of an employee's family whose name appeared in the newspapers. When the clipping was of good news, it was posted on a department bulletin board or passed along to the employee with a hand-scribbled congratulatory note, often written on the clipping itself. If the clipping was of bad news, the executive made a point of extending condolences, offering assistance or, at minimum, noting the tragedy so that help might be offered if and when it was requested or needed.

Her passing along of newspaper clippings sent a message through the ranks of the company that traveled at lightning speed: "The boss cares."

We also recommend that managers develop their own "People Report" card system to record information such as the following: spouse's and children's names, birthday, company milestones (major accomplishments), hobbies, activities, and family involvement in the community. Bear in mind that this summary should be kept confidential and that no information should be recorded that might be perceived by the employee as negative. A People Report is intended solely to remind the manager about the total scope of the employee's life.

Sort the information not only alphabetically by employees' names but also according to dates so that you'll have a ready reference for birthday and company anniversary dates as they come around each year.

As you circulate through your operation or office, carry a pocket-size tablet with you, and make notes about things your employees tell you, ask you, or suggest to you. Then follow through on your notes. Be sure to let an employee know how you've followed through on the suggestions or how you intend to deal with problems brought to your attention. Be prompt in answering an employee's questions.

As you circulate among your employees, ask how a person is progressing, recuperating, or adjusting. Search out those who are grieving or celebrating. Reach out and grab a hand or clasp a shoulder and say, "I'm sorry to hear about . . . ," or "I was sure glad to hear that . . ." You don't need to say a great deal or spend a lot of time asking for details. Your expression of concern can be a simple one: "I want you to know that I'm sorry," or "I want you to know that I'm rejoicing with you."

***VOP on the road.*** Many managers are on the road a great deal. If that is your lot in life, make it a point as you call into your office to ask about your employees. Designate someone on your staff to be your Theory R eyes and ears while you are away and to update you on the people aspects of your operation as you call in to get messages or to give instructions. If you receive word of a major crisis in an employee's life, jot a note to that person, or pick up the phone and call to give encouragement.

***VOP Point Teams.*** We recommend that a company form a Point Team. This team of people represents a cross section of the company—individuals who want to be actively involved in spearheading the accountability of the organization to Theory R.

The Point Teams at Crown International—a leading nonunionized manufacturer of amplifiers and sound equipment with more than six hundred employees—are highly structured.

Each department has a Point Person and an alternate. Every other month, the department meets with a designated Facilitator to share examples of love, dignity, and respect, and to share their concerns. The Facilitator helps the employees determine which of the corporate processes are available to solve their problems. Monthly, the Point People have a one-hour meeting with Clyde Moore, the president, to share with him the concerns for which no corporate process is available and to advise him of any processes which are not working.

In addition, a human resource staff member has been assigned specifically to see that Value of the Person concepts remain prominent and active. She trains the Point People and Facilitators and meets with departmental supervisors and managers on specific VOP issues.

At Crown International, Value of the Person behavior has permeated every area of the company. The by-products have been phenomenal. Not only is Crown International growing rapidly, but it has seen an annual increase in its market share.

*VOP newsletters.* Many companies that have implemented Value of the Person principles into their environments publish a quarterly or monthly newsletter that promotes and recognizes employee achievements and milestones (including some outside the workplace). It is a great way to uplift the people aspect of your organization.

*VOP company awards.* Consider implementing a plan to set up recognition for a Value of the Person Employee of the Month and, from those chosen, Value of the Person Employee of the Year. In one company, the Employee of the Year Award includes an out-of-state trip.

As part of a monthly recognition program, some companies have chosen to honor employees in special ways—use of a particular parking space, a photo and description posted on a bulletin board, a copy of a memo about the person posted on the workers' bulletin board in the cafeteria, and so forth.

Employees are recognized for their ability to find creative ways of expressing love, dignity, and appreciation to their fellow workers.

*VOP service awards.* Some companies recognize the community service rendered by employees to the greater community. They view this service as extending love, dignity, and respect to the corporate neighborhood and honor employees for their service in tangible and intangible ways.

*VOP employee recognition.* If you are seeking to add further means of recognizing workers, be creative! Invite workers to make suggestions about how to honor fellow workers.

You may want to recognize:

- an achievement related to work performance—high productivity, perfect quality.
- a promotion.
- a non-work-related achievement (or an achievement earned outside the work environment by a work group—such as the

league championship being won by the company softball or bowling team).
- a milestone in employment (number of years).
- excellent presenteeism.
- implementation of a suggestion the employee made.
- a particular act of love, dignity, or respect shown to another person or group.
- celebration of an employee's birthday.
- celebration of a wedding or birth of a baby.

One department at a university developed a secret pal program for one week near Valentine's Day. Each person in the department drew from a hat the name of a fellow employee, and each day of the secret pal week, the person attempted to do something nice or special for the pal. The gestures were small but, as a whole, very creative and delightful. As the week progressed, those involved became more secretive and a little more elaborate in their schemes. The head of the department noted that she could almost feel the morale of the department rise from day to day. Everybody likes to receive good surprises!

## Goal #2: Take New Look at Your Policies

Use the implementation stage of Theory R as an opportunity to review your existing company documents related to employees— personnel manuals, operations manuals, forms related to procedures and policies, and goal statements.

Adopt a people-sensitive mind-set as you read. Ask yourself, "How might this document be rewritten to reflect our greater awareness of the need for workers to be shown love, dignity, and respect?"

Be sensitive to Value of the Person concepts as you prepare new statements or work on the language of formal contracts. Keep Value of the Person concepts in mind as you write memos to or about employees.

Have you ever encountered these words in a job description: *minimum operator responsibilities*? If you put your emphasis on the minimum that you require from an operator, that's probably what you're going to get—minimum effort. In what ways might job descriptions be rewritten to challenge workers to strive for their full potential in a position?

Check the evaluation forms you use. Is Value of the Person behavior one way of measuring a person's performance? Are all managers being held accountable for demonstrating Value of the Person behavior?

---

**Goal #3: Provide VOP Training for All Employees**

Value of the Person concepts complement, blend with, and help to sustain training programs.

In many instances, Value of the Person principles also need to be a training program. Managers especially need to be exposed in a very pragmatic, systematic way to the concepts of love, dignity, and respect, and they need to be taught how to implement behaviors that affirm workers, show appreciation, and recognize employees' contributions.

**THEORY R SAYS,**

*Make sure that all employees are introduced to Value of the Person concepts.*

*Find ongoing and innovative ways of reminding all employees daily about the importance of valuing behaviors—of showing love, dignity, and respect to one another.*

*Find innovative ways of keeping Value of the Person behaviors at the forefront of everybody's thinking!*

One company that we consulted with in the Midwest set a policy that no one could be promoted to a supervisory role until the individual had attended a Value of the Person—Theory R Seminar. That was a signal sent to the workforce about the degree to which managers valued good interpersonal relationships within the plant.

Dean Skaer, plant manager of the 3M Little Rock operation (a part of 3M's industrial mineral products division), has this policy: "When we hire new salaried people, we send them to a Value of the Person—Theory R Seminar, and our new hourly hires are introduced to the program through their monthly crew meetings and my quarterly state-of-business meetings.

"When we sponsored the seminar here in Little Rock, we made it mandatory. Some were extremely skeptical, and a few initially refused to go.

"We approached the seminar as training, however, similar to other types of training we provide for our workers. Some training relates to task skills. Value of the Person training simply relates to interpersonal skills.

"When the seminar was over, we heard virtually no negative comments. A few, by their actions, let us know that they haven't bought into the concepts wholeheartedly, but over the past three years, the vast majority have been very enthusiastic in finding ways of expressing love, dignity, and respect.

"The plant was over forty years old when we had the seminar, and a few people were carrying heavy baggage. The seminar opened everything up and gave us some fresh air and a new start."

All of the programmatic ways of lifting up Value of the Person concepts discussed thus far in this chapter are aimed at one thing—raising the consciousness level of every person to the importance of love, dignity, and respect in the workplace.

## Making a Decision to Adopt or Reject

Before Theory R can be implemented, of course, the individual employee or manager must choose to adopt Theory R or reject it. The individual must decide to value others and work toward building relationships and reconciling differences with others, or the individual must choose to remain confrontational. There's really no middle ground. A person cannot be a part-time valuer of others.

Neither can a person successfully limit Theory R to one area of life. The goal is for Value of the Person behavior to be lived out every day. Otherwise, it will feel artificial and superficial.

We personally find it impossible to value our colleagues or persons we meet at seminars or in corporations and then *not* value people who clean our hotel rooms or arrange the chairs and set up the tables for our seminar sessions. To value a person is to value a person—without regard to any exterior definitions of that person's status in life.

If you choose to adopt Theory R, find ways to integrate its principles into your entire life and to personalize it so that it is natural and becomes a part of you.

## A Personal Action Plan

If you decide to adopt Theory R and to make it a part of your entire life—both at home and at work—develop an action plan for yourself.

*Such a plan is likely to have these seven components:*

*1. Commitment.* Make a firm commitment that Theory R and Value of the Person principles are going to be a part of all your interactions, habits, and policies. Make a commitment to put these principles of love, dignity, and respect into action.

*2. Investment.* Invest time and resources into keeping Theory R at the forefront of your planning and thinking. Ask yourself frequently,

- "What more needs to be done to perpetuate these principles of love, dignity, and respect?"

- "What more can I do to be a Theory R manager or employee?"
- "What more can I give of myself?"
- "What additional resources can be directed toward the workers?"
- "What additional effort can be given to help the company reach its goals?"

*3. **Attitude reappraisal**.* Challenge yourself and others to turn around the attitude of your workplace:

- What more can you do to remind yourself, or remind one another, that valuing others is the right thing to do?
- What more can you do to remind yourself as a manager to convey love, dignity, and respect to employees and peers?

Adopting a new approach is a lot like changing a habit. It will happen over time through repetition. The more you speak words of affirmation to others, the easier they will become. The more you voice appreciation or recognition, the quicker you will remember to say and do things that uplift others and applaud their contributions.

Be willing to throw away the old ways that aren't working. Be brave enough to learn new ways of communicating and to become more accessible and vulnerable.

*4. **Goals**.* Set realistic goals for yourself and others that include short-term objectives and long-term objectives that are people-oriented:

- What can you change in the short term that will benefit others?
- What more can you do immediately to show your appreciation of your employees or to give evidence of your respect?
- What are long-term goals you'd like to reach in building relationships?
- Which people would you like to get to know better?
- What about your communication would you like to improve?
- What would you like to see changed for the benefit of other people in your organization?

Many corporate leaders have a vision for their company. That vision is usually expressed in economic terms—the percentage of growth they anticipate in a year, the financial success of a new product line, the benefit to the company's bottom line if a new factory is built or new equipment is purchased.

As Reid Carpenter says, "Corporate leaders need to have a vision for the people they employ. They need to ask themselves, 'What do I want to see for my people in the next year or the next five years? What changes do I want to see in my employees' lives?' "

5. **Plans.** Plans are goals set into distinct steps and timetables. Turn your goals into plans. Consult others about the best ways of implementing your plans. Find win-win ways to reach goals. (Our earlier suggestions about Point Teams and Value of the Person recognition programs may be helpful.)

6. **Associations.** Stick with Theory R people who are committed to valuing other people. Find role models of affirming, appreciating, and recognizing behaviors within your workplace, and hold them up as examples to others. Whenever possible, hire people who will conform to Value of the Person principles.

7. **Perseverance.** Recognize that results don't happen overnight. Don't be discouraged if you personally fail on occasion to do and be a Theory R leader. Theory R leadership is a process that will challenge you for the rest of your life. Don't be discouraged if changes in your organization fail to occur instantly. Healing long-standing wounds takes time and patience. Restoring broken trust requires steadiness and faithfulness over time.

Clair Murphy, site director of 3M Cottage Grove Center in Cottage Grove, Minnesota, and a true Theory R leader, tells this story: "Years ago, in one of our buildings at 3M Cottage Grove, I had a supervisor who seemed to be in constant conflict with his subordinates. Trouble always seemed to be brewing. I said to him, 'John, why don't you just *try* coming in tomorrow and saying good morning to your workers?' Without hesitating a second, he said, 'I tried that once, and it didn't work.' "

The implementation of Theory R principles requires a certain degree of patience and even more persistence. The atmosphere in your workplace wasn't created in a day, and it won't change in a day. It can begin to change, however, in just a few seconds. You can experience a turnaround point.

**Solely Because It's the Right Thing to Do**

Theory R must be regarded not as a technique to improve results but as a new way of thinking and acting in a company. It must be implemented solely because it's the right thing to do.

It's also vital for us all to remember that none of the pragmatic methods suggested in this chapter are substitutes for daily personal interactions that affirm, appreciate, and recognize individual employees. Theory R always begins at the level of the one-to-one encounter.

We must call ourselves repeatedly back to the reason for showing love, upholding dignity, and extending respect: "Because it is right." Period.

If you make the decision that Theory R is the right thing to do, you'll find ways to implement it and sustain it. It will become that valuable to you!

# THEORY R AT WORK

Have you made a decision to adopt or reject Theory R? Why? List some of your reasons.

Now take a good look at the reasons you may have cited for implementing Theory R. Is "because it's the right thing to do" at the top of your list? Is it your only reason?

How might you implement Theory R in your workplace?

# The Relationship Between Theory R and Unions

## 18

**I**n the course of doing our Value of the Person—Theory R Seminars, we speak to groups in which both union and nonunion employees are present. The question inevitably arises: "Where do you stand? Do you come down on the side of the union, or do you come down on the side of management?"

Theory R is neither pro union nor pro management. It is pro *people*—and more specifically, pro *person*.

## Our Positions

Here are several of our positions regarding the relationship between Theory R and unions.

## First, Unions Aren't the Problem

Corporate America often blames all of our national economic woes on unions. In the American workforce, we presently have about 110 million people who are employed (out of a possible 120-million-person labor pool). Only about 16 million of these people are unionized. Union workers are very much in the minority. Unions can hardly be blamed for all the problems in our economy.

Our response to this accusation by corporate America is this: "Bad treatment of people is the real problem we face. We've seen abuses on both sides."

**Second, Unions Need Theory R, Too**

We've encountered union leaders who seemed to value their members very little. They showed very little concern for them, conveyed very little respect to them, and did precious little to uphold their dignity as workers. They had taken the traditional style of management right into the hall of their union.

Isn't it ironic that many times office employees and staff representatives working in the international union offices organize a union for themselves to represent them to—and in some cases protect them from—their international officers?

**Third, Theory R Is Not Intended to Keep Unions Out or to Bring Unions In**

Union leaders and management representatives deal primarily with the economic issues of the pocketbook—for example, wages, benefits, and paid vacation time. Theory R deals with the noneconomic issues of the heart.

Theory R calls for love, dignity, and respect to permeate not only the workplace but also the union meeting place. It calls for workers to value their union leaders and for union leaders to value their members.

**Fourth, Theory R Does Not Take Away the Right to Strike**

It does, however, lessen or eliminate the *need* to strike. Theory R sets the basis for building relationships based on trust. Thus, when the time comes for negotiations, a framework has been established so that negotiations can be conducted in a smoother, less confrontational manner. Theory R calls for an atmosphere of reconciliation that results in a win-win situation for all involved.

Union leaders sometimes initially perceive Theory R to be a management theory rather than a leadership theory or a way of life. For this reason, they are often quite skeptical of it. One skeptic was Paul Lindgren, who has been a union official for sixteen years. (Paul is presently vice president of the international union for OCAW—Oil, Chemical, and Atomic Workers.)

---

**3M Company**

Here's Paul's experience with Theory R in his own words: "Clair Murphy, the site director at the 3M Cottage Grove plant, called me one day and told me that he had a management consultant coming in for a two-day seminar. He asked me if I wanted to sit in on the seminar, and I said, 'If you think I'm going to listen to some goofy management consultant for two days, you're crazy.' Then he told me that my entire union committee was going to be there, so I decided to go. I went with an intent of blowing him out of the water in the first hour.

"The first thing I realized was that Wayne Alderson wasn't a management consultant, and next, that his program wasn't an employee-involvement program, which I personally don't agree with. Every employee-involvement program I've ever seen has actually been used to manipulate people. (OCAW has a strong tradition of opposing virtually all employee-involvement programs.)

"To my own surprise, I stayed for the entire two days of the seminar, and the longer I stayed, the more I liked what I heard— that we have to get back to putting the primary emphasis in any organization on valuing people.

"As a union leader, I like the fact that Theory R doesn't prescribe specific things to do or not to do. It doesn't prescribe simple shortcut ways but says instead, 'There are many things you *can* do that are right for people if you approach them with a desire to show love, dignity, and respect.'

"One of the foremost ways in which Theory R can work is at the negotiating table. I sat in on one negotiation not too long ago, and I listened to both sides summarize the arguments that had kept them apart for two years. I then said to them, 'I've listened to you for the last half hour, and neither one of you has even mentioned the word *workers*. You in management haven't used the word *employees* once, and you in the union haven't used the word *members* once. Why don't you both start over from the perspective of considering the people?' When they got beyond their personal fight, they began to come together and eventually worked out a good agreement."

## The Gillette Company

A person who has sat on the opposite side of the negotiating table from Paul Lindgren is Bob Wood, human relations director for The Gillette Company in St. Paul, Minnesota. Here is Bob's story: "In 1980, we at The Gillette Company experienced a strike that created an awareness on the part of management that we didn't have the cohesive 'family orientation' we once had in our plant. The company here in St. Paul began as the Toni Company in the 1940s, a small family-owned company that made home permanents. The atmosphere in that company was warm and familial. In 1948, The Gillette

Company bought out Toni, but the Toni division remained under Toni management until the late 1960s.

"In the early 1970s, The Gillette Company decided to centralize its operations. The Chicago office was closed, and many people were transferred to The Gillette Company headquarters in Boston. Old familiar faces at Toni began to retire. Automation affected the workforce. A gap began to widen between workers and management. The strike told all of us in management that things were worse than we had thought.

"We immediately began to try to put into place programs that would renew within the people a sense of participation in their company. A program called 'GO [Gillette Operational] teams' was implemented. We made some advances and enjoyed some success, but our progress was limited. Although people saw themselves as part of a team, individuals themselves were not being recognized and valued as *individuals*. We simply weren't dealing with the most basic issue: the way workers felt they were being treated as human beings.

"One day I found myself in a grievance meeting that resulted from disciplinary action that the company had taken against several workers who had a great deal of seniority. These workers had made some very costly errors, and although the errors were not willful or maliciously intended, the company was faced with a major outlay of money to rectify things. The company enacted some disciplinary measures against the workers, and hence, the grievance was filed by the workers with their union. Present at the meeting was Paul Lindgren.

"A fairly heavy argument ensued. The workers felt they were being put into an unwarranted stressful situation and were being unfairly punished for mistakes that were unintentional. The company position was that disciplinary action needed to be taken to send a message to other workers to be more careful.

"In the heat of the battle, Paul said to me, 'The problem is that you folks don't value your people.' I argued that we did, and that we also valued their jobs and our own. Paul persisted, 'You need to hear what I'm saying. You're dealing here with people who also care about their jobs, but you're not seeing them as people. You're so concerned about your disciplinary action that you've lost sight of what might have been behind the mistakes that have been made. Why did these senior workers make the mistakes they made? Maybe there's something wrong that hasn't been explored. Maybe there's something in their families or in their personal lives that caused them to lose concentration and make these mistakes. Did you ever think to ask about that? Now you're adding the stress of a threatened job loss to whatever stresses they were already feeling. You're not putting the emphasis on the people. You're only seeing their mistakes.'

"Paul went on to tell me about Wayne Alderson, and he gave me a copy of *Stronger than Steel.*\* I read the book and it really spoke to me. I saw how a man put his personal faith into action. Granted, the principles of love, dignity, and respect are not exclusive to Christianity. They are principles that are evident in just about any religion. Even atheists can buy into love, dignity, and respect among people. But for me—as a Christian—these principles were ones that were vitally linked to my faith and to what I professed to believe, at least on Sundays. I was faced with the challenge of asking myself for the first time in a serious way, 'Is what I believe truly applicable to my *job?* Can I find a way of *doing at work* what I profess to believe is important?' It was a soul-searching time for me.

"Subsequently, I sent one of my associates to a Value of the Person—Theory R Seminar to check it out. He returned and said, 'I didn't learn anything I didn't know, but these guys reminded me of everything I should be doing. Everything about them is totally believable, and they really apply what they say to the workplace. I recommend we invite them here.'

"I went to my operating committee (which included the plant manager) and called to their attention some things *they* already knew. In spite of our GO teams effort, we still had too much divisiveness in the plant, we were still spending too much money on resolving grievances, and we were still a long way away from having the atmosphere in the plant that we desired.

"I received company permission to attend a Value of the Person—Theory R Seminar, and two of the men on the operating committee joined me. One of the men had recently experienced the death of his wife and was struggling emotionally. He especially was moved by what he heard and felt. The three of us came back convinced that Theory R needed to be implemented fully at our plant, and we

---

\**Stronger than Steel* by R. C. Sproul, published in 1980 by Harper & Row, is the book that first told the Wayne Alderson story. (It is now available through Value of the Person—Theory R Seminars, 100 Ross Street, Pittsburgh, PA 15219.)

prompted our plant manager to send more members of our operating committee to the seminar, including two of our union leaders.

"The union leaders, of course, were highly suspicious. From their perspective, this seemed like just one more management ploy to manipulate workers into doing what management wanted. They came home encouraged and supportive.

"And so we began a concerted effort to expose as many people as possible in our St. Paul plant to the principles of Theory R. At present, about 300 of our 550 employees have gone through Value of the Person training.

"Last October we entered contract negotiations with both of our unions. Both were negotiations for three-year contracts. We had some significant issues to negotiate, items we had not been successful at achieving in the past. The issues had resulted in shouting matches, and rather than face a strike, we ended up pushing the issues off the table.

"Prior to the negotiations, nearly all of the people around the negotiating table had gone to a Value of the Person—Theory R Seminar. We had come to a rather informal understanding among ourselves that if we could employ the Value of the Person concepts in our negotiations—extending to one another love, dignity, and respect and attempting, above all, to do what was right for all of us as human beings—we could come out of the negotiations with an agreement that would be satisfactory to both sides. We made a commitment to try to bring about reconciliation rather than confrontation.

"Both bargaining sessions were tough. Both sides—labor and management—won some tough issues in both negotiations. And both labor and management came away with very good contracts that they were pleased with.

"Men walked out of the sessions at the end of the day saying, 'Man, these principles work.'

"People around the table were showing more respect and care for one another than I had ever witnessed in a negotiation meeting. There were differences, and they were strongly stated at times, but the overall atmosphere was one that was more supportive and positive than any negotiation meetings I had ever experienced.

"We've seen a significant drop in the number of OCAW grievances on file. The grievances that are filed are being resolved more quickly and with far less rancor.

"I've witnessed a number of reconciliations between workers. In some cases, workers who haven't even spoken to one another for twelve or fifteen years—even though, in a few cases, these workers were standing right next to each other on a line—walk up to one another and apologize to one another and make a commitment to work together. Supervisors have been making amends with their workers. It's been amazing.

"One supervisor openly admitted, 'I've been doing a lot of things wrong. I'm going to need some help in making some changes.' A man got up from the other side of the room, walked around the table, shook his hand, and said, 'I'll help you.' I had no idea at the time that the two men had been archenemies for years.

"Naturally, one of the most obvious changes to me is the change in my own life and my own approach to my work. I'm finding it much easier to ask my colleagues and employees how they're doing—and to mean it in the sense of all of their lives. I know that in asking that question genuinely, I'm opening myself up to getting a genuine answer. But I'm much more comfortable with the fact that I might get tears in response. I might hear things that will cause me to have to deal with some things I might otherwise never have had to be concerned about. I might have to expend time or energy that I hadn't planned to spend.

"Not only do I think it's OK to reach out to people, but I feel compelled to do so. It's no longer enough for me to go into the office, sign a lot of paperwork, and go home and think I've done my job. I feel a need to get involved with the people behind the paperwork. I'm a lot more aware of how divorce or chemical dependency or financial crises can affect the worker *at work*. I see people suffering who I never dreamed were suffering, not because the suffering is new but because my eyes are opened to them. I realize that there's always a reason behind a person becoming a hard case from a personnel standpoint. There's a cause for absenteeism, repeated mistakes, disruptive behaviors. I'm much more concerned with getting to the root causes than in exacting discipline.

"That doesn't mean that things have become lax or that company policies aren't being enacted. Quite the contrary. It also doesn't mean that all interpersonal problems have evaporated. Some friction still exists. It *does* mean, however, that we're all becoming much more aware of the human factors that have an impact on job performance. It does mean we're making progress, and at last, we're seeing some changes that we all know are good ones.

"I should also point out, too, that none of us consider Theory R to be some kind of vaccine against hard times in a company. We're presently facing some serious staff reduction mandates from corporate headquarters. A significant number of our people are going to lose their jobs in the next few months. Theory R can't change that fact. But the Value of the Person principles *will* make a difference in how the staff reductions take place and in how we pull together as a team in their wake.

"Perhaps best of all, we're seeing that those who make a commitment to valuing others tend to stick with their commitment. They're still displaying Theory R behaviors months after their first exposure to the Value of the Person concepts."

**Waltco Truck Equipment Company**

The union-related experiences shared by Bob Wood are not an isolated example. Here's what Rod Robinson, president of Waltco Truck Equipment Company, told us: "I first heard about Theory R at a four-hour seminar presentation in 1986. I personally decided that this was something I wanted to implement into our company. We had just been acquired by an international corporation, and I had just been promoted from a position in sales to be president of a manufacturing company. Most of our laborers were members of the Teamsters, and our relationship with the union had been quite adversarial for more than a decade. The management had a reputation of being arrogant, abrasive, and abusive. We deserved what we got from the union. During most of the 1970s and 1980s, we did not have a contract that didn't result in a strike.

"I decided that forming new relationships had to be the top priority of my new job if I was going to be able to produce satisfactory results for our new owners.

"We have three manufacturing plants where we have implemented Value of the Person concepts—two in Ohio and one in California. Every employee has been given the opportunity to attend a Value of the Person—Theory R Seminar, along with his or her spouse, on company time.

"The biggest change we've seen is how workers are relating to one another. We had numerous incidents throughout our operation where workers were holding grudges against one another. In some cases, workers hadn't spoken to one another for years. The seminar really broke down those barriers, resulting in people not only communicating with one another but helping one another. There's a much greater willingness to sit down and discuss disagreements and disappointments.

"The environment has changed to the extent that in our last contract renewal, we had a 98 percent ratification vote for the contract. The Teamsters have told me that, to the best of their knowledge, this is the highest percentage ratification vote they have ever had. I believe this is a strong indicator that the workers believe that we are being fair with them.

"Some people have said to me that we in management must have given the store away to get that kind of ratification vote, but we did not. In fact, quite the opposite. It's difficult to get 98 percent of any group to agree on *anything*, no matter how good it is, so I don't believe this vote is the result of the concessions made by the company as much as it is a vote that indicates a trust level between the workers and management.

"Probably the most rewarding by-product for me is a very personal one. The norm for most presidents is to spend much of their time dealing with problems. People call when they have a complaint. As a result, many presidents stay as far away from workers as possible in order to keep from hearing them tell of their problems. But when I want to get charged up now, I head for the shop floor. I feel tremendous affirmation from the workers out on the floor. I've also received a number of cards and letters from the wives of our factory workers, who have told me how their marriages and family life have improved since Theory R and Value of the Person concepts have been implemented in the plant. They're seeing positive results in the lives of their children. I am very grateful that a wife of an employee would feel comfortable sharing that kind of report with me."

We could fill an entire book with stories like these. When Theory R is genuinely implemented on a widespread basis, the relationship between unions and companies improves. Neither is diminished. Both are made stronger.

## Finding a Way to Work Together

As we have stated repeatedly, we never counsel companies or managers to give up their right to manage people. *Strong management is required if a company is to have order, direction, and strong morale.*

Furthermore, we don't believe that employees want weak managers. From our experiences in talking with literally thousands of employees across this nation in the past decade, we are more convinced than ever that employees want tough, skilled, straight-shooting, disciplined managers who are willing to make hard decisions and stand by them.

Neither do we say to unions to give up their right to defend their people. *Theory R doesn't take the place of a union contract.*

**THEORY R SAYS,**

*Unions and companies need to find a better way to work together for the benefit of everyone.*

Eighty percent of the time, unions and companies should get along. Their goals should be the same: to treat employees well and to build stronger companies. As Lefty Scumaci says, "Union leaders at contract negotiation time are seeking a piece of the pie. Between negotiations, they should be using Theory R to help workers build a stronger and healthier company so that when negotiating time comes, the pie is bigger!"

Probably about 20 percent of the time, companies and unions are going to be in conflict because they're trying to maximize the best interests of their clients—the stockholders and the union members, respectively. Still, even in that 20 percent of the time, union officials and company managers should be able to treat one another with love, dignity, and respect. They should openly acknowledge that they are coming from different perspectives but that their perspectives in no way reduce their value as human beings. Meetings don't need to end with hard feelings, even in the toughest negotiating sessions.

People can have philosophical differences without demeaning one another. You don't need to agree with everybody to respect everybody.

Theory R doesn't erase differences. It allows for persons with differing opinions to enjoy peaceful coexistence.

## THEORY R AT WORK

Is your company at odds with the union? What can you do to reach out to union officials and extend love, dignity, and respect to them?

Are you a manager in a plant that has some union workers and some nonunion workers? What might you do to establish harmony between the two groups?

# The Responsibility of the Individual Employee

## 19

**W**hat difference can one employee make?

What influence can a small group of people have when they're at the bottom of the organizational chart?

In one company with which we worked, a very small group of employees valued their supervisor and set in motion a chain of events that resulted in $1 million savings to their company and, very likely, gave them job stability for another year.

What did the employees do? They sent a card and a bouquet of balloons.

The supervisor's daughter was faced with a serious illness that required the family to travel out of state to a hospital that could provide specialty care for her.

The supervisor was one of the most unlovable supervisors we have ever encountered in two decades of consulting. He continually was on the backs of his employees, and he never had a kind word to say. His attitude was arrogant and condescending.

His employees, however, decided that the implementation of Value of the Person concepts had to start someplace, and it might as well be with them. They arranged to have a huge card made, which they all signed with words of encouragement, and they sent it to the hospital where the young girl was being treated. Along with the card they sent a big bouquet of balloons.

That gesture opened the man's eyes and completely turned around his approach to supervising. He came home with a brand-new attitude. He told his employees how much their kindness had meant to him. His entire department came alive, and a new spirit of cooperation bonded the employees together.

Morale skyrocketed. A new willingness to work took hold. An upward spiral was put into motion.

What did the change in attitude mean to the company? The particular manufacturing plant was faced with a shutdown in order to install new equipment and overhaul old equipment. The number of down days was critically important to the factory's productivity and profitability. Based on previous shutdowns, the company calculated that the shutdown would require two weeks.

The newly motivated employees cut that time in half. The added days of production were worth nearly $1 million of business!

## Little Things, Big Differences

Throughout this book, we've presented numerous examples of deeds that we've termed *symbolic acts*. Many people are tempted to dismiss them as trivial or inconsequential. Some have even said to us, "That's *nothing*. You weren't really making any substantive changes. A few seconds here and there don't turn things around."

But they do.

The more desperate the situation going in, the more they matter.

One of the men at Pittron, Norval Boyd—chairman of the grievance committee—said simply about Operation Turnaround, "It was like walking out of a dark room into daylight."

Little acts can signal a big change in attitude. And a change in attitude can make a great deal of difference.

Does a three-minute phone call from a runaway child make a difference in the way that child's loving and distraught parents feel? Can it signal a change in attitude that will bring reconciliation? Might it be the icebreaker toward a healing of relationships? You bet. Only three minutes. Only one call. But it can signal a change.

Does a welcome-home kiss from a spouse send a signal to a person who is used to coming home to a cold shoulder? It sure can. Only a little kiss. But what a change in attitude can result.

After years of rebuff and a total lack of communication from a former friend, does a warm handshake and a "let's let bygones be bygones" statement make a difference? Absolutely. A little thing. Takes only fifteen seconds. But it can signal a brand-new era of friendship.

## A Small Drop in a Big Pool

Some may argue that they really can't make a difference in their small niche because their massive corporation, as a whole, operates with a traditional management style.

We contend that you *can* have an impact—if only in your niche. Individual supervisors and managers have a great deal of control over the attitudinal environment of their particular work unit and their particular corner of the factory. If you are a frontline supervisor over only a handful of workers, your unit can still operate according to Value of the Person principles.

The likelihood is that your unit will begin to achieve results that will gain the attention of those above you, and rather than squash your efforts, upper levels of management are likely to express curiosity in what you are doing. Unless you are blatantly violating their policies in some way, the approach is likely to be one of "let's see what happens." When they see even more positive results coming out of your unit, you may very well be in a position to affect a larger segment of the company. Your positive influence has a good chance of spreading rather than being annihilated or overlooked.

Others argue that the complexity of their operation makes Theory R unworkable. The thinking here, we suspect, is that diversity and complexity are viewed as being close to anarchy, and the approach toward anarchy is one of exerting an iron-fist rule. From our experience in consulting with hundreds of companies, we have found no company that was too diverse to implement Value of the Person principles and to begin to do the right thing by the employees. (One company in which Theory R is being implemented has nine divisions and eight pilot plants. It produces a wide variety of products, has both union and nonunion workers, and has managers with many different styles. Theory R works there.)

It is our contention that diversity does *not* equal anarchy but calls for creativity. Theory R affects the way human beings relate to one another, not the way an organizational chart is put together. As such, it transcends the complexities of organizational charts.

Still others argue that their operations are too small for Theory R. If two or more people are involved, Theory R works.

We work with some young entrepreneurs in the Pittsburgh area—men who labor with their hands, including a sign painter, a carpet layer, a painter, a carpenter, and a landscaper. The five men started out on their own, usually as a one-person operation. They now have others working with them—three or four perhaps. We are hearing from them comments such as these:

- "We're a team. Each of us values what the other person contributes."
- "We're concerned about one another. We treat one another with respect and concern. We like to think our attitude toward one another is felt by those we work for, too."
- "It's not a matter of 'I'm the boss and you're the flunky.' We work on the job together. Each person knows that his job is really important to our total success."
- "My workers are my friends. We talk together even as we work together."

These men are committed to change in the way things are done on a small scale—and their reconciled relationships are making a difference with their clients. People are continually telling them that they've never had people work for them who were more considerate, more friendly, or more concerned with doing a good job, keeping their word, meeting deadlines, and doing so with a smile.

George Kitis is one of these young entrepreneurs. He and a crew of two helpers recently painted the entire interior of a large church in our community in record time. Staff members in the church were amazed that they finished the work so quickly and with such concern for quality. When George heard their comments, he responded simply, "We pulled together as a team."

Teams that pull together, large or small, always do a better job faster.

## How Can an Employee Value a Supervisor?

What might an employee do to show value to a supervisor and fellow workers? Here are several suggestions:

1. *Encourage attempts by management to demonstrate positive Value of the Person actions.*

2. *Take time to thank your supervisor for actions that extend value to you.*
3. *Get to know your supervisor as a whole person with real needs.*
4. *Pat your supervisor on the back for a job well done.*
5. *Be willing to communicate your concerns and problems to your supervisor.*
6. *Be an encouragement to your peers.*
7. *Get to know your coworkers as people with families.*
8. *Say "thank you" and "I'm sorry" freely and genuinely.*
9. *Willingly share your knowledge, skills, and ideas with others.*
10. *Find a way to give one gesture of decency a day.*

## A Matter of Responsibility

We believe very strongly in insisting that every employee in an operation be held responsible for getting the job done. No excuses. No backpedaling. No lame justifications. If there's a problem, someone needs to be responsible for fixing it and for doing all that is possible to see that it doesn't happen again.

When I came home from World War II, literally with a hole in my forehead where the shrapnel from a German grenade had penetrated my skull, I was an angry and frustrated young man. I rebelled against everything I could find to rebel against. I felt life had dealt me an unfair hand. I hadn't asked Red to die for me. I blamed the Germans for my feelings, the officers who had failed to come to our rescue in the trenches, and my past life as a coal miner's son. I blamed anything and anyone that I could think to blame. And no one held me accountable for my actions.

Then one of the guys I hung around with—a guy nicknamed Muscle—said to me one day, "Alderson, *you're* responsible for *your* own actions. Nobody else is responsible for the trouble you're getting into. You've got to take responsibility for what you are doing." His words hit me right between the eyes like no bullet could.

Very often, we blame others for failure on our jobs. We need to have someone come to us and say, "You're responsible. You're accountable. Nobody else. You."

Shortly after the strike ended at Pittron and we found ourselves scrambling to get back into production, I'd have managers say in meetings, "Man, we've got a real bad situation down in that area," or "This guy is a major problem in his department." I didn't know if they were fishing for sympathy or were trying to see if someone else would take on their job for them. My response to them was always the same: "Fix it. It's your responsibility to eliminate that problem. Do what you have to do to make it right, do it right, or get it right."

A manager must have that authority—to fix things that are wrong—and then the manager must be held responsible for using that authority. That's accountability. Someone needs to say, "I'm holding you accountable for getting the job done."

Workers, too, often blame their problems or negative situations on managers. Many of the problems or situations can be fixed by workers themselves—even if their role in fixing the problem means only reporting the situation or bringing the problem to light.

It truly is up to individuals to do their part. Each person has a responsibility for work performance.

You can't change the person next to you—no matter how much you may desire to do so.

- You *can* change your outlook on your job, your associates, your superiors, your subordinates, and your workplace.
- You *can* change your performance, your effort, your level of quality, your knowledge or skill base, and your quality of performance.
- You *can* determine how much you will care about persons with whom you work—and extend to them love, dignity, and respect.
- You *can* influence persons with whom you work to *want* to change their performance.

You can say to the person next to you, "I value you. I trust that you will value your own performance. I care about you as a person. I respect what you do. I believe in the worth and dignity of you as a person, and your job as being a vital job in this organization."

**THEORY R SAYS,**

*Responsibility for love, dignity, and respect rests with each person.*

One key component for the success of Theory R is a willingness on the part of each person to bring something to a work relationship. If one party chooses not to bring something to the relationship, eventually, there is no relationship.

A second key component for the success of Theory R is that each person expects more from the self than from any other person. A relationship begins to disintegrate when a person expects more from superiors or workers than from the self.

## Taking Over with Theory R

When I was a young soldier in World War II, I learned a valuable technique about how to take a town. You can neutralize a town by surrounding it, but to capture it, you need to first capture its central communication and military headquarters. To do that, you must first capture the neighborhood where those buildings are. To do that, you must first capture the neighborhood next to that one. To capture a neighborhood, you must first capture a block. To capture a block, you must first capture a street. To capture a street, you must first capture a house. To capture a house, you must first capture one room in that house.

Capturing a town begins with one room in one house. We became quite skilled at that. We would capture the first house on the outskirts of town. With soldiers backing one another up, one soldier would kick in the front door and enter the first room, and then move room by room through that house until all floors and the basement had been taken and the house was declared to be free of the enemy, either because it was empty or because all enemies in the house had been killed or taken prisoner.

How do you turn a company around? *With one worker on one line in one department in one division!*

When I look at the massive 3M Corporation, for example, I see no way in which all eighty-nine thousand employees can be won over to Theory R in a day. But I do know that in the last seven years, we've had seminars for a thousand in one plant, three hundred in another, a hundred in another, and so forth—over five thousand in all. Unit by unit by unit. That's the way a major corporation is affected.

In your workplace, begin with yourself. Share the principle with others around you. Decide among yourselves that you will be a Theory R work unit that extends Value of the Person behavior to one another. If you are a line worker, begin with yourself and others on your line. Commit to yourselves and to one another that you will be the most productive, most loving, most respected work line of workers in the entire plant. (The same goes for those who may work in an office or service area.) Even if your manager doesn't initially know what you are doing or is not on the bandwagon, go ahead and value one another!

Your improved quantity and quality of performance will get the manager's attention. Your reputation will spread throughout the company. Some of those on your line are likely to be transferred to other lines or put into supervisory positions to extend your good performance to other areas. (Managers will try to duplicate your results, even if they don't understand your motivation lies in doing the right thing.)

As you move into supervisory positions or are transferred to other lines, departments, or offices, find a way to stay in relationship. Help one another. Encourage one another. Act in Theory R ways to your new coworkers or, if you are named a supervisor, to your new crews. Create multiple Theory R work units.

Take your factory, your mill, or your organization one line, one area, one office, one branch, one department at a time.

There isn't an organization in our nation that can't be won over in this fashion.

Turning a hospital into a Theory R hospital will happen when one nurse in one group of nurses on one shift in one ward on one floor in one building commits to a new start, stays committed to Theory R, and makes an impact.

Turning a school district into a Theory R school district will happen when one teacher in a group of teachers in one grade in one elementary school commits to a new start, stays committed to Theory R, and makes an impact.

Turning a church denomination or diocese into a Theory R denomination will happen when one parishioner in one group of people in one small church in one district in one region commits to a new start, stays committed to Theory R, and makes an impact.

Theory R not only recognizes the person—its implementation begins with the person.

## THEORY R AT WORK

What can you do to implement Theory R beginning tomorrow morning?

# Making Theory R a Way of Life

## 20

**W**hile at Pittron, I sent a signal one day about valuing an employee's family. It was a spontaneous, unplanned action. I happened to be looking out the window of our conference room early one afternoon when I saw an employee's wife drop him off at the gate after lunch hour. The man jumped out of the car and ran for the door. I ran for the stairs and met him as he came back into the foundry.

I grabbed the man by the arm and said, "Was that you who just jumped out of that car and came running over here?" The man's face fell, and he started apologizing profusely. (He told me later that he had felt certain I was about to reprimand him for leaving the plant at noon.)

Just then my secretary came along, and I said to her, "I was watching this man from the window of the conference room, and do you know what he did? He jumped out of his car and ran in here without even bothering to kiss his wife good-bye." I turned to the man and said, "How could you do that? If she was still here, I'd make you go back out there and kiss her good-bye."

The man said, "I was running a little late, and I didn't want to get into trouble with my job."

I said, "Don't ever think that your job is more important than your wife."

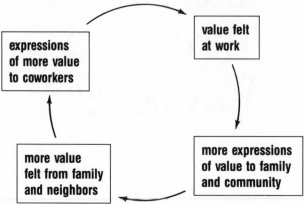

FIGURE 20.1. Cycle of benefits resulting from displaying Value of the Person behaviors at work and at home

Word of that conversation spread quickly through the plant. When you value an employee's family, you invariably value the employee.

The flip side is also true. An employee who feels valued at work tends to display Value of the Person behaviors at home. The benefits of the behaviors come back to the employee, who carries them to work the next day. A cycle is established (see fig. 20.1).

## Attitudes Carry Over

We met Penny while consulting with a hospital in our home city of Pittsburgh. During the course of our seminar, she told us about her most recent night at work. Penny worked as a nurse. Her drive home was along familiar roads with not much traffic. Her small community was calm that early in the morning. But Penny had felt anything but calm.

Her thoughts had raced a mile a minute: *I can't stand it anymore. What does he think I am, a mindless idiot he can push around and throw away? Who does he think he is—God? He's the one who made the mistake. He had no right to scream at me like that. "How dare you question me?" he said. How dare I not question him! And poor Mrs. Jenkins having to witness all of that. I keep forgetting, though. She's just the patient, and I'm just the nurse.*

As soon as Penny pulled in the driveway, she had to switch gears from being Penny, R.N., to Mom. There were breakfast to serve, children to get off to school and, somewhere down the line, an empty bed waiting for her.

"Mom, I can't find my gym clothes. Mrs. Parker said we'll get demerits if we don't have our uniform," whined Jessica, age eight, as Penny rushed around the kitchen. "You'll just have to get demerits then because I didn't have time to get the wash done!" snapped Penny.

Sara, Penny's fourteen-year-old bolted into the room, "Mom, look at me! I can't go to school with my hair like this. It's so flat! I can't believe we don't have any mousse." Penny hadn't been to the store as promised. "Listen, Sara, your hair is fine. Besides, it's about time you started to look a little more normal anyway." Sara stared at her mom for a second before running out of the kitchen.

Penny sat down at the kitchen table before she realized that Jessica was still standing in the kitchen, with big crocodile tears forming in her eyes. After a little time she said with a whimper, "If I get a demerit now, I won't get the prize."

Penny turned to see her precious little girl, and she was quickly reminded that prizes are major events in the life of an eight-year-old. In the way she had snapped at her daughters, she was no better than the doctor who had snapped at her.

Still, she found it nearly impossible to keep the way she was treated at the hospital from affecting the way she treated her family.

Yes, attitudes carry over. We can rarely leave them at work or at home.

## Attitudes Get Passed Along

Ed, a man in his forties who had worked for his company nearly twenty-five years, often felt his work cubicle was lost in a maze of room dividers. He, too, felt a little lost in the corporate structure.

One day Ed's boss came in and showed him a set of designs. "You know, I saw something like this come through awhile ago," Ed said to his supervisor, Steve. "The design looks good on paper, but it doesn't work in production. Let me make some minor adjustments that I know will correct the problem."

"Are you questioning my ability to read these designs?" Steve retorted in a loud and degrading tone of voice. Ed could feel his face turn red. He was sure the eyes of the engineers in the neighboring cubicles were turned his way.

"No, Steve," he said. "I am just trying to save us some problems down the line. I've been through this on a similar design."

"Listen," interrupted Steve, "you may think you have experience, but I just finished my graduate work on this program. I believe the best thing for you to do is to do just what I say. Your job is to produce. My job is to think, and the sooner you learn that, the better off we all will be. I suggest you get moving on this job *now!*"

Steve's loud and abrupt response hung in the air long after he left the small space, leaving behind a spirit of unrest and pent-up anger.

Ed replayed his supervisor's parting words over and over in his mind. He sat motionless for much of the next hour, consumed by feelings of humiliation and anger, not just that his idea had been thrown away but that he had been embarrassed in front of his coworkers. "Yeah, I'll give him just what he wants," Ed mumbled to himself, "and I hope he falls flat on his face."

At the family dinner table that night, conversation was stilted. Ed could contribute only one-word answers. Finally, his wife stopped trying to get him to respond, and the family ate in silence. At the end of the meal, Ed's oldest son, Terry, reminded his dad that he had a basketball game that night.

As Terry ran out the door with his high-tops in hand, he said, "Hey, aren't you coming to my game tonight? I'm starting tonight for the first time."

Ed responded, "I just don't have the energy tonight, son. I'll catch your next game, OK?"

Terry was hurt but made a brave effort to cover his feelings. "Yeah, Dad. Sure."

Ed couldn't see that his son's expression was an exact mirror of his own earlier in the day.

Yes, attitudes get passed along.

---

## Feelings Don't Know Work from Home

We met Bob at an executive seminar, and he told us about his life as we conversed together in a New York City boardroom.

Bob rises every morning at five o'clock to make sure that he beats the traffic and is at his office between 6:30 and 7:00 A.M. A sixteen-hour day is not unusual for him, taking into consideration executive dinners to entertain clients or meet with other executives. He also travels a great deal. Is Bob a workaholic? Not from his perspective. He simply puts in the hours he needs to put in to maintain his job.

Karen, his wife of twenty years, would disagree. She felt, not surprisingly, that Bob gave all of his best time to the job. She was the one who had to raise the children, attend their events, and be there to give them encouragement, solace, and advice. Even when Bob was home, he didn't seem present in mind and heart.

During an unusually tough week, Bob answered the phone at about eight o'clock one night. "Bob, where are you? We were supposed to go to a dinner and a movie tonight. Just the two of us. You promised."

Karen's voice was not sympathetic. She was angry and tired of waiting, tired of feeling forgotten. Bob responded, "Listen, I'm sorry, but dinner and the movie will have to wait until tomorrow. You know how pressured I am this week. I have to get these reports finished tonight. Go ahead and eat without me. Why not take one of your girlfriends with you? We can do something tomorrow."

Bob used the same tone of voice that he used in conducting business deals—authoritative, firm, absolute. Karen didn't respond. Bob reviewed the papers in front of him for a few seconds and then said, "Karen, are you there?" No answer. He asked again, "Karen, are you there?" This time she said, "I'm here, Bob, but I don't know for how long."

It doesn't really matter where a person is on the corporate ladder or what job the person does. That job and the life at home are bound together. Feelings from one area of life inevitably fall out on the other.

Yes, attitudes alter relationships.

## Attitudes Know No Boundaries— Neither Should Valuing

When it comes to our feelings, emotions, and ideas—the unseen intangibles of our lives—there are no sharp boundaries, distinctions, or pigeonholes. Rarely can we separate how one person treats us from how we will respond to the next person who crosses our path. What happens in one relationship nearly always affects what happens in the other relationships of both parties.

If this is true for attitudes, the behaviors of love, dignity, and respect must also become such that they know no boundaries.

What we do at work, we should do at home. What we do at home, we should do at church. What we do at church, we should do in the community. What we do in the community, we should do in the workplace. That's the only true way to live with integrity and to build character that is strong and consistent.

## Somebody Has to Start the Cycle

If the cycle of valuing behaviors is not currently in your life, it's up to you to start it rolling. There are two points at which this is possible. Take a look again at the cycle in figure 20.1.

The two areas dealing with expressions are behaviors that are up to you! You can begin the process.

If you want to feel valued, start valuing! Be creative about it. Reid Carpenter and two of his friends were.

## Are You Willing to Ask for the Next Slow Dance?

Reid tells this story about a way in which he and two other men expressed value to their teenage daughters: "I have a teenage daughter, and the fathers of two of her friends and I were having a conversation one night. One of them said to me, 'I just don't know how to relate to my little girl anymore. She's grown up and is interested in things other than spending time with me. I'm losing touch, and I don't know what to do.'

"I said, 'Be here at nine o'clock on Saturday night, and I'll tell you what we're going to do.' The men showed up the next Saturday night, and I drove the three of us down to the high school where our daughters were at a school dance.

"They asked, 'What are we doing here?' I said, 'We're going to walk into that gymnasium. And the next slow dance, each of us is going to find his daughter and ask her to dance. Just one dance. We don't have to say a word. Just dance, and when the dance is over, thank your daughter for the dance, then walk away, and we're out of here.'

"Now this took a lot of courage on the part of these men. But we followed through. Our daughters, of course, were shocked. All the time we were dancing with them, they were whispering to us, 'What are you doing here, Dad? I'm so embarrassed. How could you do this to me?'

"But after we had left, other friends of our daughters came to them and said, 'Wow, your dads are great. I wish my dad would care enough to do something like that.' We ended up being heroes. Best of all, we had found a way of telling our daughters that we valued them!"

There's something you can do *today* to show your children and your spouse that you value them. There's something you can do to say, "You're special. I value you. I love you and appreciate you. I respect who you are."

Everywhere we turn we see gaps in our society:

## Closing the Gaps

- Gaps between unions and management
- Gaps between workers
- Gaps between managers and persons they supervise
- Gaps between students and teachers
- Gaps between parishioners and clergypersons, and between the church and the marketplace
- Gaps between nurses and doctors
- Gaps between voters and their elected officials

On the personal level, we see gaps in marriages, gaps in friendships, gaps between parents and their children, gaps between brothers and sisters.

In the Old Testament of the Bible we find these words: "So I sought for a man among them who would make a wall, and stand in the gap before Me on behalf of the land, that I should not destroy it; but I found no one" (Ezek. 22:30).

What does it mean to make a wall and stand in the gap? It means to be a bridge builder, a peacemaker, one who closes in the wall and breaches the break in it with one's life.

Closing a gap costs something. It means putting your reputation on the line, being willing to take a risk to do what is right. There's usually a price to pay—at least initially—in terms of time and effort.

Closing a gap means being vulnerable to others.

Closing a gap means being a peacemaker.

Those who will close the gaps, however, are true heroes. They are the ones who bring about reconciliation. And reconciliation flows from love, dignity, and respect.

We'd like to end by having you ask yourself two questions. The first is, "*Can* I implement Theory R at work and in my home and neighborhood?" If you are honest with yourself, the answer is, "Yes, I can." The second and more important question is, "*Will* I?" Only *you* can answer that question.

## Two Parting Questions

To contact Wayne Alderson and
Nancy Alderson McDonnell, write:

**Value of the Person—**
   **Theory R Seminars**
100 Ross Street
Pittsburgh, PA 15219

Or call:

(412) 562-9070
FAX: (412) 281-2312